The Hope of Happiness

Helen Oppenheimer

The Hope of Happiness

A Sketch for a Christian Humanism

SCM PRESS LTD

334 02054 9

First published 1983
by SCM Press Ltd
26–30 Tottenham Road, London N1

Filmset and printed in Great Britain at
The Camelot Press Ltd, Southampton

To
Henrietta   Matilda   Xanthe
Adam   Neil   Ivo

CONTENTS

Preface   ix
1   Does Happiness Matter?   1
2   Does it Pay to be Good?   9
3   According to Human Nature   18
4   Who Chooses?   26
5   Autonomy and Authority   35
6   Choosing and Finding   45
7   Valuing   56
8   Claims   69
9   People   77
10   Being and Doing   85
11   Mattering   92
12   One-way Love   101
13   Minding   111
14   Liking   124
15   Attending   132
16   Worshipping   140
17   Images and Idols   147
18   The End of Man   156
19   Hoping   167
20   Glibness, Gloom and Glory   176
Notes   190
Index   203

PREFACE

None of this book has appeared in print before, but several of its chapters started life as lectures or talks in various places, and I owe large debts of gratitude to all those people who invited me, entertained me and listened to me so kindly. The book began with four 'Pastoral theology lectures' called 'Flourishing and Fulfilment' given in the University of Durham in 1974 and I have the most happy recollections of my visit there and especially the enjoyable hospitality I was given at Trevelyan College under the auspices of its then Principal, Miss Joan Bernard. A visit to the Theology Department at Manchester University at the invitation of Professor Ronald Preston also stands out in my mind with much gratitude. Professor G. R. Dunstan has given me kind encouragement at several stages. Various people have read chapters of the book in typescript and of these I am especially grateful to Mrs Lionel Butler and Professor Dorothy Emmet. In innumerable ways my husband has helped me throughout.

I have indulged in rather a large number of notes in the hope of acknowledging gratitude to many other people, living and dead, for their written words.

I have retained the convention of using capital H for He and Him for the Deity, as a hint that He is not anthropomorphically masculine.

Helen Oppenheimer

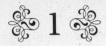

Does Happiness Matter?

Of course happiness matters. The question is why Christians are so apt to suggest the contrary. Two reasons stand out. First, we are stale. It is not fair to accuse us *en bloc* of being lukewarm; but we seem to have lost the art of expressing our faith in a way that gives people anything to be happy about. Second, we dare not make happiness important for fear of being mercenary and presumptuous, and forgetting that Christianity is supposed to be about self-sacrifice. These reasons are not altogether distinct, but let us take them separately to start with.

The dreariness of Christians is nothing new. Gabriel Marcel said in a lecture called 'Some Remarks on the Irreligion of Today',

> I realise perfectly that the words 'grace' and 'salvation' give some of you a heartbreaking feeling of staleness. There is nothing new in them for voice or vision. The air around them has been breathed so long that it has become stifling.[1]

He said that over half a century ago, and it still strikes home. Many Christians do not give the impression of believing anything very remarkable and reiteration of the basic doctrines of faith seems to fail to revive them. Ronald Knox neatly turned Milton's line round: 'The sheep look fed up and are not hungry.'

Not surprisingly there ensues a tendency to try to demolish some of the standard structures which seem to have lost their purpose, in the hope that their collapse will make room to build something fresh to take their place. Even less surprisingly, instead of being stimulated by this treatment, many of the faithful react defensively, sheltering in the ruins and trying to shore up what they can. The result is literally unedifying.

Some Christians, taking to heart the spectacle they see of indifference and destructiveness, cry out for God to raise us up a prophet to denounce this sinful generation. They forget that the prophets of old were generally raised up among God's people who were conscious of being God's people and expected his favours. It is not much use to proclaim that the Day of the Lord will be darkness and not light when nobody is expecting a Day of the Lord. They forget too that painting a gloomy picture, from the right or the left, of collapsing standards or prevailing selfishness, is the surest way to make it come true. They think that they can safely denigrate where they know they love; but what they say may cover up their love so effectively that nobody could find it and its absence is presumed.

Nor has the twentieth century been without prophets, inspired with a positive vision of what Christianity is about. For many, Teilhard de Chardin has fulfilled this role. Anglicans should not quickly let Austin Farrer be forgotten. Nobody could recall us to a less stale faith than Karl Barth. But if already these giants are part of history, and the spectacles that they gave us to look through are misting up again with everyday steam and grime, there may be scope for a sort of cleaning and polishing operation to allow us to look more clearly at what there is to make us happy.

But is 'happiness' the right word? Even before we come to ask whether the Christian hope is merely mercenary, 'happiness' can already seem a thin and inadequate lever to prise open the riches of the Christian faith. It is worth taking hold of simply as a convenient start. It has plenty of partial synonyms, useful as variations: pleasure, contentment, prosperity, flourishing, well-being, satisfaction, enjoyment, delight, felicity, fulfilment, blessedness, joy. All these in Christian thinking have been worthy concepts with honourable histories, but 'happiness' is the most suitable to begin with, as it can cover anything from getting what I want at the moment to entering into eternal life. It need not imply approval or disapproval, nor require any moral or philosophical point of view. It can span the whole range of the greater and the less, the intense and the calm, the earthly and the heavenly. So we can use it with the minimum of confusion to ask questions about the meaning of life.

Of course it would be really naive to suggest that Christians will become less jaded by being told to be happy. There is a kind of artificial rejoicing whipped up to cover dryness, like synthetic cream on cakes, which is no kind of substitute for the real thing. The spirit of delight which will 'never come for pity' will certainly never come for nagging. Delight must almost always take us by surprise; but maybe the surprise could consist in seeing that delight is, after all, worth expecting.

But if we offer people delight, it seems that we are only trying to rescue our old stale morality with a mercenary morality. How dare we expect virtue to be rewarded? It has always been dubious to expect goodness to pay in this life, but nowadays it seems unlikely that it ought to pay at all. Because of the prevailing horror of other-worldliness, the promise of future Christian happiness has become a particularly difficult idea for our contemporaries. We have come to understand that 'pie in the sky' is the wrong sort of substitute for pie on earth, that crude other-worldliness can corrupt and the more rarified kind can make us neglect our duties here. Our generation has been almost obsessed with the dangers of thinking too much about heaven; but caution overgrown can itself become dangerous. In turning our backs on reward, we may only reinforce our staleness. We risk becoming prigs, too busy being good to notice God's kindness.

When St Augustine preached at Hippo, he sometimes made his congregation cry out 'with longing for some vision of beauty not yet granted'.[2] He could assume that heaven was what they deeply wanted although they might be distracted by worldly things and that it was part of his vocation to help them find it. He was not afraid of eloquence, the eloquence of promises more characteristically than of threats. He offered 'a vision surpassing all earthly beauty, of gold or silver, of woods or fields, the beauty of sea and sky, of sun, moon, and stars, the beauty of angels', and went on,

I said once before: Empty out that vessel that is to be filled; you are to be filled with good, pour away the evil. God would fill you, shall we say, with honey; where will you put it if you are full of vinegar? What your vessel held must be poured away, and the vessel cleansed . . . so that it be fit to hold – did we say honey? Gold? Wine? Speak as we may of that which cannot be spoken, call it what we will, its proper name is – God.[3]

One wonders if this would evoke any 'disclosure situations', in I. T. Ramsey's phrase, with a congregation today. Perhaps it would. Perhaps Augustine's preaching is unappreciated at present only because it is widely unknown; but if it could stir people still, it would have to be by awaking longings which have become strange even to good men. The difficulty which confronts the Christian church today is not just that people have stopped believing in heaven: they have largely stopped wanting heaven. A large part of the cry for *relevance* is apt to be the cry to give us something other than heaven. The problem cannot be dealt with merely by renewed affirmations that in the end there is nothing but heaven to be had, so people must take it or leave it. We cannot opt out of contemporary difficulties so neatly.

At present, any talk of fulfilment which at last places our goals in another world than this is apt to be ruled out of court as somehow both irrelevant and unworthy. So we not only lose enthusiasm for it but also manage to feel virtuous for doing so. Uninterest takes the credit for disinterest, and unselfishness has become more important than hope. Perhaps the time has come to look for a corrective, remembering always that correctives are in their nature one-sided and sooner or later will need re-correcting. There is more at stake than human disappointment of a good time coming. We are concerned here with the ultimate goodness of God's universe.

At least it may be said that for Christians simply to acquiesce in the assumption that this life is all is to tie our hands behind our backs at the outset in a needlessly defeatist way. If we will not even try to project the pattern of Christian morality on to the other side of death and resurrection, then it is hardly *Christian* morality we are talking about. For believers, goodness unrewarded is not the only alternative to instant results. There is room for the connection of goodness and happiness according to God's purpose to be complicated, to be real but not immediately obvious. A fresh look at the place of happiness in the Christian gospel could be both valuable in its own right and a dispeller of discouragement.

But surely this is precisely a bribe? If we can only get over contemporaries' lack of interest in Christianity by making them feel that after all we are on to a good thing, then we really are encouraging them to be mercenary.

A thoroughly unworthy view of the Christian church seems to be emerging: either we nag about morality so that the faithful become stale, or we offer heavenly prizes so that they become corrupt; or, worse, we offer boring heavenly prizes so that they become staler than ever, and threaten them with penalties so as to drown both good news and morality.

Here a good platitude is in place. It is God we are supposed to be talking about, not a system of morality called 'Christianity'. If we fix our minds upon what we believe about the God we are supposed to worship, we may be able to find out whether happiness is important in His sight. At least we may say that *human beings* are important. The Christian faith is essentially a humanist faith, paradoxical as this may sound.

To make this assertion is after all an aggressive way of re-stating the doctrine of creation: that God seemingly values people enough both to make them and save them. Our creed is about the trouble God took to fashion a world of people. The work of Christ was never a raid on an alien universe; God saves what He first created. Believers talk about the cost of this in words that they have blunted, but its meaning is sharply definite. We cannot think of the Cross as an unexpected emergency.[4] So we can measure the value of creation by what it cost to perfect it. 'If in your own reckoning you have held yourselves cheap because of your earthly frailty, now assess yourselves by the price paid for you,' said St Augustine.[5] Because creation has a cross in it, we are not just God's hobby or menagerie: we are worth more than that. The fulfilment of human beings, whatever that means exactly, is wanted by God even at a great price. To try to defend and fill out a little this manner of speaking, not as the whole truth but as a proper emphasis for the present time, is the object of this book.

The attempt to set out a kind of theological humanism or humanist theology, a way of believing in God which makes human beings important, is likely to be looked at askance both by sceptics and Christians. Sceptics will expect it to be naive and Christians will be suspicious of deep-rooted selfishness.

The sceptic cannot believe that we can talk usefully about *ultimate* fulfilment; many Christians think that we should avert our gaze from any such idea for the sake of our soul's health; and both sorts of criticism are responsible and need recognition as well as refutation.

The next world can easily come to seem better forgotten. We have no right to suppose that we can say cheerfully to people whose lives we have failed to make tolerable, 'Never mind. It will be all right in heaven. God will wash away all your tears.' They will simply not believe us. It is more human to stand by them here and now, knowing that it is never safe to postpone our ideals. Even among believers, it is unwise to be too ready to brush aside present troubles. When we are talking to one another about how to lead Christian lives, then the war on selfishness, the taking up of the cross and dying daily, are an emphasis we forget at our peril, on pain of being both mercenary and shallow.

Yet in spite of all this, there remains the persistent conviction that there is more to be said. There is an end to which all this is the means. When we are commending the gospel, we have something positive not negative to offer: a wedding invitation, a hidden treasure, a homecoming, something worth any sacrifice to achieve. Repentance leads to celebration not to mortification. The one whom we call the man of sorrows was called by his contemporaries a gluttonous man and a wine-bibber. His longing was to drink new wine with his friends in the kingdom of God.

There is no need to say either, on the one hand, 'Cheer up. The present doesn't matter,' or, on the other hand, 'Never mind. Go on with your own selfish life. God loves you as you are and He will forgive you and make you happy anyway.' What needs to be said is rather, God has something to *give*, which is what humanity is for. The end of everything is not loss but gain. The universe was made for God's creatures to glorify Him and *enjoy* Him for ever.[6]

This specific belief in the worthwhileness of creation is thoroughly traditional, not any kind of accommodation to current worldliness. What matters, of course, is not whether the doctrine appeals to us but whether it is true; but if it is true it would seem an understatement to call it important. Is the universe really a sort of artefact? Is there Someone behind it who wanted there to be human beings? Is that Someone in any way accessible? Is He on our side? The Christian faith has affirmative answers to all these questions, but the message has a curious tendency to go by default. Christians take their Maker for granted, sceptics assume or conclude that this world is all there is; and so the idea of the Creator's satisfaction with His handywork remains more or less unremarked and unconsidered, as either too obvious to mention or too unlikely to be credible. If these beliefs are not to die away from human consciousness for lack of attention, it is worth making a conscious effort to mention the obvious, to uncover and look at the most basic tenets, not in order to try to demolish them nor to prop them up, but simply to appreciate them. Then it could begin to seem worthwhile again for people to make the strenuous efforts needed to find out whether the Christian commonplaces are actually true, and how they relate to the way we ought to live.

It would be false to suggest that to appreciate the wonder of creation as such is unfashionable today: far from it. Christians are prominent in that growing movement of thought in which nature is respected, studied and cherished as a heritage not a mere environment. They have opportunities to develop piecemeal a kind of scientist's Canticle of the Sun, not trying to force the universe into a ready-made mould but cataloguing it in its given immensity and intricacy as God's handiwork and possession. The earth is not to be presumed upon nor exploited, certainly not for any short-term human enjoyment. To 'consider the heavens' is more than ever to confront human littleness with the scope of the divine mathematics; and the question which still follows insistently is 'What is man that thou art mindful of him?' If mankind is after all meant to be the crown of a creation on such a scale, not of a little three-storey affair; if the Son of God was made man in this vast scheme of things, then we have now even more reason for wonder than the Psalmist or the early Christians who quoted his poem.[7]

But the pity is that here, looking at the universe with twentieth-century eyes as a greater marvel than ever and needing the more urgently to enquire about man's place in it and man's hopes, Christians have somehow lost the honourable name of humanist. A Christian, one would think, should find in his theology more comprehensive reason than the unbeliever can have for setting a positive value upon humanity. He could be more humanist than the sceptical humanist: both in general, because God Himself became man, and in particular, because each individual human being is the brother for whom Christ died. Yet humanism has come to mean 'a practical decision to live on the assumption that man is on his own and this life is all',[8] and for a Christian to call himself a humanist has become shocking, not nowadays as a presumptuous claim to deep learning in the classics, but as a repudiation of belief in God. It may be too late for the word 'humanism' to shed this negative connotation; but it is not too late for Christians to enquire hopefully into the positive principle that humanism stands for, the value and importance of human beings and human fulfilment.

Does it Pay to be Good?

We are asking about the place of happiness in our beliefs and about what sort of fulfilment we can offer to our contemporaries; but first, who are 'we' to offer? It is not just that somebody will retort sooner or later, 'And who are you to talk?' The question 'Who are *we*?' is one which it is worthwhile to keep asking ourselves and other people. *We* are always being told about our situation: that we are stale, that we seem to have lost the art of expressing our faith, though we have had prophets and we believe certain things about God. Once one starts watching for this generalizing use of 'we', one seems to find it everywhere, and maybe one falls back upon 'one' at the price of formality and ugliness.

It would be inconvenient to manage without 'we', but the habit is worth watching lest it lure *us* into slipshod thinking, particularly when it takes the form of a confession of sin. We pollute the environment, we oppress the stranger in our midst, we neglect the Third World, we think about nothing but pay-packets, we perpetuate our divisions, we are inward-looking: who? Are these precise self-accusations or polite ways of attacking other people?

Sometimes we find a 'we' with which it is easy to identify. 'We have left undone those things which we ought to have done.' 'From all blindness of heart; from pride, vain glory and hypocrisy . . . Good Lord, deliver *us*.' But it is sensible to keep asking, can *we* readers of a particular book or members of a particular group associate ourselves with these statements made in our name and, if so what ought *we* to do about it? If the author would say 'I' or 'you', or make it clear how widely he is drawing the net of his 'we', the rest of us would have a better chance of making an honest response.

So, to take this advice, let me say that the 'we' I have immediately in mind consists of those Christian people who are concerned not only with trying to live by the gospel, but also with thinking about it in such a way as to be the more able to explain it to other people. For good measure, we may ask, 'What other people?' Of course nobody can be heard by everyone. Let us hope to address some of our nearer neighbours and especially those who seem to share a recognizable moral point of view, whether or not they call themselves Christian: who believe in justice rather than injustice, who know how to give good gifts to their children, who would rather be kind than unkind, but who do not want unreasonable demands to be made upon them.

Sooner or later, it is going to be time to make what seem to be unreasonable demands upon them in God's name. So it is important to be clear in our own minds about how what we are going to ask is related to what we believe we have to offer.

The word 'offer' immediately jars. It suggests a bargain. It leads straight to the crude question 'Does it pay to be good?' At one level, the question must simply be rejected: to be good on the understanding that it will pay is not to be good at all. Unless morality *can* mean going against everything we think will benefit us, it is not morality but expediency. Convenient as it would be for the human race at large if we could convince some bad people that behaving well would be in their interest, we must turn our backs on any such consideration. If we have any glimpse of what real virtue means, we must fall in with those austere moralists who keep insisting that to give a selfish man a knockdown argument for being good is to corrupt him, not to improve him.

But that is not the whole story. We must also call morality to witness that virtue and happiness are not at last to be taken apart. We know, of course, that a man must be good even if it hurts: that is part of what goodness means. But, on the other hand, there is also the ancient insight that in a sense a good man *cannot* be harmed: that his goodness is his true well-being which only wrong-doing can damage, and this too is what goodness means. The need to go on insisting upon this link between virtue and happiness may be easier to see in the negative. It is not very paradoxical to connect badness and *un*happiness. A bad man, surely, is harmed just by being bad. If we think we have some clue about what goodness is, we cannot admit that a wicked man can be truly or ultimately happy, or that it could be in a man's interest to let himself become thoroughly selfish. For one thing, he would be so lonely. Our pity for real depravity is more than a sentimental compensation for our own cowardice. Wordsworth's instinct to 'grieve' for the tyrant[1] is humanly satisfactory.

It is not a long step to affirm the positive conviction that to follow goodness with all my heart must somehow be in my real best interest and constitute my true happiness. This is not necessarily a religious statement. It is not because God will sort out people's deserts in the end. Rather, we feel sure as human beings that goodness itself is somehow to be our fulfilment. Nor are we just saying 'virtue is its own reward'. It is not that feeling good makes us feel happy, but that being good somehow satisfies and enhances our natures.

So we have to keep trying to do justice to two seemingly contradictory truths, that we are to do right even if we suffer for it and that it is better *for us* to do right. We must both deny and affirm that we can see the point of morality.[2] In the name of our best insights, we have to perform a balancing act of a kind with which Christians are not unfamiliar. Notoriously it is heresies that are simple, refusing the complexity truth is apt to demand. Belief that morality is what we need and yet is distinct from all our wants and needs has something of the same paradoxical awkwardness as belief that God is both Three and One, but the reason for holding on is the same: that to lose one side would be an over-simplfication.

It might seem now that the answer is obvious and only looks difficult because we have already forgotten to ask 'Who are we?' Of course morality is good *for us*, but *us* may not be *me*. Have we never heard of the greatest good of the greatest number? There is no denying that utilitarianism as a way of understanding the basis of morality has an enormous initial plausibility. Of course great sacrifices may be required to produce great goods, but surely always great goods for somebody: not sacrifice as an end in itself. We may well feel convinced that virtue is meant to pay, but this conviction gives me no right to expect that my virtue will pay me: not because happiness is unimportant or virtue unprofitable, but because I only count for one. So utilitarianism presents itself as a lively candidate for the post of chief moral theory, for believers and unbelievers alike. It claims that the whole point of morality, earthly or heavenly, is to bring about happiness. This can seem self-evident or a dangerous heresy. There is no need to be side-tracked by the mathematics of whether we may sacrifice forty-nine per cent for the sake of fifty-one per cent. At least the claim deserves looking into, that it is *consequences* which truly determine whether actions are right or wrong: consequences judged by benefit. The sacrifice of my own good, it is affirmed, can only be justified in these terms.

In Southey's poem 'After Blenheim', old Kaspar's grandchildren wanted to know what was the point of the 'famous victory' which was supposed to explain why they kept finding human skulls in the garden. Little Peterkin asked the right question: 'What good came of it at last?' In this frame of mind, utilitarianism can come into its own and the traditional ethical mistrust of benefit in the name of principle can seem unnecessary. On the contrary, one begins to wonder whether bringing about happiness is not a sort of summary of what the Christian Golden Rule is really about. John Stuart Mill claimed as much:

> If it be a true belief that God desires, above all things, the happiness of his creatures, and that this was his purpose in creation, utility is not only not a godless doctrine, but more profoundly religious than any other.[3]

That is all very well, but we have to notice the 'if'. It is relevant that Mill did not himself have faith in such a God. Devout believers have characteristically been repelled by the doctrine of utility; and it seems unlikely that there is nothing but prejudice behind their resistance. Surely they are right that the heart of Christian morality is not to be so easily analysed. Is the holy God concerned with making things agreeable? Even if an unbeliever is prepared to measure goodness by usefulness, surely a man of faith must measure usefulness by goodness?

As usual in ethical controversy, there are caricatures at war with one another here. The Christian is supposed to obey the implacable will of God however horrible the human consequences. He will betray his friends to a tyrant rather than tell a lie and blithely refuse an abortion to a raped twelve-year-old. Meantime the utilitarian in unprincipled expediency is supposed to ignore every dictate of honour and integrity for the sake of immediate satisfaction. He will cheerfully shoot a few scapegoats in the interests of law and order and study how to alter people's genes to make them stupidly contented. Each presents the other as both immoral and opposed to common sense.

Yet perhaps the gap between Christianity and utilitarianism is not so wide as it can be made to look. At least some of the unhelpful terminology can be avoided. 'Utility' today sounds stodgily uninspiring. 'Pleasure' sounds trivially titillating. Either can suggest a heartless calculus of benefits unattractive to the god-fearing and just as unattractive to those who would simply claim to be humane. 'Happiness' is still a more convenient word. It allows greater elbow room and gives the argument more scope.

We can make a more substantial concession to the utilitarian. We can refrain from accusing him of being a selfish hedonist. He says that what ultimately matters is to make people happy. He does not have to mean trivial or sensual kinds of happiness, nor need he put his own happiness first. He may consistently devote his life to the lasting good of mankind: that is exactly what on his theory he *ought* to do, whether he is religious or not. Far be it from Christian moralists to discourage him. They have enough troubles on their hands, without using the deliverances of the contemporary conscience that happiness matters as target practice. It seems fair to say that people who seriously pursue happiness need be no more self-seeking than people who consciously pursue virtue and in practice it will often be the virtuous ones who seem more self-centred.

Yet without being essentially *self*-indulgent, the doctrine of 'greatest happiness' has an intrinsic tendency to be indulgent all round. Cruelty seems so obviously the worst sin, kindness the most real virtue, that it becomes difficult to make room for those moral convictions which are made of sterner stuff. Here we are approaching the real reason why Christians are doubtful about giving happiness such an honourable place. They need not think of the utilitarian doctrine as selfishly mercenary and yet somehow it remains inadequate. What it cannot allow for is any clear moral insistence that some sorts of things really are wrong and not to be done however beneficial it might seem to be to allow them. Could it ever be right to torture the innocent, whatever harm is threatened if we decline?

The utilitarian in turn can allow a good deal to the man of principle. He can almost always show that moral integrity tends to produce good, claiming that this is why we want it. Likewise he can make a good deal of room for moral rules, as useful and even essential to save people from constantly calculating and miscalculating consequences. But in the end the throughgoing utilitarian must say that the consequences justify the rule and may justify breaking it, not that the rule justifies the consequences even when they are thoroughly unpalatable. There still remains a conviction that there is more in moral duty than he can allow, that truth and honour and steadfastness and special loyalties have claims upon human beings which cannot be resolved without remainder into their potential usefulness. To make 'What's the harm?' or even 'What's the advantage?' one's ultimate moral question is potentially as shallow as to reply unbendingly 'Never mind harm and benefit: God has forbidden it' is narrow-minded. The appeal of the kind of virtue which says 'I will *not* do evil that good may come' is capable of being felt by unbelievers as well as Christians, and cannot be dissolved into a mixture of platitude and confusion.

For example, Professor Bernard Williams has told a story of a botanist called Jim who arrives in a small South American town just as twenty protesters are about to be executed.[4] The captain in charge offers Jim the guest's privilege of shooting one of them himself, in which case the others will be let off as a special mark of the occasion. All the villagers are begging Jim to accept the offer: but should he? Professor Williams' point is not that he certainly ought to refuse, but that the answer is not obvious; whereas, if utilitarianism were true, it would be obvious and any consideration of Jim's integrity would be morally irrelevant. Jim is precluded from simply saying 'But that would be wrong', and we are precluded from admiring him if he does say that. For the utilitarian, if Jim refuses he has actually done wrong. Surely this over-simplifies what we believe as much as an inflexible rule-morality does, though in the opposite direction.

Instead of resorting to a head-on clash between principle and expediency, an Anglican Christian will characteristically look for ways of saying that both can be honoured. Not surprisingly, such a solution has already been weightily propounded. It has been propounded by a great eighteenth-century Christian divine whose reputation as a moral philosopher is still high today, perhaps higher among philosophers than among theologians: Bishop Butler of Durham. What he says about goodness and human nature is more subtle than a mere taking sides over whether virtue is to be thought of as profitable.

Butler does not encourage us as human creatures to presume to take up a utilitarian stance. Our ignorance is too great. We are not to suppose that we can decide what is right or wrong by calculating the 'overbalance of happiness or misery'.[5] Our part is to obey conscience. Butler does not rule out the possibility that God, who sees all, may be a sort of grand utilitarian; though it must be admitted that he does not make this possibility sound very exciting. 'Were the Author of nature to propose nothing to himself as an end but the production of happiness, were his moral character merely that of benevolence; yet ours is not so.'[6]

The attraction of Butler's view is that the conscience which we are to obey is no alien imperative but the voice of our true nature. Though Butler does not theorize about what moral school of thought the Almighty belongs to, this understanding of human beings builds into them the kind of significance which ought to be congenial to a utilitarian. We are capable of being happy and capable of being harmed, and this fact is not irrelevant to morality but central to it. Vice is 'a violation or breaking in upon our own nature'.[7] Moral laws are not arbitrarily imposed upon us from outside ourselves but have to do with what is good for us and bad for us.

Butler's account of human nature starts, as it were, at ground level. As human beings, we all have a variety of 'particular passions',[8] wants and aversions, likes and dislikes, which are the raw material of our moral lives. Neither self-love nor love of other people could get started unless there were specific things human beings minded about. These particular passions are not morally bad nor good but neutral. It is a 'strange affectation' to explain away their neutrality and look upon 'the whole of life as one continued exercise of self-love'.[9] A good person is not without particular passions but is able to integrate them into a satisfying whole.

It is at the next level that self-love comes in; but so, parallel with it, does a natural love of others. Our basic concern for ourselves is not the whole truth about the way we are made. Human beings, in Butler's scheme of things, have also a real built-in benevolence, just as real as self-love, inclining them to try to make their fellow-creatures happy. Both principles alike, self-love as well as benevolence, are often inadequate and need to be fostered; and conversely, both are apt to overreach themselves and need to be checked. In allowing self-love its place alongside benevolence, we really are in line with the Golden Rule. More benevolence, not less self-love, is what we need.[10] Neither is absolute: both are under the authority of conscience, 'the guide assigned to us by the Author of our nature'.[11]

The utilitarian's mistake is that he thinks of benevolence as self-justifying and indeed finds it hard to think of self-love being subject to anything but benevolence. Yet one does not have to be particularly religious, nor a victim of one's upbringing, to acknowledge the rule of conscience in Butler's sense. To be governed by conscience is not a matter of listening to divine whisperings or reiterating what one's parents always said, but of something like integrity as Professor Williams brings it in, integrity in the sense of not regarding one's deepest commitments as expendable.[12] This wholeness of personality has everything to do with happiness but can leave behind the oversimplification of self-affirmation versus self-denial. 'Act as you please, as you think most fit,' says Butler; 'make that choice, and prefer that course of life, which you can justify to yourselves, and which sits most easy upon your own mind. It will immediately appear, that vice cannot be the happiness, but must upon the whole be the misery, of such a creature as man; a moral, an accountable agent.'[13]

In this way of looking at things, what conscience requires arises from the way we are made and from what we deeply want and need. 'Had it strength, as it has right; had it power, as it has manifest authority; it would absolutely govern the world.'[14] If we find this convincing, we shall want to say that to do right is to go with, not against, the way the world is made, and that wrong-doing is cross-grained not just forbidden. We find ourselves, whether with satisfaction or surprise, inclined to talk about 'natural law'. Morality does not so much 'pay' as 'make sense'. It makes sense in the end in terms of happiness.

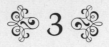

According to Human Nature

To follow Bishop Butler's approach to morality is promising because we can make happiness morally important without letting the idea of goodness be subordinated. We can refuse to be led into a shallow morality which identifies goodness with expediency, or into a mercenary morality which identifies goodness with self-interest. We can keep a firm grip of the principle that moral goodness is not to be *identified* with anything other than itself. Goodness is goodness and definitions only define it away. Its link with happiness needs to be made more subtly than by way of definition. That is where Butler's notion of human nature comes in, as a promising way of showing how goodness belongs with wellbeing, without dissolving goodness into what makes us happy. Instead of attempting the impossible, a definition of goodness, we can set about *characterizing* it, giving it body as it were, in terms of what befits human beings, what enables them to be properly human. So we begin to work towards a concept of *fulfilment* which, we hope, will focus goodness and happiness together in a sort of stereoscopic vision which neither alone can achieve.

Now we need to be careful. Any such 'natural law' theory that makes goodness a matter of what is fitting for human nature is suspect to many moralists, and not without reason.[1] It needs defence, not mere assertion. As G. F. Woods pleasingly put it, 'all the words which are used are as elusive as goldfish in a bowl. They are most satisfying when no effort is made to handle them.'[2] It is easy enough to hint at moral depth just by being vague and to imagine that an argument goes a long way when it is merely circular. On the face of it, this argument is circular already. To say that goodness is what befits the creatures we are, avoids defining goodness in non-moral terms simply by saying nothing. Of course goodness must be what befits us, but this goes no way towards illuminating what does befit us or what will fulfil us. It looks as if we could fill it out, to taste, with anything or nothing.

Talk of 'following nature' or of 'obeying the law of nature' will raise many hackles. Moralists will expect an immoral obedience to merely biological impulses, justifying all manner of self-indulgence and promiscuity. Scientists will expect a naive use of analogy in which stones and planets obeying the law of gravity are called upon for our edification.[3] Humanists will expect an inflexible adherence to outworn moral assumptions in which clerics take it upon themselves to tell us what our nature demands.

But there is no need to be so hasty as to suppose that the concept of human nature will let us simply read off what goodness really is, still less reassure us that we know already. What we have is a question mark, a starting point for *asking* what goodness is. Properly understood, natural law morality works only by not being a theory at all. We might perhaps seek scientific respectability by calling it a 'methodology'. It is a way of looking at the world in a hopeful expectation that some sense can be made of it. It is not so much informative as encouraging.

This attitude is particularly congenial to those who affirm that the world has a Creator, but it does not have to drive believers and unbelievers apart. On the contrary, it can be a link between human beings who assert, what is after all quite a lot to assert, that our common humanity means something and therefore that morality has a point. With these assumptions there is some sense in asking what meaning and what point. Then, when Christians and sceptics diverge again, they will at least understand what each other is talking about.

For Christians today to dismiss the natural law tradition, whether because they know little about it, or because they know a good deal about it and think of it as more Stoic than Christian, or because they do not like what they see of it, would still be to miss opportunities. It would be to neglect in the present a chance to find common ground with other human beings who are made in the same way as ourselves. And just as much, it would be to neglect in the past the roots which the idea of a law of human nature does have in our own religious tradition. The refreshing conviction of the essential normality of goodness, of a harmony between what is right and what works, is not alien to what we believe as Christians: it is deeply embedded in the Old Testament record of human beings coming to know the God we still worship.

Anglicans have characteristically fed their faith on the psalms, with their recurring emphasis on earthly well-being as the proper result of doing God's will and itself pleasing to God.[4] The good man 'shall be like a tree planted by the waterside: that will bring forth his fruit in due season' (Ps. 1.3). To suppose that it is now time to outgrow this notion could be a piece of adolescent impatience, not of real maturity. Even the agricultural concern need not seem irrelevantly primitive and pre-industrial now to a generation with a renewed interest in feeding the hungry. 'The folds shall be full of sheep; the valleys also shall stand so thick with corn that they shall laugh and sing' (Ps. 65.13) means more than the nostalgia of an indoor Christian whose hands are more often inky than earthy: it could be a real promise to be re-claimed if mankind could manage to stop abusing the earth it lives in.

Nor is the notion of what befits human nature as hopelessly uninformative as all that. It is not a sort of enormous hold-all into which practically anything can be put. The extent to which people's ideas of what is right and fitting do or can diverge has been exaggerated, and relativism has had its own way too much.[5] The modes in which people can work out their own salvation, individually or corporately, are not infinitely various. There could not be a moral system based upon dishonour, deceit and debility.

C. S. Lewis' hero Ransom, newly arrived upon Mars, sees some of the inhabitants approaching by boat and is comforted to see that it looks very much like an earthly boat; until he pauses to wonder what else a boat could look like.[6] In the same way we may well wonder what else a moral system could look like. There are limits to diversity. It is not just chance that we have the moral rules we do have: even though anthropologists may bring us word of strange customs and philosophers may amuse themselves by imagining moralities in which not walking on the lines of a pavement or clapping one's hands every two hours are considered important.[7] Sometimes natural law can seem to be left far behind; but to such oddities we can give an answer which is a little more than a brisk 'what nonsense'. We can say that to give these strange samples of morality any significance we should have to link them with ideas that do make sense in terms of the human beings that we are, ideas such as reverence or discipline or corporate unity. If we cannot do this, they are not samples of morality.[8] The notion of what befits our nature is not just a slogan but sets some real limits to what we can call moral.

But surely there have been and still are horrible moralities which could never be brought into one system? Human sacrifice and the burning of witches are not theoretical inventions and have presumably been considered right and proper by those who have done them. When horrors are commended and thought fitting, as distinct from wickedly perpetrated, it is for reasons which latch on to what we can call morality. This enemy is not 'one of us': his sufferings do not count. This sacrifice is necessary so that strength can flow into the next generation. This old woman is in league with the devil: the penalty must be the highest. Mercy would be a weakness, worse for everyone in the end.

It may be practically pointless and even dangerous to argue about human nature with people who hold views like these, but the argument is not logically pointless. We still seem to inhabit one moral world. We would hope, if only circumstances were more propitious, to find out and be able to show which ways of being human really are best; which systems of morality are indeed fulfilling. We would expect to discover this eventually by finding that people are actually fulfilled. So instead of jumping straight from goodness to happiness, we first try to make sense of morality in terms of fittingness, and then of fittingness in terms of fulfilment. Of course we must keep in mind that 'fulfilment' is not a plain factual concept like 'fullness'. To believe in natural law could be to hang on nonetheless to the conviction that fulfilment does have something definite to do with fact. Whether people are fulfilled is not a mere matter of opinion but is, in the last resort, recognizable.[9]

Christians have an authoritative image to help here. If we look on ourselves as children of God, we can consider what is good for human beings in terms of what a father wants for his family, and see more clearly that utilitarianism is nearly but not quite adequate. Of course parents bringing up their children will by no means reject the idea that they are aiming at their 'greatest happiness'; but they will be uneasy and start making qualifications if it is suggested that this is the whole story. Certainly contentment is not all one asks for one's children; and there are inhuman sorts of happiness which it needs no calculation to repudiate for them. What matters is that they should become their true selves and fulfil their promise. Talk of natural law is at its best when it encourages this emphasis on what is right for human beings because they are human.

What all this has in common with Bishop Butler is a solid appreciation that happiness does matter, in independence from the utilitarian notion that the way to achieve it is to calculate the consequences of our actions. We have to recognize the complaint that this way of making sense of morality as that which befits the creatures we are does not give us much specific guidance about what in fact we ought to do. In practice, it is only fair to admit that when moralists make definite announcements purporting to be based on human nature, the results are apt to be unconvincing.[10] The gain we may hope for in talking like this is different. To borrow Bishop Butler's language about the moral constitution of human beings allows us, not to set up particular laws, but to state problems in such a way as to do justice to their complexity. It may be patience we need rather than ready answers. We cannot say simply that nature tells us what conscience requires. What we hope eventually to be able to say is that conscience will tell us what nature requires, because 'what nature requires' means something real.

Still it may be complained that Bishop Butler's account of human nature solves no moral problems. At least it allows us to do justice to their intractability. Butler is not wont to draw our attention to such alarming problems as the unfinished story of Jim and the Indians,[11] but he should be able to help us to understand ethically both Jim's wish to comply and his reluctance to do so. An analysis of the case in Butler's terminology might go something like this.

Jim's natural repulsion and fear at the situation in which he finds himself are 'particular passions'. As a peaceful botanist, he really wants just to run away, or perhaps he is angry enough to long to knock the gun out of the captain's hand and take sides directly with the miserable, subjugated Indians. But these are unregulated impulses, evidently hopeless in this situation. Self-love and benevolence speak with one voice here, which would be no surprise to Butler, to tell Jim to keep calm.

Now in the story it is benevolence rather than self-love which is controlling Jim's aims: the plain wish to do good to other people directly, not as a means to some good of one's own. The question, once we refuse to go all the way with the utilitarians, is what Conscience will say. We are really asking whether it adds anything significant to our account to talk about conscience at all? In answer, it may be suggested that what conscience is apt to say first is 'Hold on'.

Moral theories that make difficult problems look easy must surely be mistaken. A man of principle is inclined to say that to shoot the Indian is simply wrong and never mind the unhappiness refusal will cause. A utilitarian is inclined to say that not to shoot the Indian is simply wrong and never mind the principle which is no more than a rule of thumb. Maybe, after all, Jim's conscience will vouchsafe the utilitarian answer and Jim will decide to shoot the one Indian as the least bad course open to him. But he is not stuck, as an utilitarian seemingly must be, in this answer. This could be a case where benevolence is over-adequate, needing to be heeded but perhaps not obeyed. Perhaps this is a time when conscience 'magisterially exerts itself'[12] to insist that what natural goodwill wants here is not fitting conduct for a human being. Bishop Butler's terminology of human nature under the authority of conscience can allow us to honour the integrity of a man who, in good faith, cannot see his way to do the evidently benevolent act. Conversely, we can honour integrity without making it an arbitrary tyranny. We need not reduce benevolence and the happiness it aims at to the status of a mere temptation. Conscience will disallow any idea that Jim is good just by having high principles, still less by 'meaning well', if his principles and his well-meaning are horrible for everyone else.

Certainly it seems anachronistic to imagine Butler entering into the agony of helping to solve Jim's problem; but there is a wisdom in not trying too decisively to sort out contrived situations. It is real problems, not imaginary ones, that have real answers. It takes a novelist, not a moralist, to make fiction real enough for human judgment. If Jim shoots an Indian, it will be the whole detail of the situation and the interrelationships of everyone's points of view that will determine what his action really is: a co-operation in a willing sacrifice (maybe one Indian stands forward); a desperate though excusable lapse from virtue; an unconscious expression of a suppressed blood-lust; a hearkening or a deafness to God's word; a bold acceptance of the logic of the situation; a piece of rank folly bound to lead to disaster? (Perhaps the captain never meant to keep his word, or the family of the slain man will start a blood-feud.) The story could be worked out in any of these ways and more. Only by being worked out in reality can it have an actual solution.

How does it help then to bring conscience in? Unless somehow the idea of conscience can be given more content, it seems to be no more than the name of a problem. Partly, that is what it is. This way of talking about moral questions is a way of showing that there *is* a problem to which utilitarianism is too simple an answer, just as a plain dogmatism of rules is too simple an answer. But perhaps the notion of conscience as a regulating principle of human nature can do a little more for us. It could be the name not only of a problem but of a sort of faith, that real questions can have real answers.

Such a faith is not necessarily, though characteristically, religious. It is a faith in the creative capacity of human beings: a Christian will say, of human creatures. It would let us keep open the sample problems offered for our decision, and not succumb to the temptation to provide advance recipes, whether of principle or expediency. As Butler put it,

> From his make, constitution, or nature, man is in the strictest and most proper sense a law to himself. He hath the rule of right within: what is wanting is only that he honestly attend to it.[13]

To say 'conscience must decide' could be a way of saying, 'I must decide and I can decide if I put my heart into it.' To handle moral problems creatively is to face them in their recalcitrant reality and bring to bear upon them all the resources of common sense and goodwill which it is our human duty and need to accumulate all our lives; in the hope that these resources will be backed also by some kind of inspiration from within or without. As Oman put it long ago in *Grace and Personality*,

> To be independent moral persons, legislating for ourselves, is not only not hostile to true knowledge and right sense of God, but is the imperative condition without which God can neither be known nor served.[14]

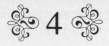

4

Who Chooses?

'I must decide.' It is an attractive notion that morality is about choice: a much more attractive notion, to many contemporary thinkers, than the idea that morality is about obedience to the law of nature. I am arguing that the two notions are in accord. It is not perverse to develop an emphasis on choice out of a natural law morality like Bishop Butler's. I am carefully not saying that the law of nature, whatever that is, will give orders to my conscience like a memorandum to an official. That way round we first beg all the questions about authority and then find no scope for choice. But conscience is not a subsidiary agent taking and giving orders. It is no less than myself as a moral creature. So the way we can travel from a morality of what is fitting for human nature to a morality of choice is by affirming that conscience can and must decide what *is* fitting for human nature, assuming this to be a real question which I can hope to answer. To obey conscience is to go on to put these decisions into practice; and of course human beings are fallible at all stages.

A sceptic or a Pelagian may take up the statement that conscience decides, that *I* decide, what befits my humanity in an aggressive way, making it an excuse to set me up on my own apart from God, but for Christians, on the contrary, this will be just the moment to build in all our ideas about God's grace. I 'can decide' because God is there in my conscience, not dictating to me or deciding for me but inspiring me to be myself. To say this is no platitude but a definite affirmation of belief.

So having begun with the idea that morality is something to do with realizing our true natures, we move on to do justice to the idea that realizing our true natures has everything to do with making choices. Natural law morality has a bad name for seeming to belittle human choices. It is supposed to be either static, as if nature were permanently fixed; or mechanical, as if nature were a computer printing out automatic answers. But for a Christian to say that goodness has a footing in nature is to appeal to creation, to the way things and people are made; and we can see for ourselves that creation is complicated, untidy and mobile. If we cannot take 'nature' to have at least the dynamic growing richness of the organic world we know, it is hard to see what point there is in using the idea. A natural law morality that does not make room for the more exuberant kinds of creativeness may not be exactly a contradiction in terms, but is surely letting its hands be tied behind its back. Our natures will not be fulfilled by inertness.

Christians believe that nature is not only exuberant but created by God, and that human beings in particular are made 'in God's image'. So they can be prepared to find themselves particularly at home with a morality which allows human beings a creativeness akin to God's. If we are small models of God, we may expect to be entrusted with some of His dynamic character. We are clay in His hands, but we are also supposed to have His spirit breathed into us.

But what about obedience? We are made to obey, not to branch out on our own. This has been emphasized ever since the story of God's creation was first told: but obedience is not automation. We may say it is more like tending God's garden than parading for drill. When it comes to finding out what obedience requires of us in practice, we must think of our God as Creator of this complicated universe that we live in. To obey such a God seems to imply for us, who are made in His image, no lifeless conformity but scope for imagination and inspiration. Our faith need not oblige us to approach problems about what to do like a set of exercises with the answers all at the end of the book ready to be looked up.[1] Instead we must realize that often the answer is not anywhere at all yet, but has to be made. We must respect the raw material we have been given and try to make something worthwhile of it. Deciding really is deciding, not totting up anything. There is no short cut to the knowledge of good and evil, and to look for short cuts can be one sort of disobedience.

Of course 'being good' includes resisting temptations to disobey, as one set of moralists always remind us; and of course it includes making people happy, as another set of moralists insist; but neither of these models does justice to creativeness of choice. Shall I become a lawyer? Shall we get married? Should I encourage her to have an abortion? Ought this handicapped child to be placed in an institution? Shall we move house? How can these people get on better with each other? How shall I cast my vote? Can I forgive her? What all these real questions facing human beings have in common is that when the decisions are made, whether according to principle or consequences, the working out of the answers begins not ends. They are not done with a yes or a no. Somebody has to make them good, develop or redeem them. An act, well-intentioned or ill, is hardly ever 'done when 'tis done'. Even the characteristic time-seizing choices of the gospels, 'come', 'repent', 'follow', are not complete with a yes, though the chance may be lost with a no. Presumably Judas had once said yes to the sort of opportunity that the rich young man rejected, but his yes ended in a despairing no. Doing right or wrong is not like throwing a pebble into a pond and watching the ripples spread. It is more like joining in a dance.

But how impromptu is the dance? And for whose pleasure is it? It is time to drop analogies and face the question, the fundamental question, of how far we are to take the morality of choice. For one reason why choice has been so popular of late among moral philosophers has been a deep, and moral, distrust of the whole idea of making obedience an important moral category at all. Since the Nazi concentration camps, to say 'I acted under orders' is a dubious excuse. On the contrary, there is another notion to which our contemporaries respond: the notion of *autonomy*, the moral freedom to choose our own goals as well as shape the means to them. But this is a concept in the presence of which religious moralists are bound to feel on edge, anxious if not actually hostile, for fear lest the authority of God is going to be impugned. Even if Adam and Eve could be creative in the Garden of Eden, they could not be autonomous. There is a real divergence here.

One proper Christian reaction is a robust confidence that God can look after His own authority and that human beings will serve Him best, not by cautious attempts to placate or protect Him, but by following the moral argument where it leads, in the faith that if we do this with energy and integrity it will, in God's universe, lead us home at last. So it is incumbent upon us not to reject out of hand the insistence of some contemporary moral philosophers that the choice of right and wrong is one's own through and through. It is no good merely to label them overweening. If we differ from them, we ought to take some care to see where and how. There are several layers of agreement to be uncovered before we reach stark disagreement.

Choosing for oneself can come into morality at several levels. First, it is common ground that a moral agent is a free agent. He must not be *coerced*: he must act for himself. If people are given no choice, their moral responsibility is destroyed. As Christians put it, God wants people to choose to serve Him freely and is prepared even to risk their rebellion. Secondly, we do not want a moral agent to be *naive*: he must understand for himself. He must not give unthinking obedience. Thirdly, a moral agent is not be be *inert*: he must decide for himself. He has real work to do which he cannot expect somebody else to do for him. The argument of this chapter so far has been that the free choice to obey God will demand going on to make many choices about *what* to do to obey God. We are indeed His servants: are we perhaps civil servants in His ministry, with policies laid down by statute but plenty of decisions to make in their execution? A Christian, of all people, ought not to be prejudiced against the idea of the free moral agent. Nor need he have a special enthusiasm for ready-made moral answers. It is nonsense for him to be averse to freedom or creativeness.

It is the next level which is uncomfortable for Christians, the level at which the moral agent is supposed to be *sovereign*, not under orders at all. Here, not before, is the awkward ethical sticking-point. The problem is that however splendid human freedom and creativeness may appear, they must in any Christian scheme of things give way at last to what God decides is best for human fulfilment. It is excellent to be what Kant called 'a legislating member of the kingdom of ends', but if the 'kingdom of ends' is also the kingdom of heaven, there must be a final appeal against any human decision. God's royal assent is no rubber stamp.

Insist as we may that the sovereign will of God is not tyrannical
or mechanical, and that it is for us to work out our own salvation,
it is still for God to allow that we have worked it out properly and
to recognize when His will is being done. For faithful believers
all true morality, however diverse it may be as it develops, must
sooner or later *converge*. We may claim to be humanists and
emphasize fulfilment, but still a fulfilment which is pre-
ordained. The end of man is not self-realization but to glorify
God and enjoy Him for ever. If it matters totally that we should
find our peace in God's will, it cannot matter totally that we
should find our own morality. Does this mean that Christian
fulfilment is essentially prefabricated? If it does mean this, does
it matter?

Certainly any talk of a single end of man, a human nature
somehow laid down for us, is apt to sound naive today. It does not
easily hold its own in sophisticated company. If Christians want
to insist that all real values are bound to converge at last and find
their consummation in the will of God, they seem to be
committed to a distinctly intractable and cut-and-dried sort of
morality. Our fulfilment seems eventually to be forced upon us.
We have to imagine a kind of ideal point at which all our diverse
aims and goals will somehow neatly coalesce and be fulfilled.
But if so, what has become of the great principle of the Autonomy
of Ethics? How can we freely choose a compulsory end?

A comprehensible Christian reaction at this point is to say that
the whole discussion is preposterous: of course Christian
morality is compulsory and intractable. The moral agent is not
meant to be entirely his own master. Human beings, we are
reminded, are rebellious creatures who have abused their
autonomy, and that is the meaning of the story of the Fall. Indeed,
sophisticated moralists are exactly what Adam and Eve represent. They wanted to find their own fulfilment and that it seems
is just where they went wrong. So we have a head-on clash
between the trustful believer whose highest aim is to serve God
and receive His ready-made blessings, and the high-minded
sceptic who approves of Adam and Eve and disapproves of
religious morality, not because he wants to be free to be bad, but
because he does not hold with predetermined values.

Ecumenically-minded Christians do not like head-on clashes
with unbelievers. They prefer to feel sorry for them. They can

hardly comprehend a sceptic who glories in his unbelief. They are more inclined to look upon him as a man forlorn and lost without the meaning which faith gives to the world, like a child who (as Professor Hepburn once put it) 'has awakened not in the familiar, friendly nursery in which he fell asleep, his parents within easy call, but in a desolate wilderness where no one knows of him, no one answers his cry'.[2]

It is tempting to patronize unbelievers and then blame them when they do not want our sympathy. If at this stage we merely reaffirm undefended our traditional ethic of obedience, we shall miss the moral point of those serious sceptics who believe that the loss of faith is a liberation: who do not want the meaning that Christians give to life, the ethical certainties and dogmatisms of the Christian church. These thinkers believe that it is up to human beings to find their own meanings, even to construct them, not to accept them as given.

Those who make this stand are not simply being awkward. It is not a question of trying to set up the rights of moral agents, a sort of 'creature's lib'. It is a matter of the irreducible character of goodness itself.[3] So far we have paid a due deference to the principle that moral goodness is not to be identified with anything other than itself, but we have not yet faced it head on. To insist upon the Autonomy of Ethics is an attempt to safeguard what is special about value. 'This is good' must not be allowed to disappear into 'This is how things are' or 'This is how things will be'. For many thinkers the main thing to say about ethics is that *ought* must never be reduced to *is*, not even to 'This *is* God's will'. Facts and values have to be different kinds of concept.

There are three great names which are much bandied about at this stage. First and foremost there is Hume, who pointed out, in one of the most quoted passages in modern philosophy, that as long as we put nothing but *is* into our arguments, we cannot expect to have the right to draw out *ought*.[4] To say that there is a God or that the world is like this or that does not immediately show that anything is good or our duty: there is a stage missing in many moral proofs. If we say 'Remember now thy Creator', we need to show that we mean more than 'God is watching so look out'. To believe that certain states of affairs will as a matter of fact fulfil human needs does not allow us to go on and make free with the high moral connotations of 'fulfilment'.

Secondly, John Stuart Mill is made into an awful warning for falling into this very error and confusing the 'desired' and the 'desirable'.[5] It can be argued that Mill himself was being more subtle, but the mistake itself remains a trap for the unwary. To say that something is desired (by anyone, even God) does not establish that it is worth desiring. That is another step, which no amount of information about the bare facts will entitle us to make. If 'I like it' does not entail 'I ought to do it', how can 'It is God's will' entail 'You ought to do it'? Of course it does entail this for believers, but only because they are building in assumptions which ought to be made explicit. So Christian moralists need to be careful what they say in case they seem not to know the precept 'Thou shalt not get an *ought* from an *is*'.

Thirdly, there is G. E. Moore, who gave a name to the dread error of defining goodness in non-moral terms. Since his painstaking exposition of the argument,[6] philosophers have had a lively fear of committing 'the naturalistic fallacy'. Religious and secular theories alike come under this axe. Duty must not be reduced to benefit, nor goodness to usefulness, nor right conduct to obedience. The Autonomy of Ethics means that values and facts have to be independent of each other. 'Eat up your crusts to make your hair curl' leaves me free to say 'But I don't want my hair to curl'. 'Behave or I'll spank you' has as little to do with real morality. Any kind of pre-ordained goodness in this world or the next which we must at last conform to rather than choose is suspect, according to this way of thinking. Moral theories which treat values as matters of fact, as things we can find in the world like objects, have been given the name of 'naturalistic' theories.

For many moral philosophers this battle has been won. Of course the picture is not simple and theories which put the emphasis the other way have had authoritative exponents;[7] but it would be fair to say that what is called 'non-naturalism' has been in the ascendant. 'Naturalism' is often assumed to be discredited, a Goliath who has succumbed to the sling of David Hume.

What non-naturalist moral philosophers are determined to do is keep facts and values apart. To do this they have developed and refined a distinction between 'describing' and 'evaluating'. To describe, in this technical terminology, is to state a neutral fact, such as 'This is red', or 'She put arsenic in his coffee'. To evaluate is to go further and cease to be simply factual: 'This is a glorious colour', or 'That was very wrong'. The point of making this distinction is to give morality a real purchase on human life. Bare facts, it is pointed out, are just facts, to which people can merely reply 'Oh yes'. A fact is, so to speak, inert: we know as a piece of information that kindness is enjoined upon us, but why should *I* bother to be kind? It takes more than a statement of fact, it takes a live value, to guide my actions. I must not only recognize but choose what is good if I claim to understand the meaning of goodness. So choices, not facts, are set up as the heart of morality.

The early results of this way of thinking were to make morality look merely subjective in a way totally unacceptable to religious belief.[8] 'This is good' was supposed to mean something about me, not about 'this'. 'I like this', or 'This gives me a feeling of approval', were what moral statements were really saying. So moral language seemed to be reduced to expressions of taste or emotion and objective values seemed to have evaporated. When we tried to state moral truths all we seemed able to do was say something like 'Hurrah' or 'Please'.

Those days have gone by. It is quite wrong now to caricature contemporary moral philosophy as if it were simply 'subjectivist' or 'emotivist'. On the contrary, consistency and rationality have come into the front of the picture again. The moral theory which is called 'prescriptivism' faces the problem of how we can make morality come to life for us, make it 'our own', without making it only too much our own, a merely subjective matter of taste. The solution which is offered is that characteristic moral language does not merely express our own feelings or our likes and dislikes, any more than it merely states facts. What moral language does is *prescribe* our choices to other people. So choice is indeed set up as fundamental to value, but if it is to be moral choice it cannot be private or arbitrary. Moral choice is capable of being generalized, of being commended to anyone else in like circumstances. If I say it is right to tell a lie, not just convenient to tell a lie, I am recommending you to lie to me as well as choosing to tell a lie myself. The key word for the prescriptivist moral philosopher is 'universalizability'.

Christians have no right to think of all this as external to their proper concerns. It is far from being an aberration of hostile sceptics. The current non-naturalism is not anti-Christian, and certainly not in the person of its most distinguished exponent, Professor Hare. Moral philosophers have every right to complain if they find religious believers simply joining battle with them, not listening to what they have to say, on the assumption that they must be a destructive influence. To try to keep values distinct from facts is not an immoral enterprise. Those who attempt it are firmly on the side of goodness.

The question is whether all this reasonableness and responsibility conceals a deep-seated incompatibility with what Christians need to say about the will of God. It is suspected, with some reason, that Christian moralists are shaky on this distinction between describing and evaluating; and so perhaps they are. In a way, they have to be. They are determined to make statements like 'God shall be all in all', which cannot be placed neatly on one side or the other of the fact/value line. It cannot be a neutral statement of what is going to happen about which we can then make our own moral judgments. Nor can it be a moral evaluation which commits us to no statement of fact. When God's will is done in earth as it is in heaven, the *ought* and the *is* may be said to converge. If Christianity is the ultimate truth, it seems that this convergence must be somehow *bound* to happen and we *bound* to approve it. Value and fact must coalesce at last: so a Christian can hardly help being some sort of ethical naturalist, whether he wants to be or not and whether he can justify his position to philosophers or not. He cannot go all the way with the autonomy of ethics. Yet nor can he brush it aside.

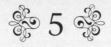

5

Autonomy and Authority

'I went shopping and I bought . . .' is a cumulative family game to stave off travel sickness on longish journeys. A similar reiteration now, at a like risk of adding a tedium of its own, may help us to keep a grip of the argument so far. Happiness matters: though staleness and the fear of being mercenary may mask this truth. When we let ourselves emphasize happiness, we may be tempted to take 'the greatest happiness of the greatest number' as the whole story; but natural law, unfashionable as it is, can offer a more adequate picture of the fulfilment for which human beings were made. Carefully explained, natural law gives no cut-and-dried regulations but a conviction of the normality of goodness, an assurance that there is some point in trying. It does not circumscribe choice but demands it. We have the potentially creative task of finding out what conscience requires.

So far, so good; but choice, given an inch, will take an ell. To put choice at the heart of morality sounds constructive; to say that we are to choose our own morality sounds outrageous; yet somehow the one statement slides into the other. Likewise, to insist that values are independent of facts (the Autonomy of Ethics) sounds admirable; to say that value is something each person must choose for himself (the autonomy of the moral agent) sounds much more dubious, but tends to follow. The attractive and promising realization that a person is not some sort of robot but a living, choosing being can lead on into the denigration of everything that is controllable. Continental existentialism, stressing choice as pure spontaneity, has taken this very far. True morality has had to be an arbitrary opting without structure or criteria, on pain of 'bad faith'. In Britain, the emphasis on choice has not been existentialist: we are to live by principles, not from moment to moment; but it has been stressed that in the last resort our principles must be our own, subject only to consistency among themselves. Professor Hare quite bluntly took this as his starting point, the very basis of his problem, in *Freedom and Reason*. 'We are free to form our own moral opinions in a much stronger sense than we are free to form our own opinions as to what the facts are.'[1] This is the freedom which he has set himself to reconcile with reason. In this way of thinking, it is not just a wrench to give up our own autonomy: it is actually unethical. We cannot lay our moral responsibility upon anybody else.

All this is convincing, even inspiring, for the humanist, but for the anti-humanist it only serves to confirm his worst suspicions that to begin by asserting the importance of happiness is to end unrepentantly in a free-for-all, in which 'all we like sheep have gone astray and are turned every one to his own way'. What has become of God's will in all this? Does it count for nothing? How can we so proudly make values 'our own' without making it a matter of chance if they are also God's? Yet values that are not our own are not values to us.

If Christian humanists keep their heads they will have plenty more to say: but they had better say it with precision. They may reasonably object to the crude theology which makes God's will something simply distinct from human wills in this clear-cut way. Does God not will *through* our wills? Unfortunately the sorts of things Christians want to say about God's grace are not necessarily going to have much impact at this stage in the argument. To assume prematurely and superficially that we can simply rely upon God to bring our recalcitrant wills into line with His can look like papering over the cracks in our morality. To offer union with God's will as a kind of prefabricated fulfilment can easily look, from the point of view of a secular moralist, like a temptation luring people away from the self-realization which is both their right and their duty. To remind ourselves that we are meant to be 'in' Him and He 'in' us is theologically accurate but morally difficult. It can look confusingly like pantheism which sinks human autonomy for good in the divine being.[2]

What Christian morality is up against here is not the attitude of a group of unsteady disciples or awkward dissentients, but a developing orthodoxy which has increasingly been putting the onus of proof upon those who hold out against it. According to this orthodoxy it is the authoritarians who are the new heretics and must now learn the error of their ways. In this atmosphere a Christian who has doubts about autonomy may feel nervous about even trying to formulate his uncertainty, let alone giving it weight. A humanist-minded Christian can feel trapped here by history, conscious of an over-authoritarian church down the centuries, anxious not to become identified with an illiberal tradition. If eventually one is going to criticize and limit the doctrine of autonomy, it is both honest and diplomatic to appreciate it on the way, to proceed by doing justice to its merits.

The morality of choice has a lot to offer. It sees human beings as active people, not just as puppets. It is a dynamic morality, both as a theory and in its application. Choice lets value come to life and bridges the threatening gap between inert 'fact' and moral 'act'. It gets rid of the silly question with which the plain man can pester moral philosophers: 'I know that is right, but why should I bother?'

In applying this morality in practice, we find ourselves concerned with the sorts of things people really mind about. This way of 'doing ethics' is much more lively than the dry discussion of pedestrian duties like returning borrowed books, to which philosophers were prone between the wars. A good many of Professor Hare's examples are political, having to do with such matters as race and the treatment of prisoners. He has concerned himself, as a moral philosopher, with social questions such as abortion, town planning,[3] and education. For him morality asks 'What am I to do?' where it really matters; and religious moralists can happily agree that when we make choices we are at our most human.

The current stress on autonomy is not a bee in philosophical bonnets but a responsible programme for the betterment of human life which claims serious attention. Of course hardly anyone is fully autonomous in practice. Most of us accept our morality mechanically from other people and find this quite satisfactory; but when we stop to think we are supposed to realize that autonomy, not conformity, is the proper ideal, and that 'heteronomy', the rule of others, will not do for responsible moral agents. We are reminded of Mark Twain's Huckleberry Finn, whose failure to see this, portrayed in straightfaced irony, provides a classic example of heteronomy. He helped a runaway slave to escape and was tormented by his conscience for not resisting the temptation to make free with somebody else's property.

It has to be admitted that the case for autonomy is apt to be put more sensitively, with more regard for real humanity, than the case for a downright moral authority. The philosophical journals teem with articles in which ethical theory is worked out with the responsible care of people who are not unaware that what they write may have practical bearings. It is not suggested that we are to choose our principles 'as we choose our hats and ties',[4] rather that we discover in practice 'what considerations really matter to us, or, what amounts to the same thing, who we really are'; and that 'such discoveries are possible only to the extent that we are autonomous'.[5] The 'heteronomous man', who always looks to someone else, will not have the vigour or courage to develop a worthwhile morality. Autonomy need not mean making up our own morality as we go along. Huckleberry Finn's bothersome conscience has been taken in hand by Professor Jonathan Bennett: 'What Huck didn't see is that one can live by principles and yet have ultimate control over their content. And one way such control can be exercised is by checking of one's principles in the light of one's sympathies.'[6]

So autonomous morality is attractively presented. Like any orthodoxy, it has to consider how to hand on its way of life to the next generation. Here, at this important meeting place of ethical theory and actual reality, the anti-authoritarian doctrine can claim a strong position. It has plenty to say about the upbringing and education of the young. Professor Hare has applied his 'prescriptivism' here with delightful clarity.[7] He has taken the problem of young hooligans as an example, and suggested that their elders' bafflement is due to a philosophical mistake. The old-style moralists have been trying to teach right and wrong as facts not as choices. In other words, they have been holding a naturalist theory of morality and are not distinguishing properly between describing and evaluating.

More in sorrow than in anger, and with his tongue gently in his cheek, Professor Hare characterized 'descriptivist families', who have 'quite failed to diagnose the disease which afflicts them'. Their children 'know perfectly well that all sorts of things, from growing their hair long to extra-marital sex and to murder, are wrong; but they do not see that that is any reason for abstaining from them'.[8] They have, as it were, a list of conduct which their elders would describe as 'wrong'; they can use the word entirely correctly; but there is a gap between this factual knowledge and their own actions. So the remedy becomes apparent: to teach them to choose what is right and wrong like good prescriptivists. Once they see that moral problems are their own problems which nobody can answer for them, morality will come to bear upon their lives.

Here at its moment of triumph autonomy runs into its great difficulty. If we teach people to choose, they may choose differently. Moral judgments may diverge. We must hope they will not diverge too far. Professor Hare's critics have given him a lot of trouble over the moral status of the fanatic, the man with whom it is no use arguing because he just chooses differently from the rest of us. It has been presented as an unattractive but needful part of a morality which insists on autonomy to allow even the fanatic to choose his own values, to be a hooligan or even a racist or a terrorist provided that he is prepared to take the consequences, to be in his turn a victim of his own prescriptions if 'universalizability' works out that way. If we appeal to choice, to choice we must go.

Humanly speaking, this sounds acceptable. It answers to what we are actually inclined to think about people with deeply-held moral convictions which seem preposterous to us. The only way we can argue with them, as distinct from bandying commandments or resorting to force, is by trying to show them the full implications of their views for themselves and others; and if that fails reason is indeed stuck. So the likelihood remains, if we care about autonomy, that morality may become a good deal more diverse than some of us will find comfortable.

There is a good deal the prescriptivist can do to keep the divergence of morality under control. He must go on insisting that what is prescribed must be prescribed universally. It is no good his children choosing hooliganism unless they are prepared for my children to be hooligans too. If they want their chaos to be allowed within a framework of order, they must be prepared both to back up the order where they believe it is good and to tolerate other people's chaos on the same terms as their own. An imaginative prescriptivist can make a great deal of play, both emotionally and logically, with the argument, 'How would *you* like it?'

Professor Hare has taken this argument so far in his latest book[9] that he has explicitly become a kind of utilitarian: at some risk to his prescriptivism, as he himself recognizes. At the end of the book he even wonders whether it is worth going on refusing the label of 'descriptivist'.[10] Yet he still does refuse it. He will not allow ethics to be a matter of fact, however much our prescriptions in matters which affect other people are bound to converge. Objectivity in morals still has to be suspect in the name of choice. There is still what he calls the 'amoralist escape route', which lets someone avoid utilitarianism, quite consistently, by refusing to make moral judgments at all.[11] More importantly, Professor Hare will still found his 'rational universal prescriptivism' not on stable upstanding 'values' but on 'shifting facts about people's prescriptions'. So he ends by reaffirming choice as 'the liberty we all have to prefer what we prefer'. 'Reason leaves us with our freedom,' he concludes, 'but constrains us to respect the freedom of others, and to combine with them in exercising it.'[12]

So it is prescribed that we shall learn to respect the moral freedom of other people. Like other moral lessons, this proposed twentieth-century one is admitted to be not easy. In an essay explaining the work of the Farmington Trust at Oxford, John Wilson put the case disarmingly: 'The educator will find it hard to set aside his own likes and dislikes . . . and pursue single-mindedly the educational goal of getting the pupils to see for themselves what is good and bad.'[13] It is, to say the least, a hard thing to learn to look on one's own values as prejudices, but the bait we are offered is that the next generation shall learn to make functioning moral judgments for themselves, to grow into their own standards rather than putting them on like someone else's clothes.[14]

Those who have been offering us this bait have taken trouble to explain that they are not belittling moral knowledge or denying objective values. It is not moral answers that are impugned, only second-hand moral answers. Indoctrination, however well-meant, is excluded as a way of teaching morality, but it does not have to be concluded that choice is merely subjective. The values we are teaching people to look for are still allowed to be real, but we are forbidden to teach them directly. It is skills not ideas that we are to impart. The analogy of the scientific method and the way it arrives at sound answers is given.[15]

The same moral approach has been made familiar to students of psychology. For instance, Derek Wright's standard book, *The Psychology of Moral Behaviour*, has things to say which fit in nicely with prescriptivism. He sorts out different moral types and the one he praises is the 'altruistic-autonomous' character, who 'chooses the rules he lives by, and feels free to modify them with increased experience':[16] as, presumably, Huckleberry Finn ought to have done. Schools, Wright believes, can develop such autonomous characters, if they are places where pupils find in the staff 'unanimity over the importance of commitment to basic moral principles coupled with diversity of judgment about their application'.[17]

Dispelling a lingering recollection of a description of people who 'sweat with conviction about nothing in particular', one is tempted simply to go along with this because one does not want to be dubbed an 'authoritarian personality'. Wright ends his book, 'There has also been the more daring hope that it might edge some readers towards a greater autonomy in their own moral life . . .'[18] and it is not easy to resist such a challenge, particularly when as a Christian one is conscious of being in an exposed position. Religion is not being attacked; yet one knows uneasily that it has often been open to attack here, and if as a Christian one is ready to give warm approval to autonomy, maybe the critics of the Christian tradition in this matter will be willing to let bygones be bygones. But doubts recur and there comes a point where it looks like cowardice or laziness, not toleration, to keep on squashing them.

Must diversity always be admired? The 'open society' is a splendid ideal, but without any wish to play God or to run other people's lives one can still be haunted by a discontent with the apparent conclusion that it does not matter *what* is chosen so long as the moral agent chooses freely and responsibly. Is 'you

choose' being given too much advantage over 'we know'?
Prescriptivism has been caricatured as 'my morality – neither
right nor wrong but *my own*'.[19] Has morality anything to get its
teeth into if our values are allowed to be self-generated and self-
justifying? That way moral scepticism lies, in Professor Renford
Bambrough's sense of the inability to 'recognize the existence or
the possibility of such a thing as moral knowledge'.[20]

Christians can hardly be moral sceptics in this or any other
sense, but it is not easy to keep belief in moral knowledge and
belief in autonomy alive both at once. Professor H. L. A. Hart, in
an interesting article on Professor Hare's *Freedom and Reason*,
has put the problem in a nutshell: 'If the thing that matters
when a man is faced with a moral problem is that the answer he
gives should be the right answer, how can we say that the thing
that matters is that the answer he gives should be *his* answer:'[21]
The whole difficulty is akin to the old dilemma 'Is it my duty to
do what *is* right or what I *think* is right?', but for a believer it has
a sharper edge. Does God mind what we choose as well as how
we choose it? Is He on the side of right answers or autonomous
decisions? Surely His will has a definite content: He commands,
not only commends, if only we can find out what. This foetus
ought, or ought not, to be aborted. This valley ought, or ought
not, to be flooded for a reservoir. However sure we are that God
can redeem our choices, we dare not say that it is all one to Him.
In making up our minds, we are trying to ascertain something
real which is the will of God.

What then guarantees that autonomy will bring us, on our
feet, to the same place at which authority would wish to round
us up? If you and I fundamentally disagree about values, I can
call you a fanatic; but we cannot call God a fanatic. Can we
count on the Almighty turning out in the end to be a liberal
Protestant?[22] If we seem to find Him tyrannical, what appeal
have we? Or if He is *too* liberal for some people, have they also
the right to their opinion? What are we to say on behalf of our
God to Nietzsche, or maybe to a modern Muslim, who main-
tains that the Christian style of mercy is soft?

It is a moral answer we need. The problem is not changed,
only sharpened, by having God brought into it. It is still the
problem of how to maintain any convictions about the substance of morality if we also care about moral autonomy. What

Christianity does here is keep us insisting that we must care about *what* is good, because we believe God cares. We cannot happily relinquish any definite content to our ethics, even for the sake of autonomy.

As Christians we are bound to try to redress the balance between the morality we choose and the morality we find; but we need not suppose ourselves to be alone in this enterprise. Philosophers as well as Christian moralists have been voicing concern here:[23] notably Bernard Williams who is far from being entirely happy with the morality that decides on principles instead of acknowledging them. The morality we choose 'seems a cheat, presenting itself to us as too like something which it is not'.[24] He goes on to speak, of 'discovery, trust, and risk' instead of decision.[25] Surely a Christian may well warm to this.

Likewise, Brenda Cohen has characterized 'the liberal's dilemma', in the specific context of how we are to bring up our children. How is the liberal 'to place these things about which he had deep and unshakeable moral conviction out of reach of the toleration and situationalism to which his position appears to commit him?'[26] Lying may be a matter for our own moral decision: racism decidedly not. S. I. Benn, after arguing persuasively on behalf of autonomy, has put the other side crisply: 'Of course, autonomy is not an exhaustive characterization of a personality. . . . If Cesare Borgia turned out to have been no less autonomous than Socrates, one would still be hard put to it to share Machiavelli's unqualified admiration. Autonomy may not be an all-embracing excellence, redeeming all the rest.'[27] Somehow or other we must make room for the substance of morality as well.

And of course the substance of morality will in any case make room for itself. Even the morality of autonomy cannot leave people free to fill in the content of morality for themselves, pride itself as it may upon doing so. The idea of a formal ethical theory which remains cleanly neutral between particular values is a chimera. No theory can help setting up certain characteristics of a worthwhile morality: for instance, flexibility, tolerance, reasonableness. We cannot be sure it is not doing this at the expense of other substantive qualities which we ought to be loath to relinquish.

To be value-free is not as easy as some people think. It can mean letting values creep in surreptitiously instead of acknowledging them openly. This is a lesson we need to keep learning and applying. Some of us first absorbed it from books which were new in the sixties, such as Paul Halmos' *The Faith of the Counsellors*[28] and Dorothy Emmet's *Rules, Roles and Relations*.[29] The lesson is not by any means out of date. In education, in journalism, in legislation, in medicine, we can still be threatened by pseudo value-free judgments which are dangerous because they involve 'a concealed, rather than an open and explicit, domination, one which is the more difficult to evade because it is not exercised by any particular individuals'.[30]

The danger is hard to fight without merely retreating to overt authoritarianism. As usual, we are between Scylla and Charybdis. If the whirlpool of autonomy does not sink us, the monster authority will gobble us up. It is a question of where we think the greater danger lies. The present argument is designed as a counterweight to complacency about the whirlpool: not to suggest complacency about the monster. It is intended as a corrective, and correctives ought not to claim finality.

Do we choose or do we find our morality? If we want to reply that the true answer is a matter of emphasis, we are not just saying that there is no true answer. It is a delicate matter to discern and express the truth in such a way that it can be received undistorted among the variegated preconceptions, sound and unsound of which human minds are never bare. One thinker's main point is another thinker's concession; one man's insight is another man's platitude. Of course we choose and of course we find, but how are the choosing and the finding to be fairly related?

6

Choosing and Finding

If we want to give *finding* its proper place in morality without belittling *choosing*, the best plan is to sort out the problem. Moral questions seem to arrange themselves in a sequence. At one end, choice prevails: What am I to do for a living? Where am I to give my loyalty? At the other end, we seem to have no choice at all: Is murder wrong? May I blacken my friend's character? The controversial range is in the middle: Must my loyalty, once given, be lifelong? Is abortion murder? What rights have human beings?

It is this middle range which is so hotly disputed between autonomy and authority. Each wants to overrun this important territory and annex it: for choice on the one hand, or duty on the other. The choosers want their decisions, say about abortion, to be responsible; the dutiful are unable to treat abortion as a matter for decision at all. So unprofitably at odds with one another, these moralists cannot join forces against the simply irresponsible and unscrupulous. But before the whole of morality is made into a battle-ground, choice can have quite a large area assigned to it. There are at least some moral questions which are not pre-determined. Human beings have to make decisions for themselves about satisfying and unsatisfying ways of life, and here anyway autonomy is thoroughly at home.[1] How are we to live? What is worth taking trouble over? What are we to aim at? Is activity or contemplation more important? Is excellence or peace more worth attaining? Are we to admire firmness or gentleness? Do we want roughness or fineness, informality or formality? Do we belive in splendour or simplicity? Does ambition add a spice to life? Is adventure a glorious end in itself, or a fearful contingency? How important is orderliness?

Surely we want to say that these kinds of questions are for human beings to decide and they have a real choice. It would be morally insensitive, not just practically unrealistic, to expect everyone to give identical or even converging answers to them. People are not single-minded, let alone unanimous, in settling them one way or another. They do not particularly want to be. Some would say these are not moral problems at all and simply detach them from the moral scale. Yet these questions matter morally. They are not mere matters of taste, if matters of taste are 'mere'. There are values here and where there are values it is defeatist to deny that there is morality.

Whatever we decide presently to say about finding, we have given choosing a significant place. We may invite agreement from moralists of different persuasions that choice leading to diversity is positively and importantly good at this end of the scale, that the world would be drearier and less worthwhile without it and therefore that here at least choice is to be welcomed into morality, not grudgingly tolerated.[2] Whatever destination we believe humanity ought to be looking for and however religious our approach to it, we do ill if we try to force everybody into one pattern of life on the way; and scarcely less ill if we wash our hands of the patterns they set about shaping, as if these simply did not matter. To exercise this kind of choice is one of the most 'moral' things human beings do. They need every encouragement to do it well.

All this sounds quite easy to agree with, but its consequences could be exacting. We cannot keep our notion of autonomy as a sort of pet, to bring out of its hutch and take for a run when we feel like it. Politically, the argument cuts both ways. Busybodies should take it to heart as a stringent demand to respect the free choice of other people. But some of us are only too ready to settle down in that blithe unconcern about others which is stigmatized as *laissez faire*. When we become aware that there are people who are simply not in a position to exercise these admirable life-shaping autonomous choices, we may find that something frankly political has to be done about it.

So, even in emphasizing choosing, we have slipped in finding. Morality, in its nature, makes demands upon us at all stages.

Soon we work our way on into the more central and controversial areas, where our choices and our obligations are hardest to relate, where the struggle between autonomy and authority is at its most urgent and least manageable.

This middle range of the scale is where the great moral arguments belong; and many of them have to do with sexual morality. There is no need to be surprised or apologetic about this. It is easy, indeed facile, to pour scorn on the human tendency to equate immorality with sex, but human beings are not always as silly as they seem. Of course sometimes they appear to be obsessed with sex, but they would be more unrealistic to try to make sex peripheral. 'Male and female created he them.' The making of a person by conception, birth, upbringing and relationships is the making of a man or a woman by men and women. Our duties, our expectations, our happiness and unhappiness are all profoundly coloured by the way we learn to understand ourselves and each other as masculine and feminine. What could be more to do with morality than this? Some see it all as a mass of perdition; some are able to recognize the image of God; some feel themselves engaged in an entirely human enterprise; some are at ease, some at odds, with their own natures; but nobody who applies moral categories at all can decline to apply them characteristically here. Partly overlapping with the sexual questions, partly distinct from them, are the strenuous enquiries about the boundaries of life and the ways we can honour and dishonour our fellow beings. What makes a life worth continuing, and at what cost? Who is to choose? When we have considered people's rights, what consideration do we give to their wishes? What is the shape of our responsibility here?

For behind all the particular discussions is the recurrent question about the scope for decision. Nobody is going to say that the rightness or wrongness of abortion or euthanasia is a matter of taste like the choice of a hobby: but how far is it from being a matter of taste? Have we arrived in a distinctive world of hard right and wrong, or are we still, though in a more fundamental way, talking about chosen styles of life? We cannot just decide for ourselves whether monogamy is best; or can we? It is not only Christians who are reluctant to make choosing the whole story. Somehow or other, like it or not, we have got to begin to reckon with moral truth not only moral options.[3] If I say 'I don't know anything about morality but I know what I like', I am being outrageous, not merely Philistine. Moral goodness, whatever it is, is not optional. But having said this, we are still pulled both ways. We cannot leave choice behind. We cannot make morality a simple conflict between obedient 'goodies' and disobedient 'baddies' or we beg the really perplexing questions about what ought to be done.

Of course in practice we live and make most of our decisions in terms of norms laid down by our society. Without norms we should probably go mad. But does norm or decision have the last word? Does it make sense to talk about choosing our own norms? This is where Professor Hare has been wont to take sides so firmly with choosing even at the expense of finding.[4] He has been much concerned to insist that we cannot make people agree with us morally. If an inquirer persists in asking, 'But why *should* I live like that?' there comes a time when the decision has to be thrown back to him:

> We can only ask him to make up his own mind which way he ought to live; for in the end everything rests upon such a decision of principle. He has to decide whether to accept that way of life or not; if he accepts it, then we can proceed to justify the decisions that are based upon it; if he does not accept it, then let him accept some other, and try to live by it.[5]

Here is the morality of choice at its most weighty; and here it is time to remember the objections. These fundamental 'decisions of principle' sounded splendid, until someone asks how they can possibly be made. It is high time to attend to the philosophical criticism that any such decision is essentially arbitrary. If reasoning has to come to an end, we are left with sheer commitment, taking sides freely but not rationally, plumping for a morality we cannot justify.[6]

So far, so bad. It is still quite tempting to think we must just accept this. If we have any claim to be humanist, the morality of choice looks sufficiently convincing and attractive to invite us to put up with its inconveniences. Our excitement about the important decisions we have to make combines readily with our respect for autonomy to let us be persuaded that all morality culminates in choice, even if this means that our moralities diverge. Relativism does not seem altogether unattractive, if it gives us an assortment of options. 'Any diminution in this variety' said Professor P. F. Strawson, 'would impoverish the human scene. The multiplicity of conflicting pictures is itself the essential element in one of one's pictures of man.'[7] Unless we are worried about what God will think, we can at least try to glory in the maturity and authenticity of our moral ways of life.

But so far is not the whole story, even humanly. We have not yet allowed for the full range of morality. It is no wonder that up to now the necessity for moral choice has been in the foreground, when the whole point of this central area of the moral scale is that this is where answers, though urgent, are not obvious and do not compel agreement. Sooner or later the morality of *finding* comes into its own. Already racism has given pause to liberal tolerance.[8] 'Choose your own values' evidently has its limitations. There is a whole range of cases, not just a handful of exceptions, where we simply are not free to do our own deciding. Here we are inclined to say with the old-fashioned intuitionist that we do not choose but see. It is all very well to imagine fanatics, to make allowance for variegated moralities, to refuse to judge other people; but still when we hear about somebody tormenting a child, betraying a friend, driving recklessly, or spreading malicious rumours, we are coming across something which we are bound to say bluntly is wrong.[9] To say anything else is at best cold-hearted and at worst corrupt. Extenuating circumstances may indeed extenuate, but they do not make conduct of these kinds a matter of choice.

We seem to have arrived at the sort of morality which we find and cannot make for ourselves or for anyone else. Even sexual morality, so persuasively portrayed since the advent of contraception as a matter of chosen lifestyles, has its clear prohibitions. We are not likely to start approving of rape. 'False Sextus who wrought the deed of shame' is not going to appear in an heroic light, though we may adjust our condemnation somewhat to give less weight to impurity and more weight to using a woman as an object.

This morality we discover rather than invent[10] appeals to us as human beings not only as believers in God. It does not have to be all negative. We may need reminding, but we are not going to disagree with the positive judgment that where we see misery, hurt and despair we ought to be willing to do what we can.[11] To turn one's back on someone in pain or starving is a real dereliction of duty. A person or a society that does not even try to comfort and help people in trouble is worse than a person or a society that shows human compassion. Our toleration of different ways of life, individual or corporate, does stop short of full relativism.

This means that when we come to think again about moral education, there are some matters which we cannot with integrity treat as open questions. It may be a marvellous example if a teacher is ready to change his own attitude about pacifism or sex if that is the way the argument goes;[12] but not, surely not, about bullying or cheating. Suppose that while he is excited by the diversity of moral opinions in his class, a tradition grows up that the big boys systematically torment the little ones for sport. They are quite happy to universalize their moral judgments about this. The small boys knuckle under obediently, awaiting their turn in the fullness of time. Are their parents being paternalist if they complain to the headmaster and ought they to accept his reply: 'It's all right: they are all fanatics. They are choosing this way of life freely'?

The school example may not sound quite fair, because pupils, by definition, are immature. They are not yet old enough to make their own moralities. Perhaps we are, or ought to be. Once we are grown up, do we still need to be told that choice has limitations? It may sound either tiresome or just platitudinous to make a great point of these. Do we really need to be reminded that fraud and torture are wrong and belong to ways of life which are not to be chosen? The answer is that to spell out the obvious is not always superfluous. Perhaps it may really help, when we meet a fanatic, to have some confidence in the judgments about moral reality which we share with our fellow human beings so that we can make some sort of stand upon them. There are mad worlds we need not enter, or only as it were with oxygen masks to rescue their victims.

More diffidently, a little more may be said. To take a rest from time to time on solid obvious morality may hearten us for cautious forays back into the disputed central area. It is not impossible that too much is being claimed for choice there; or rather, that too many of the choices are being pre-determined in one direction. Open-mindedness ought to have the confidence to look both ways. It helps if there is something in both directions for it to look at. If, on one side, I have learnt to value my autonomy, I am less likely to give way to mindless conformity. If, on the other side, I know that some sorts of actions really are wrong, I am protected from supposing that my own choice can ever be all that matters.

Balanced and peaceful as this may sound, the trouble is that the morality of finding and the morality of choosing cannot really settle down side by side, allowing each other fair shares. Each in its nature has to claim sovereignty over the whole field. We can survey the land and appreciate the strengths and weaknesses of each, but it hardly seems possible either to make an apportionment between them or to give them joint rule.

What we can do is try to look at the entire question in a different way. The problem has arisen out of a determination to do full justice to autonomous choice, which seems to have brought us into collision with the idea that values are *given* to us and are not for us to choose. But is it after all a necessary assumption that if choice is important, what it chooses must be values? Could this assumption be reconsidered?

The idea that autonomous human beings must choose their own values seems obvious because of an even better established assumption, that at any rate they cannot be allowed to choose *facts*. Facts at least seem definitely given to us. They are 'hard facts', 'bare facts', 'neutral facts', on to which we (may be) have the right and duty to superimpose our own valuations. It has been a philosophical commonplace that facts are fixed, whether or not the values we attach to them can shift. A ship has been wrecked by the forces of wind and sea. That is a fact. The survivors say 'How terrible'. That is an evaluation. Centuries later, archaeologists dive down to the hulk and fish up interesting remains. Their evaluations are quite different. 'The good, beautiful shipwrecks where we have wood and treasures are one in a thousand,' they say to the newspapers: so offering philosophers 'good shipwreck' as a change of example from 'good knife', or 'beautiful sunset' to illustrate their fact/value distinction.

But are facts fixed? That ship was wrecked, but no doubt its captain tried hard to save it. Perhaps he nearly succeeded. What he decided to do or not to do was of the greatest concern to himself and his crew. He could decide to give this or that order to his men and in a sort of way they had a choice between obedience and panic. They had some scope for autonomy, until their fate overcame them: but surely it was an autonomy of doing not of valuing. They could hardly choose for the shipwreck not to be terrible; they could choose to endure it valiantly. They could change what happened, though in this case not enough to help. They could even in various ways change their attitude to what happened: 'I will be brave.' 'I will not let this deter me.' Thoughts, after all, are facts. What they precisely could not do was change the value of what happened. Their courage was exemplary, their panic was regrettable, the loss of the ship was grievous, the finding of it was interesting. As history adds fact to fact, the values to be found in them grow more complex, but the only way to alter values is to set about altering facts.

It is often in human power to do just that, to make history eventually tell quite a different story, not in the disreputable sense in which totalitarian governments get the books re-written, but in the encouraging sense in which people refuse to remain stuck in unpromising situations. The true story of the facts can be changed not only by what we decisively do but by the attitudes we take up. What we keep saying comes true. People thrive on appreciation and pine when they are starved of it. A teacher can encourage a rather ordinary pupil into distinctiveness. A statesman heartens a nation into economic recovery or victory. An uncouth girl grows up suddenly into a beautiful young woman when somebody falls in love with her. These examples are almost too obvious, but they are not examples of unchanging facts being given new values.

But sometimes the facts are only too plainly fixed. That is when human beings are sometimes able most triumphantly to create value out of them. Are we not to say that here at least they are really choosing values? The illness is incurable, the disability permanent, the hero is dead; and yet faith or courage seem to give a kind of accolade to the facts, making disaster into triumph. 'Come, come, no time for lamentation now, nor much more cause.' Has the philosopher now no right to say 'I told you so: first fact, then evaluation'? The case is not so clear as it seems. Only when something new has *happened* to the complete picture have we any right to make these exultant or soothing judgments. Otherwise we run the risk of being naive or glib or insensitive. Wilfrid Owen has taken to task those who

> tell with such high zest
> To children ardent for some desperate glory
> The old lie *Dulce et decorum est*
> *Pro patria mori.*

Whether a death can be sweet and noble, whether a sorrow can be an inspiration, whether a disaster can be a triumph, depends upon all the facts and is not an open question.

The accolade is a good analogy. It is a happening, not just a reappraisal. 'Arise, Sir George' creates a change of status, if it is said by somebody with the right authority. Similarly, we may say, it takes authority to give any set of facts a new status. So the experience of affliction can give the authority to create something new out of the affliction. 'Blossoms of grief and charity bloom in these darkened fields alone.'[13] Until they have bloomed, we have no right to say they have, though maybe we can do something to cultivate or cherish them, or simply to train our eyes to discern them.

It is not so paradoxical to say that our autonomy consists in choosing facts and not after all in choosing values. Of course, 'choosing facts' is an odd way of putting it. It sounds as if the facts were spread out in front of us and we picked one or two like biscuits on a plate. More seriously, it sounds as if we were proposing to make free with our data, with what is *given* to us, in a thoroughly unsound way. A scholar, a historian, a scientist, is forbidden to make his own choice of the facts. A politician or an administrator does so at his peril. But that is not the point. Future facts are not yet 'data'. Not all history has already happened. Human beings are doers as well as watchers. What they do is exercise choice in the present and so determine, carefully or carelessly, successfully or unsuccessfully, what the facts are going to be. We are constantly laying down new deposits of fact, data for the future. Respect for facts does not mean that people cannot or may not alter the facts, any more than respect for law means that law cannot or may not be altered: far from it. It does mean that we may not say things have altered when they have not. When we do alter them or watch them altering, we shall be able to find fresh value in them.

Choosing is certainly an odd concept. The idea of freedom is particularly apt to 'tease us out of thought'. Somewhere between the arbitrary and the fixed there is this mystery of human choice, somehow both continuous with what has gone before and newly creative. If it is completely determined and predictable like machinery, or undetermined and dependent on chance like the tossing of a coin, it is not real choice. It is surely not a bit of both, like a machine that does not work very well. But we need not embark upon the 'wandering mazes' in which Milton's devils 'found no end'. What needs to be said about human autonomy is that however freedom of choice is to be philosophically explained, it is primarily freedom to *act*: in other words, to affect what the facts are going to be. We are seldom as free as we should like: but that is the central meaning of freedom. Autonomous beings are doers.

If I want something to eat, I do not choose whether that is greedy or not; I choose whether to go and get an apple from the kitchen, or whether to refrain. If I eat the apple, there is one less apple in the kitchen and in the world. As I am not Eve, let us hope the world will never notice. What will sooner or later be noticeable is whether my nibbling or refraining boosts or damages my morale, strengthens or sours my character. Choices have results, small and big. We impinge upon the world, positively and negatively, building or destroying. As autonomous agents, we exercise our choice upon the facts, sometimes by selecting from existing alternatives, sometimes by inaction, sometimes by being able to make something new. What else would we expect, if we are made in the image of God, and the God in whose image we are made is God the Creator? To exercise choice in making new facts is what it means to be creative. In this sense, God the Creator chooses facts. Then He sees that they are good. As Austin Farrer put it, in making the things He 'made them worth what they are worth'.[14]

To say that even God chooses values is more confusing than illuminating. His command is 'Let there be light' or 'Thou shalt love the Lord thy God', not 'Let light be valuable' nor even 'Let love be valuable'. He ordains that something shall happen: 'Do this.' He does not decide that love shall be good and hatred bad, so that if He had chosen otherwise it would have been so. We may say, if we like, that He 'chooses' love: but what our tradition has said is that He *is* love; which is one aspect of saying that He is the ultimate good. Hatred is fundamentally perverse, not because God says so but because it could not be otherwise. What God makes is not values but a world of facts in which we can discover values.

Moral philosophers have been afraid to talk about discovering values, in case they should be committed to the notion that values are extra objects like needles in haystacks. We must agree that to find values is not to find some mysterious kind of fact. It is difficult to be accurate here, but with diffidence it seems possible to say that what we find are the variegated and developing meanings of the facts, sometimes obvious, sometimes subtle, sometimes unexpected, sometimes controversial. What we choose is how we are going to respond, what we will welcome, what ignore, what we will endure and what we will try to alter. We can choose to some extent how much we will see and in what light, but we cannot by our choice put value into fact or remove it. Our creativity, like our Maker's, lies in what we bring into being, in what happens because of us. Our decision can indeed create value, but not as it were by nominating it. It would be more accurate to say that we cultivate value by what we choose to do.

The sceptical humanist, who acknowledges no divine Creator, can join in saying most of this with us. He also is making our world and finding values in it. We can work back with him along the whole way we have come, looking at duties, at problems and at lifestyles. We can begin with some common understanding of obligation and arrive at similar difficulties. We can share his horror at the cruelties human beings inflict upon one another; point out to each other the people who need our help; argue about how to apply ethics to politics; discover what meaning other people find in personal relationships; acknowledge the limits of our understanding; differ probably both about the facts and how to interpret them; accuse each other of being blind, irresponsible or lop-sided; learn to respect each other's point of view; appreciate each other's idiosyncrasies; and wonder what the other can possibly see in his leisure enjoyments. In all this we are engaged upon the same enterprise. We are making choices and seeing what comes of them in terms of facts and values.

Valuing

The theory of given facts and chosen values seems to have collapsed, if it is true that our real autonomy is a matter of doing rather than of commending. We can have another look at the prescriptivist's ultimate 'decisions of principle', and realize, with relief rather than disappointment, that after all perhaps they are not really required of us: at least, not in the sense of creating morality for ourselves. It is only fair to quote again the actual words of Professor Hare rather than knocking down some summary caricature:

> We can only ask [the inquirer] to make up his own mind which way he ought to live; for in the end everything rests upon such a decision of principle. He has to decide whether to accept that way of life or not; if he accepts it, then we can proceed to justify the decisions that are based upon it; if he does not accept it, then let him accept some other, and try to live by it.[1]

We warm to this in so far as we do believe in autonomy. But what is it after all to 'accept a way of life'? Surely it is to choose how to live and what to do because we find, not 'decide', that this way is right, satisfying, laid upon us, desirable, necessary. Someone else may choose differently; we make our own moral decisions, but we do not make our own moral principles.

To assert this brings to the point of clear disagreement a long-standing discontent with Professor Hare's declaration at the beginning of *Freedom and Reason* that 'we are free to form our own moral opinions in a much stronger sense than we are free to form our own opinions as to what the facts are'.[2] Of course to doubt this is asking for philosophical trouble, though maybe less so than a few years ago. Professor Renford Bambrough in particular has doughtily defended the idea that morality is after all 'a branch of knowledge' and that 'Hare crosses the wires and muddies the waters' in denying this.[3]

What needs to be reiterated now is that moral autonomy is not being attacked. We choose how to live. We choose what to do. This way of speaking, far from denigrating autonomy, allows well for the various kinds of autonomy people actually have. Some people exercise their moral freedom, or fail to exercise it, within the systems in which they were born; some extricate themselves partially or totally from the ways of life in which they were brought up; some walk into new moralities with their eyes open. To remain may be autonomous; to change may be mechanical; and either may lead to moral satisfaction or remorse. In all this, it is more accurate to say that people shape their *lives* by their positive and negative choices than to say that they shape their *values*. It looks as if value confronts us or steals up on us and we are not expected to determine it; what we are required to choose is what we shall help to make happen. This way round is more congenial to Christians, who are bound to be chary of 'home-made' values for fear they are not up to standard or even come to pieces in their hands.

We had better not be too quick to indulge in unlovely triumph. Congenial arguments are not always as safe as they seem. It is hardly credible that moralists have all been barking up the wrong tree when they have sung the praises of an autonomy of *valuing*. Can we really say that the moral notion of people exercising their freedom by making evaluations is reducible, without remainder, to values found and only actions chosen? Surely there is still a creative human activity of judging? A culprit must be punished, a candidate has passed with honours, a child is naughty, an operation is a reasonable risk, a poem is moving, a landscape is enchanting, a story is thrilling, a picture is a masterpiece, a soldier is a hero, a saint is holy, a vocation is genuine, a plea is sincere, a way of life is satisfying. The court, we say, 'found'; but can it only 'find'? We have partly judge-made law: have we partly man-made values? It is only fair to pause and try to do more justice to the complexity of the ideas which cluster around the concept of making evaluations.

It is too easy anyway just to say 'Judge not' as if that settled the matter, putting a stopper on the philosophical problem. Dogged piety here takes hold of the wrong point. Judging as such is not a dubious activity like fighting that we may be inclined to hope perfect beings would never need to do: quite the contrary. What judging needs is authority. Human beings have no individual authority to declare each other's standing in the sight of God. We are fellow creatures, and God is the Judge of all of us. So we have been sternly warned against going about trying to judge one another. Even humanly, to claim a right to judge brings us under judgment. Someone who says 'Mozart is trite' reveals more about himself than about Mozart.

But not all human judging is presuming. There are judgments, including value judgments, which human beings in various ways do have the authority to make, which it is their right and even their duty to make. We are not always meant to say 'I cannot tell'. Judgment can be a proper exercise of human autonomy.

Sometimes the authority to judge is given, divinely or humanly: to the church or to a parliament, to magistrates, doctors, generals or examiners. Sometimes it is tacitly assumed or acquired: by a parent, or an expert, or a natural leader. About all these and especially about the moral authority which human beings must have simply as such if after all their autonomy is not to be meaningless, we need to ask 'What are people doing when they exercise these various kinds of right to make judgments?' If 'good judgment' is just reading off something which is there already and is not a real matter of choice, we seem to make a poor thing of the honoured notion of wisdom, divine and human. Has 'the spirit of wisdom and understanding, the spirit of counsel and might, the spirit of knowledge and of the fear of the Lord' (Isa. 11.2) nothing to do with evaluation? Surely there is a practical wisdom which is more than passively receiving information?

Human beings, of course, frequently do something which is called 'making' value judgments. No doubt there is apt to be a good deal of *hubris* in this, but it was perhaps a bit unfair of Austin Farrer to pour scorn on the 'wonderful activity called "valuation"' and ask, 'Well, and shall I ticket the throne of glory, shall I assign my Creator n units of intrinsic merit and p units of relevance, and decide in consequence to spend three minutes in prayer to him every other night?'[4] God forbid: but that is not quite the point. Pricing is one simple humble form of setting a value on things and there is no need to let it get out of hand. Evaluation is much more than pricing and only a cynic is in real danger of thinking otherwise. The simple folly of reducing everything to market value is fairly easily detected. If evaluation as such is presumptuous, it must be open to more fundamental criticism than this.

Putting prices on things, far from being the best example of the activity people generally mean by 'evaluation', is hardly at the beginning of it. 'This picture should fetch so many pounds in the saleroom', in its place, is as suitable and useful a statement as 'strawberries are so much a punnet'; but these are very minimal judgments of value, hardly getting beyond plain statements of fact. They do not even claim to answer the question 'Are they worth it?' We can go on to say 'It is a fine example of his mature work' or 'The good ones are all on top', still without needing to exercise any particularly sensitive appreciation. By the time we reach the kind of 'evaluation' which claims to put in the values, we shall be a long way from pricing; and only here do human values begin to look like serious rivals to divine values. The sin of Adam was not an ambition to keep a shop.

Are values for choosing? All this ground is staked out in philosophical distinctions, not always helpfully. The value/fact distinction itself is more treacherous and slippery than we might suppose. The technicalities of 'descriptions' and 'prescriptions' have created prejudice as much as enlightenment. We might hope to limit the problem by distinguishing 'moral' values from values of other kinds, but that could be more of an impoverishment than a help. On the contrary, there is no harm in taking the idea of moral judgment as widely as we please and maintaining that all serious judging is a kind of moral activity, well or badly done.[5] What then does it do?

Let us try a different distinction, suggested as commonsense not as a technicality. Let us divide judgments, roughly but conveniently, into decisions, verdicts and true evaluations. The point of doing this is to show that decisions and verdicts, at any rate, need not be a trouble to the argument. They can be sorted out, on the lines already indicated, into making things happen (decisions) and finding that something is so (verdicts), giving judgment real scope for choice without requiring it to choose values. We can surely do justice to the autonomy and even the creativeness of the wise judge along these lines.

Decisions do not announce that a thing is good, but *do* something.[6] When they come into effect they make a difference to the facts. 'I will have that one.' 'Endorse his licence.' 'You may have time off to go to the party.' 'Up, Guards, and at 'em.' Practical wisdom is in its element here and of course practical wisdom has to do with choosing well; but it does not have to create the values it establishes. Its model is the divine fiat 'let there be light', not 'let there be value'. Characteristically, this sort of good judgment is exercised in giving instructions that something shall be done. 'Render unto Caesar the things that are Caesar's, and unto God the things that are God's.' In some famous examples the instructions are never meant to be obeyed, but it is still fact, not value, they would impinge upon. The waves will not stop for Canute, Shylock never takes his pound of flesh, Solomon's swordsman does not divide the living child in half, nobody casts the first stone at the woman taken in adultery; but situations are altered. We may certainly say that values emerge, attitudes are affected, truth is brought to light. What we do not have to say is that values are chosen.

But nor do judgments which are verdicts choose values. However delicately they discriminate, their job is to find and not to create. What a verdict sets out to do is discover and state what is already the case. 'She is his mother.' 'He died by misadventure.' 'This task is within my capacity.' 'There was some negligence on both sides.' 'He is guilty.' 'This candidate's paper is B+.' 'They deserve a treat.' 'This one is genuine.' However 'evaluative' these judgments turn out to be, there is still no need, so far, to talk about values as subject to choice.

Unfortunately, the neatness of this division of judgments into decisions and verdicts is too neat. For one thing, decisions and verdicts themselves shade into each other. There is a characteristic kind of judgment where the facts of the case are not in dispute but their meaning has to be weighed. Is this (carefully described) course of events to be called 'negligence' or not? Is this purported contract valid? Who is the rightful owner of this property? Here real judgment, real discrimination, is called for. As Professor Hart pointed out in a classic article 'On the Ascription of Responsibility and Rights',[7] it is 'a disastrous over-simplification and distortion' to say that the judge in such a case simply reads off his judgment from the facts. He does more – he *ascribes* – he has 'a wide freedom' to interpret and decide. We might seem to have an elegant legal model for moral judgment, swinging us right back to the idea that we first establish the facts and then decide how to evaluate them. But there is no need to be swept away. We can still say, quite toughly, that the *logical* distinction between verdict and decision holds good, even if in practice they run into each other. Where 'finding' stops, 'deciding' begins, and decisions are still decisions about what to *do*. How are we to distinguish between malice, negligence and accident; or between generosity and extravagance; or between gentleness and weakness? When does a child become an adult? What is undue influence? Is this comatose patient alive? Is a foetus a human being? Is artificial insemination by donor a kind of condoned adultery? What constitutes obscenity? If we cannot *find* lines we need to *draw* them. So we make 'evaluations' in the sense of 'appraisals'; we may also creatively exercise our autonomy; but we shall still not be creating value, except the value of our hard work or flash of inspiration. When we have drawn a line or refused to draw one, then we find ourselves bound by various claims. What all this shows is not that values are for people to choose, but that there is more doing than we may have thought in judgments that look like finding. It complicates what we have been saying so far, but need not upset it.

The real difficulty is that, even when we have said all this about decisions and verdicts, there still seems to be a kind of judgment left over. There remains an awkward residue of cases where it still looks as if people somehow put value into existing facts. We have not abolished true evaluations, only reduced them. 'He is guilty' is a finding: but what about 'This dress suits you' or 'His predicament is harrowing' or 'That is a most moving piece' or 'What a lovely present'? On the face of it, value not fact is being made here by human judgment. We seem at last to be pushed into saying that there is an area where values are for people to make.

It is better to labour this point than to brush it aside. Sometimes it is the toughest objections to a theory that are most help in modifying it in a satisfactory way. So having arrived in this area, let us explore it hopefully not reluctantly, asking what this notion of creative evaluation really amounts to.

The work of creative artists, great and small, need not disturb us. When they put value into the world, it is by making things, facts, which turn out to be valuable. They design or compose, they paint or carve, they sing and play, they plant and water, they cook and they write, and in all these kinds of activities they shape their raw material into significance, maybe into kinds of significance of which their contemporaries had not dreamed. Sometimes it is given to them 'out of three sounds' to 'frame not a fourth sound, but a star'.

It is not makers but appreciators who endanger our scheme of values found and facts chosen. What are we to say about connoisseurs, experts and enthusiasts, in so far as they are doing something positive but not actually making new things? What about art critics and gourmets, bird-watchers and musicologists, yachtsmen and horsemen, hermits and lovers? All these are proclaiming in their different styles that the object of their attentions is valuable. They are not creators like parents or artists, teachers or builders, actors or farmers or conductors, who by their skills shape the world of facts; yet they are good examples of practical judgment. Are we to call them creative also and, if so, is it values they are making? Certainly their judgments seem to be characteristically their own. If these people are simply finding values that are already there, why do they so often fail to find one another's? It is not just that athletes have no great wish to tramp round museums; that a craftsman is sure that his work is more real than a scholar's; that I am asking for something quite different from a tall ship and a star to steer her by. We can differ about values even when we are seemingly directing our attention the same way. Critics are capable of disagreeing fundamentally among themselves. Your true love is not beautiful to me. Yet we are not dealing with unimportant whims. We are pursuing variegated visions of our own, humble or sublime. In valuing things according to our own choice, we

are choosing to value. We may say, significantly, that we are
giving priority to this or that. It is only a step further to say that
we are choosing values and that here at last individual choice,
not predetermined goodness, comes into its own.

In a way this is nothing new. We began by trying to do justice
both to finding and to choosing.[8] The values we assuredly find
have emerged out of a vaguer context where a good deal is for
people to choose. We have been emphasizing that there *are*
values we find. The more we stress them, the less we can say
that all evaluation is a matter of choice. So we have expressly
limited the role of choice in the establishing of our values. What
the argument so far has done is try to show that to concur in all
this need not be to limit or belittle our moral autonomy. There
is plenty of scope for autonomous choice which is not the
choosing of values. Hence all the emphasis on the choosing, or
rather making, of facts.

But if, as we now seem driven to allow, there is still a residue
which we do need to think of as the choosing of value, we are
back in the difficulty that the two sorts of morality, found and
chosen, cannot happily settle down alongside each other. Each
needs to be sovereign. We have only re-drawn the frontier,
without ending the dispute. If any morality is 'found', it makes
nothing choosable seem truly moral. If anything in morality is
choosable, we seem to have taken a step towards making values
a matter of taste.

The trouble with matters of taste is that they have a way of
creeping back into morality. If anything is just a matter of taste,
sooner or later everything seems to be. I like curry: you do not;
nobody minds, even if I say to myself 'That's good' and you say
'That's nasty' when we eat it. We do not feel we have exactly
contradicted each other about something objective, the 'goodness' of curry. But still 'That's good' is in its small way an
evaluation, certainly not just a pun. It is a step towards the full-
blown moral meaning of 'good'. We can see this by contrasting it
with 'That's dear', which also is not just a pun but which hardly
begins to approach the emotional meaning of 'dear'.

Matters of taste are the beginning of valuing. Taste moves
gently towards 'good taste'. If we are used to disagreeing quite
happily about curry, we can move on to disagreeing about
something more high-powered, say modern art. Neither of us

wants to be intolerant, so we say 'I suppose it is a matter of taste.' But then is the appreciation of the ancient and great also a matter of taste? In some ways we want to say it is, in some ways not. We can argue about all these matters and offer reasons for our choices, but in the end we can hardly maintain that greatness is a measurable quality like fatness. Certainly, we have a reluctance to say that it is wrong to prefer Tintoretto to Rubens, or Bach to Beethoven. So it seems that we must choose what we will value, profoundly as well as trivially, and not be anxious if our evaluations diverge. To find somebody else who values as we do is maybe an uncovenanted mercy, not something we have the right to expect.

So gently we are softened up to say this kind of thing about morality too. If it is all right to agree to differ over mankind's most sublime creations, can we not also agree to differ about our human concern over how to live? If we aspire at all to liberality of mind, we find a continuing reluctance to say that other people's significant ways of life are wrong. But then where has objective morality, let alone God's will, got to? The fatal split between the values we find and the values we choose is still endangering our own moral edifice.

It was as well to give this worry a full run for its money, but now it is time to say quite firmly that too much emphasis on 'only' matters of taste is defeatist even in aesthetics. Instead of letting choosing take over more and more from finding, we can reverse the process. The point is that the world is much richer than we sometimes let ourselves think. There is far more to be found in it than any of us can do more than begin to discover. What wonder then that our findings diverge, including our findings of values?

If we clear our minds of the prejudice that to make an evaluation must be to put value into something, we can notice that taste, at any level of sophistication, has to do with perceiving. I like curry, partly because human tastebuds and digestions are so constituted that spices are suitable for them, partly because on a particular occasion I tried it and found it enjoyable. I did not nominate it to be good. I may be said to have made a discovery. Until then I was missing something. There are many such discoveries that I shall never make, some that I am incapable of making. I cannot imagine what people see in pickled gherkins, but I am willing to believe that here I am continuing, probably permanently, to miss something. Their taste is valid and mine is limited.

When I want to encourage somebody to enjoy something I enjoy, whether I am walking round a picture gallery with a friend or feeding a faddy child, I ought to realize that argument is not going to be much help: I cannot prove that there is value there to be perceived. But this does not mean that I am asking for acts of willpower. People cannot simply choose to like things. What I say is 'Do look at that', or 'Try it', 'Give it a chance', 'See whether you can find something in it after all.' We show each other things and begin to perceive more. 'See how the elaborate details are set in a simple arrangement.' 'Notice how that blue enhances that green.' 'What a subtle mixture of flavours.' We do not want a philosopher here to try to make us keep facts and values rigidly separate.

Sometimes we find that people are almost literally living in different worlds. One really cannot see what another sees, any more than a human being can enter into his dog's three-dimensional world of important smells. They may become exasperated at each other's limitations. So with the best intent they try preaching themselves little sermons on tolerance, saying if they can, 'Oh well, it is really a matter of taste.' Unfortunately, sooner or later this kind of tolerance begins to endanger our profoundest convictions. It threatens to make everything subjective, even what really matters. But there is no necessity to move this way. What is needed is not to acquiesce in this creeping relativism, but to make an adjustment of scale.

Of course what we perceive is limited. Only God appraises the whole creation from every point of view in its total and glorious complexity. We each have a small window on this immensely diverse world, a window out of which we choose to look: but what is out there to be discerned is not a matter of choice. So we can get our exasperation right. If people pull down the blinds or look out through bullseye glass or tinted spectacles, they will miss or distort what we want them to see. But generally we can be grateful, not anxious, when perceptions diverge.[9] It is a good thing that there is somebody looking north while we are looking south. It is a still better thing that there are people with binoculars who can show us things we never imagined.[10]

But what about the people who are seemingly looking the same way and yet contradict each other's evaluations? How could this happen so often if evaluation were a sort of perception? One critic says the play is profound, another that it is sentimental: are they finding these qualities or putting them in? The way to answer this is to consider how we actually react to these situations when we are not afraid of some philosopher calling us naive. Surely we usually go on arguing? If we are too timid to say that one critic is right, we shall still go on asking which is the more convincing. We are much less inclined than is often supposed simply to acquiesce in divergence. We can evaluate evaluations and criticize criticism and the criteria we use are, for instance, whether someone was really attending;[11] whether his vision was distorted; what aspects of the whole he has picked out; whether his interpretation sheds light on what is there; whether, in fact, he has shown discernment. We can properly appraise evaluations as perceptive or insensitive, honest or hasty; not as kind or cruel, loyal or selfish: in other words, for what they draw out rather than for what they put in.

If this has to be called 'intuitionism', so be it. One jibs at the label because of its association with dubious claims to incorrigibility, with 'feminine intuition' and all manner of irrationality. It is by attacking 'intuitionists' that Professor Hare still shows himself as a 'prescriptivist'. But the truth behind intuitionism may sound better in the words of Iris Murdoch: 'I have used the word "attention", which I borrow from Simone Weil, to express the idea of a just and loving gaze directed upon an individual reality. I believe this to be the characteristic and proper mark of the active moral agent.'[12] She illustrates her meaning in a passage now famous:

> I am looking out of my window in an anxious and resentful state of mind, oblivious of my surroundings, brooding perhaps on some damage done to my prestige. Then suddenly I observe a hovering kestrel. In a moment everything is altered. The brooding self with its hurt vanity has disappeared. There is nothing now but kestrel. And when I return to thinking about the other matter it seems less important.[13]

She comments, 'It is so patently a good thing to take delight in flowers and animals that people who bring home potted plants and watch kestrels might even be surprised at the notion that these things have anything to do with virtue.'[14] To adopt her emphasis on 'attention' in this almost contemplative sense should be a good corrective to what might otherwise be a one-sidedly busy morality of creative choice.

Talk about valuing in terms of perceiving need not be invalidated by the wry thought that one could also tell quite a different story about the kestrel. I creep out of my mouse-hole on a beautiful sunny day, looking for crumbs. Then suddenly I observe a hovering kestrel. The warm feeling of well-being disappears. One swoop: and there is nothing now but kestrel. The real world is large and rich enough to include the terror as well as the beauty of predators, the goodness and the nastiness of curry, just as it includes the famous incompatible 'sense-data' philosophers have worried about, the stick bent in water, the round and elliptical penny. These things are a matter of point of view. They are still found rather than chosen.

If evaluating is rightly taken as a kind of perceiving, I may look and see and judge, and offer the results to my fellow human beings; but I am not authorized simply to dig in my toes and say, 'Well, I just *see* that this is right', when to anyone else it is perfectly apparent that I am only giving a voice to the accumulated prejudices of my upbringing. What we are talking about is not a magic way of 'value-spotting', but a kind of patient and skilful focusing of fact and value together.

Take, for example, the story of the Ancient Mariner. He was released from his agony and the albatross fell off his neck at the moment when he found himself blessing the water-snakes as beautiful. This might seem to be a perfect illustration of the theory of facts as found and values as chosen: of evaluation as imposed upon neutral 'description'. But if we *attend* to the poem, it may yield a different impression. At no stage is the evaluation something added. There are two descriptions of living creatures in the water, in the ordinary rather than technical sense of 'description'; and both descriptions *are* evaluations. 'Yea, slimy things did crawl with legs/Upon the slimy sea.' That was what the Mariner saw first. But then somehow he sees something different:

Beyond the shadow of the ship,
I watched the water-snakes:
They moved in tracks of shining white,
And when they reared, the elfish light
Fell off in hoary flakes.
Within the shadow of the ship
I watched their rich attire:
Blue, glossy green, and velvet black
They coiled and swam: and every track
Was a flash of golden fire.
O happy living things! no tongue
Their beauty might declare
A spring of love gushed from my heart
And I blessed them unaware . . .

The horror departs: not by his choice but by his renewed perception.[15]

Claims

It may seem a far cry from a response to the pleasantness of curry, or even the beauty of water-snakes, to the stringency of moral obligation. It is all very well to lump all these together as 'values'; but if value can be anything from the optional to the extremely compulsory, it may not appear to be a very promising concept for understanding what really matters in life. My likes and dislikes in the way of food, or even the concerts I attend or stay away from, can hardly be expected to tell me much about my duty to tell the truth even if it will get me into trouble, or to help somebody in distress. The argument needs to be expressed more tautly. It is an *a fortiori* argument. If the ethic of choice is inadequate even where it may seem most promising and we discover value much more than we invent it,[1] how much more is *moral* value *there* to be found, irrespective of our choice? We can insist upon this in good company. I. T. Ramsey pointed out as long ago as 1966 that there is an element in the logic of moral judgment 'which even Hare's lucid and brilliant exposition neglects: a claim-acknowedging element'.[2]

So, with some trepidation, we turn the prescriptivist analysis round. We explain how morality comes to bear upon us, not by saying that we reach out across the fact/value chasm and grab values, but that values, large and small, reach out and grab us. Our positive activity of evaluating is met more than halfway by *claims* and our part is not so much to choose as to respond. Our response of course is always selective, never complete. The development of our sensitivity is part of the development of our humanity. There are some values which it simply is inhuman to miss, others which it takes a rare discrimination to find. There is no need to limit this kind of sensitivity to the sophisticated and articulate, any more than sensitivity of hand or eye is so limited. Nor is it something that we either have once for all or fail in. It can be trained; and people can enlighten one another.

Sometimes it may be important to emphasize our freedom to give or withhold our response, but at present, as autonomy is so much in fashion, it seems more necessary to do justice to the contrary emphasis. Refusal to respond can be an abuse of freedom which eventually diminishes one as a person. It may not be illogical to neglect the claims that are made upon us, but it is worse than illogical: it is ultimately inhuman. Professor Hare himself, in the midst of stressing our own choice, has spoken of the 'shallow stagnation' which afflicts us when we 'content ourselves with the appreciation of those things, like eating, which most people can appreciate without effort, and never learn to prize those things whose true value is apparent only to those who have fought hard to reach it'.[3]

That sounds as much like finding values as choosing them, but clearly is not to be presumed upon. Its context forbids us to suppose that careless talk about an activity called 'claiming' which things mysteriously do would be acceptable to a prescriptivist philosopher. It comes in a paper called 'Nothing Matters' in *Applications of Moral Philosophy*, in which Professor Hare delightfully demolishes the notion that 'mattering' is something to be found going on in the real world. He tells ruefully of how a young Swiss guest, on reading Camus' *L'Etranger*, hospitably placed in his bedroom, was seized acutely of the existentialist idea that 'nothing matters', for he realized that he could find nothing of the kind going on. The story has a happy ending, for Professor Hare cheered him up by convincing him that he was making a logical mistake: looking for an activity called 'mattering' and finding nothing doing it. 'My wife matters to me' is not 'similar in logical function to "My wife chatters to me"'.[4] The activity which does go on is not mattering but valuing, and most human beings do it all the time. So he easily persuaded his young guest that in this sense plenty of things mattered, for he valued them.

But if we need to be careful in talking about mattering, then presumably we must be equally careful in talking about claims.

Certainly we do not want to say that there are claims somehow going on their own, hitting us when we come into range. But it is fair to point out that claiming is, quite literally, an activity in a way in which mattering is not. 'I was first', 'That's mine', 'It's not fair', 'Surely I deserve better than that', are claims, justified or unjustified. So to talk about moral obligation in terms of response to real claims is at least grammatical. The question is whether this model of values as claims can be extended beyond these legalistic or juvenile examples without becoming intolerably metaphorical. Does Beethoven's Pastoral Symphony or a magnificent sunset say 'Attend to me'? Does an unconscious sick person say 'Look after me'? Does a lie say 'Don't utter me'? Is that what we mean by the objectivity of value?

To this we may dare to give an answer which Addison gave in a celebrated poem, that though the universe may be literally silent it is not inert. 'What though no real voice nor sound' speaks to us out of the heavens (or, as we may add, on earth), 'in Reason's ear' there is more to be listened to than speech. Of course it is metaphorical to say that a suffering animal makes claims upon us: but so it is metaphorical to say that we grasp what the trouble is. Even 'understand' is a metaphor: but a theorem we can understand is as real in its way as a bus shelter we can stand under. From our point of view, the claims which have to be expressed in figures of speech are at least as demanding and objective as the claims that lawyers can handle. Whether we ever arrive at a literal statement does not matter here, but the structure of morality does. What we are struggling to affirm, with more or less help or hindrance from metaphor, is that values impinge upon us from outside and are not something we add to the world. They are built into things not painted on to them.

But of course 'things' are not the point. The time has come to affirm bluntly at last that it is *people* that make claims upon us.[5] There is no need to make the case more difficult than it need be by giving the impression that values are not only objective but also impersonal. It is not a question we need go into, whether there could be value out of all relation to persons. Primarily and fundamentally it is to be found in persons, or at least in sentient beings. If there is any 'built-in' value, it is here. Whatever persons are, they are not value-free.

This is the point to which the whole argument so far has been tending; and it is a point finely balanced between the obvious and the controversial. If there is any morality which is found rather than chosen, it is based upon the idea of a person; and in a way this could not be otherwise. A person is a being that is capable, one way or another, of being made glad or sorry. We may not like this emphasis, or the interest in happiness and unhappiness to which it tends to lead, but we cannot make it morally irrelevant. The meaning of 'person' as a *wanting* being has something to do with the notion of a moral claim. There could hardly be a morality which was not a variation upon this theme. Moralities of obedience, however bizarre and even unpleasant, are not impersonal. They are based upon the will of a lawgiver. Moralities that recognize no lawgiver concern themselves directly with human satisfaction and dissatisfaction. Even Kant's austere insisence on duty for duty's sake makes it our duty to treat persons as ends not as means.

It is not conceivable that morality should lose all touch with the idea of moral goodness pleasing somebody. Moral views may diverge very far, both in form and in content, and in acknowledging this divergence we may feel impelled to take many steps towards relativism; but there remains this inevitable point of contact. So we have a kind of minimal 'personalism' which ought to be too obvious to mention, except that it is as well to make one's assumptions plain. To build a more substantial personalism upon this foundation is a delicate exercise but a promising one.

The project is to show that the idea of a person as a *claimant* can mean something definite. It can be more than an almost vanishing point of contact between divergent moralities. It can be a place where we may actually expect convergence. It can draw different moralities together. Such a substantive personalism is not obvious. It is easier to affirm it than to prove it. It can best be established by making affirmations cautiously, building up a structure, in the hope that it will so to speak prove itself when the edifice actually stands up, not like a card house but like a building to be lived in.

Talk about diverging or converging moralities could be intolerably slipshod. Is a 'morality' an ethical theory like utilitarianism, or a system of laws like the Torah, or a way of life as lived by the Bloomsbury Group or the Trobriand Islanders? These are divergent enough, but they can hardly converge as they are not on one level to start with. Personalism cannot knock their heads together and tell them to compose their differences. If personalism is to be some sort of rival morality, it will first have to make up its mind which level of theory or practice to operate on; and then it will find itself competing at that level with whatever views are there already.

But personalism does not have to be a kind of morality. The notion of a person could be looked on as something *given*, a concept to hold on to when thinking morally at any level. What I am suggesting is that if we do hold on to it we can make sense of a great many different moralities and even find ourselves agreeing with most of them; and where we have to disagree, we can give reasons and not say 'I just choose differently from you' or 'It must be a matter of taste.' For instance, if we take the idea of a person as a kind of touchstone we can appreciate the utilitarian's concern for happiness and argue with his seeming lack of concern for integrity. We can take heed of claims that human life is sacred and so come to see abortion and euthanasia, war and capital punishment as difficult, not easy, questions. We can enter into people's need for definite laws to live by and ideals which are absolute, not optional. It can become something more than a cliché that heretics, and not only heretics, are right in what they affirm and wrong in what they deny. We can be impressed rather than alarmed at the varieties of ways in which people can seek and find satisfaction.[6] We shall not find it necessary to deny that there is such a thing as human nature;[7] nor that it can express itself in innumerable valid and worthwhile forms of society; nor that there is a great deal amiss with humanity so that there are always desperate possibilities of things going wrong.

In particular, if we take a firm hold of the concept of a person, there need not be fundamental divergence between the moralities of Christians and unbelievers. Convergence is possible here too, or at least both groups can see the point of each other's affirmations. The agreement they need is that if value is indeed to be *found* anywhere it is to be found in persons. They do not have to turn their backs upon each other and choose between two sorts of values, divine and human, but attend to the persons we find. Christians believe that God is, so to say, the height of Personhood: He is the heart of value, and the existence and the value of every other person derives from Him.[8] Human beings are planets, not stars; but in the night-sky their brightness is no less real.

To put it another way, the unbeliever can find just the same kind of value as the Christian but not so tidily arranged. For him there is no question of one great worshipful Being for whose sake we honour all the others.[9] There are innumerable valuable people claiming our regard. But so, in practice, there are for Christians. What we find around us is what the unbeliever finds. Some people are more attractive and some seem to have special claims; but they are all ends in themselves if we are to be Kantians; they are all capable of happiness and unhappiness if we are to be utilitarians. Our morality is the way we respond to these claims, the kind of priority we give them, whether we specialize or generalize, and the kind of reasons we give for action or inaction. There is plenty of scope for diversity including theoretical diversity, but much less for incomprehension if we have begun with the notion of a person as a being who makes claims upon us.

We can understand the egoist who specializes in himself and the mystic who wants to be alone with God, though we may point out to each the good reasons why these attempts at an extremely limited personalism are likely to topple over into concern for other people. In a more ordinary way, we can comprehend the diversity of people's attempts to organize the miscellany of claims they find made upon them, the chaos and the over-simplifications and sometimes the sensitivity of people's moral responses. Belief in God is the simplest way of making personalism coherent, but personalists who do not believe in God are talking the same language.

But is personalism any more than an enormous begging of the main question about the value of people? What is this 'value' that is to control morality and judge moralities? It is easy to talk about 'respect for persons' as the fundamental moral attitude, and find nobody, Christian or sceptic, to say us nay; and so to continue in a relaxing uncertainty about what we are really affirming. Some personalists really believe in *agape*, some in immortal souls, some in equality, some in freedom; and these ideas, appealing in their different ways, are not the same idea. They might even conflict. If we are to make a covenant between them it ought to be an explicit covenant.

Why respect persons? Sometimes, of course, because they are wise or good or brave: but what is in question here is the sort of attitude we are meant to take up simply because they are persons. In the end the Christian answer will have to be 'because God made them', but that ought to be a way to summarize understanding not to block it. As Christians and unbelievers are living in the same world, they ought to be able to explore some of it together. It is not as if Christians had a sort of direct line to God so that they could comprehend Him first and His creation second. To find value in people for God's sake is an advanced not an elementary moral lesson. It is quite in order that we should first love the brother whom we have seen. The question is what kind of basis this gives us. Is a personalist morality, if it is to get started at all, dependent upon the happy chance of finding people lovable; or have we the right to say that there is something about people as such which demands our regard?

The word 'regard' covers a slide we have just made from basic 'respect' to 'love'. It is natural, maybe too natural, for a Christian to talk about love. On realizing this, one could apologize and retreat, trying to express what one wants to say in terms of the more non-committal 'respect' for the sake of the unbelievers. But it would be both more true to the facts and more fair to the unbelievers to try to keep the whole range. 'Respect for persons' is all very well but does not take us very far. It is not only Christians who are aware that there is more to life than respecting one another's rightful claims or even one another's integrity. If we are asking about the value of a person, we want to leave room to think about superlative not only workaday value.

This is not making the problem more difficult. To claim more, not less, often helps. As a way of getting morality started, a claim that people ought to be loved is more convincing than a claim that they ought to be respected. Love, even self-sacrificing love, comes more easily to us than plain cold ethics. 'Respect for persons' is so non committal that it is difficult, as it were, to make it stick. If someone says, 'Why should I respect other people if it means I must inconvenience myself?', it is notoriously hard to give a compelling answer. (That is one reason why philosophers have been so inclined to emphasize *choice* as the only way to give morality a purchase on fact.) But suppose someone says, 'Why should I care about other people?', he has taken up a more unstable position. He is, in a way, denying his own nature. Almost certainly, he does care already. But if he seems not to care, we can call him inhuman, with a good deal of confidence that he will not like it. We can appeal to his hard heart by showing him joy or suffering more easily than we can appeal to his indifference by showing him 'respect-ability', which in this meaning is not even a real word.

This kind of talk about love as basic to human nature we might call 'strong personalism'. We have been taking persons as essentially claimants. Now we fill in a rich rather than a weak notion of what it is they claim. In doing this we may hope both to be more true to the facts and to make better sense of morality. To insist that it is a warm regard not just a cool respect that our fellow beings intrinsically claim from us leaves less room for the question that short-circuits morality, 'Does it pay?' If we can let love come into the picture, we know quite well that we are not primarily concerned with paying and not paying. So, if this is really what morality is about, we cannot wriggle out of it with a 'Why should I?'

What we are trying to do with this strong personalism is ground morality in the way persons are made. 'Made' need not beg the religious question. It could mean either the impersonal forces of evolution or the sovereign fiat of God; or, more satisfyingly, the creative power of God working through evolution. Whichever of these makes sense to us, we can say as personalists that our very existence involves valuing and being valued by one another. To put it bluntly, we are getting an *ought* from an *is*, and this is entirely in order so long as we know what we are at. We are looking on persons as living claims, beings whose value is ready built into them not added to them. To miss this value is to miss a large part of the meaning of 'person'.

So far, so good. But all this has only clarified the problem. We have kept coming to the brink of asking and must now ask in earnest, whether we can ascribe value in this way to every person and to persons as such. Can value somehow inhere in a person, *as* a person, not only as somebody's friend or lover or child? What are people to be valued for?

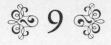

People

There is no difficulty about finding reasons for valuing people. In a way the most obvious fact about persons is their value. But the obvious can turn out to be a wobbly stepping-stone. It looks secure enough – in talking about value we are certainly talking about something fundamental and characteristic which has to do with the very meaning of the word 'person'. But as soon as we try to specify what that something is, we find ourselves talking about characteristics which persons can have in varying degrees: reason, or self-consciousness, or feeling, or relationships with each other, or even humanity. So one person might be of inestimable value and another of very little value or none: which is not at all what we want to say.

At this point, we begin to track down a kind of moral or metaphysical snobbery. Identifying snobbery is like peeling an onion. The outer skin which really must come off is the simple hypocrisy which is concerned with people's usefulness to us, not their value at all. Within this, once we have started to be critical, we can discern layers of real valuing for bad reasons: regarding people, or for that matter hating them, for their social standing or wealth; or (not much better) for their beauty or brain power. All these, our sense of fairness insists, are unsatisfactory grounds for value or disvalue. They are somehow extraneous to the 'real' person. We ought not to take heed of them in bestowing our regard, still less in withdrawing our regard if fortune later removes what fortune once bestowed.

Then once we have started on this argument it can begin to seem just as bad to value people for their lovableness or friendliness or creativity, or even for their kindness or wisdom. We may loftily adopt the sentiments of Jonathan in Handel's *Saul*, 'Birth and fortune I despise', and then still more loftily check before we continue, 'From virtue let my friendship rise.' Regard, we start to say, ought to be 'unconditional', not associated in any way with good qualities we should like people to have. We are to respect people 'as people'. But what is there in a person to hold our regard, if all question of attractiveness or even goodness which can be ascribed to one person rather than another is ruled out?

When moralists make assumptions about the sacredness of life, or the value of all rational or all sentient beings, it is as well to ask some awkward questions about whether this value is a matter of form or of content. A formal principle applies in general, but may amount to remarkably little. A particular statement gives us something definite to go on, but only in the particular case. So it is necessary to keep asking, even of people whose positions we honour, are they *defining* a person as a being that is to be valued? Or are they expressing a faith that every being we can recognize as a person will turn out to have some minimal good qualities worth valuing? Or are they merely laying down a principle of fairness, that we ought not to treat one person differently from another without showing good cause? Any of these positions may be in order, but not unnoticed slides from one of them to another.

Confusions have beset the practical controversies here. The affirmation that persons are valuable as such is less help than one might suppose in setting up a particular living being as deserving protection. If 'All persons are valuable' is used to block the move, 'This one is not valuable in the way you say', it cannot *also* block the move 'This one is not a person after all', without begging the question. This trouble has bedevilled the arguments about abortion. To one moralist, a foetus is a person and it is obviously wrong to kill a person. To another, a foetus is a person but not all persons are sacred. To another, persons are sacred but a foetus is not a person. To another, persons are sacred and a foetus is a person, but ideals cannot always be realized. Another may be disinclined to talk about the sacredness of persons, but still hold to the belief that abortion is profoundly harmful. If the arguments are even to join, let alone be resolved, the notions which cluster around the value of personal life need closer attention. Pursuit of the detailed moral issues would need an urgent look at the connection between the concepts of 'human being' and of 'person', maybe taking into account animals on the one hand and computers on the other.

The present discussion is at an earlier stage. We are trying to see what it can *mean* to say that a person is valuable as such. For this purpose we can take anyway some persons as 'given'. The human beings we meet provide us at least with good examples of 'persons'. That is, we can conveniently use 'person' as primarily the singular of 'people', and leave on one side questions about the boundaries of the concept. What are we saying when we call a person valuable?

It is no wonder that religious believers are inclined to make the value of a person a matter of divine appointment. If people are somehow *ex officio* sacred, we hope we have found a more real and less abstract way of respecting them than bald calculations of equality. We spread on to the unlovable and even on to the unaware the infinite regard we feel is morally apt for any member of this curious class of beings that think and feel and love. Because God will have it so, the drunken tramp or the handicapped foetus is as valuable as Michelangelo. But unfortunately we gain this moral certainty at the cost of begging all the questions and cutting our lines of communication with those who think otherwise.

To define persons as sacred, even theologically, is to abandon personalism, because it makes it impossible to give any character to their sacredness. They can be, indeed have to be, counted as sacred whether or not they turn out to have any specifically valuable qualities. Of course, for believers, persons are valuable in the end because God makes them so and for no other reason whatsoever, but if we assert this prematurely we seem to make humanity colourless and God not only inscrutable but arbitrary. God loves us 'unconditionally': does He also love us 'indiscriminately'? He loves people as such, but He has also made people as such: it dishonours Him to think of the exercise as pointless.

What we have lost in this formal way of valuing persons simply because they are persons is the hard-won idea of a person as a living claim. Instead we have reverted to the notion of values as chosen: but now it is God who does all the choosing and it only remains for us to fall in with His choice that persons are to be deemed sacred, however little findable value they seem to have, indeed however little value they really have even in His eyes.

So let us presume to wonder what God sees in people; or rather (with a due recollection of human sinfulness) what He will see in them when they are redeemed and creation is fulfilled. We need not imagine that we are really God's farm, producing for His consumption so many units of praise or sacrifice on a quasi-economic footing. We are no 'use' to God in that sort of sense. Nor does God need us as lap dogs on which to lavish His affections, or as specimens in His collection. We must be more humanist than that, more aware that God is able to make creatures to be worthwhile for their own sakes, or we shall find ourselves both irreverent towards God and morally unintelligible to those humanists whose scheme of things leaves God out.

Can we say then that what God the Creator values is His image in us? We seem to be like pennies stamped with the Queen's, or Caesar's, head; or maybe, if we hesitate to ascribe to ourselves any intrinsic worth, we are like banknotes to be honoured because the bank is known to be sound. Our value on this view is entirely authentic and entirely derivative from God's own value. The unbeliever's currency is the same as ours, but he has as it were gone off the gold standard. We might suggest that human attempts to restrict the sheer number of God's creatures are a sort of monetarism: a specific policy against a dreaded inflation, which will eventually turn out to have been a good or a bad idea in God's eyes.

More seriously, we can compare a thoroughly rational, sensitive, well-integrated human being with a crisp newly-printed pound note: agreeable to deal with, but not a whit more valuable than the crumpled, dirty, torn note that we hardly like to touch. In one way, the value of a pound note depends entirely upon its shape and size and the printing upon it; but in another way it is entirely independent both of the excellence or otherwise of the artist's design and of the way that design has stood up to wear and tear. Even if it comes in two, we can stick it together again, and there is no sense in trying to make an invisible mend as if we were restoring a picture. Does the value of a coin depend upon how it looks? Does the value of a person depend upon particular characteristics? In a way yes, and in another way no, if we look on people as sent out into the world stamped with God's image and superscription. We have it on good authority that He will search high and low to find a lost one.[1] The intrinsic equality of all human beings as such, in which secular humanists also believe, could hardly find a better analogy.

But the analogy has a fatal flaw, if it is used not just to illustrate but to explain our value. Suppose a small boy drops his pocket money down a drain. 'Never mind,' says his kind father, 'I will give you another one.' If he does not learn to take care, his father may become irritated or impoverished; but as long as there is a constant supply of coins forthcoming, the boy has no reason to cry for the particular one that has gone for good. 'It was a lovely shiny new one,' he laments, but that is just sentimental. An old dull one will buy as many or as few sweets. Likewise, when a banknote becomes bedraggled, the bank will still honour it, but sooner or later, even in Italy, it will call it in and issue a new one. That is not the sort of honour we owe to human beings. They can never, since Noah's rainbow, be returned for cancellation.

We might almost say, holding our breaths in expectation of a liberal thunderbolt, that the whole point of persons is precisely that they are not equal. One is not as good as another. No human being is worth less than another in God's sight, not because they are all worth the same, but because each one is irreplaceable. Not surprisingly, parenthood is the clue. The alternative to making favourites among our children is not to love them 'all alike': it is to love them all differently, so differently that comparisons of 'amounts' of love are not just odious but impossible.[2] Even finite loves can be incommensurable. All the less does infinite love do sums and put living creatures into equations. Persons are not units of value. No one can adequately stand in for another. If one is lost, the loss is irreparable.

So we are forced back upon the increasingly mysterious question: What is this 'value' that each one of us has as an individual not as a sort of thing? The special qualities some people have are as agreeably irrelevant as the newness and shininess of a coin; and yet it is the 'specialness' of persons that we are trying to track down.

The answer is not staring us in the face, but is even nearer home. Each of us knows as a matter of plain fact what it is to be 'special'. To see what mattering means, I do not have to be young and beautiful, rich and powerful, witty and eloquent, brilliant or efficient, learned or athletic or musical, or even sane, but simply to be Me.[3] Fact and value are united here if anywhere. I know at first hand that if I were snuffed out something irreplaceable would have gone. My difficulty is not to apprehend my own value but to put it in its proper place, maybe an entirely insignificant one behind a pillar, so to say, in God's temple. Even if I am a lost sheep, there is not much difficulty in imagining the Shepherd leaving all the others to come and look for me. One's own failings are lovable, one's own peculiarities are interesting, one's own talents are important, one's own embarrassments are ghastly, one's own virtues are solid. We avert our eyes from all this because we have been taught that it is wicked to be self-centred, forgetting that repressed self-centredness is likely to be at least as dangerous as repressed sex. It makes more sense to start with ourselves as we are and use our consciousness of ourselves to illuminate what a self is. By being me, I know what it is to be irreplaceable. I acknowledge my own claim, because I am also the claimant.

The next step follows on directly, though it will need a little care to get it right. What we have to do is ascribe this same irreplaceability to other people. If we can do this we know, really know, what the intrinsic value of a person is. This knowledge is not reserved for religious believers. Of course, if we are religious we believe that whatever value persons turn out to have all comes from God who created and sustains them. But the understanding of the value of persons is independent of the understanding of God; so believers and unbelievers can talk the same language.

But now if they are not careful, they will soon find that the language they are talking is simply the language of equality again. 'All these other people are as good as me. They have the same right to consideration, as creatures of God or just as human beings.' It is better to say that much than not to say it at all, but it entirely misses the point about the value of persons: nobody else is as good as me; nobody can replace me; I am completely special; and I cannot replace anybody else; every single person matters uniquely. The thought is terrifying, but convincing. I cannot imagine what it is like to be Beethoven, or Himmler, or St Teresa of Avila, or an Australian aborigine, but I can imagine what it is like to mind what happens to somebody else in the way I do mind what happens to me. It is often beyond us to enter into one another's hopes and fears and contents and discontents; but it is not beyond us to understand what it is for someone else to be thwarted or satisfied, terrified or delighted. This is the sort of claim we are talking about as the foundation of the value of persons. It is a sort of claim which, if we acknowledge it at all, can by-pass mere respect and introduce us in an elementary way to love.

It will be quite difficult to keep a hold of this understanding, even apart from the sheer practical difficulty of being good enough to live up to it. What is not easy is to keep this way of thinking sufficiently concrete. The person who matters is a particular person, not an abstract idea of a person. I do not love myself for my good qualities, but nor do I love myself because of some generalized respect for persons. I mind about myself as the self I am, who is like this rather than like that.

This notion of loving *as* is important because it can make the link we need between my mattering and other people's mattering. If your particular qualities are taken to be the reasons for me to love you, then my self-love (which has no need of reasons) seems uncomfortably unique. Our special unreasoned loves for our separate selves run parallel without needing to meet in mutual lovability. Only God or a saint, it seems, can reliably bridge this chasm between self-love and love of others by loving *another* person simply as such: an odd enough idea anyway. But if we forget about valuing anyone for reasons, but say that all valuing, whether of oneself or of somebody else, can be valuing as a person with qualities, we need never put different selves asunder in this way. I can value you as the person you are and you can value me as the person I am. The person I mind about, *with* my qualities rather than either because of them or abstracted from them, is the very person that you can mind about too. You are not dependent upon the chance of merit in me or the miracle of sanctity in yourself to be able to value me in my irreplaceable reality, which is like yours and yet unlike yours.

If we like, we can call this kind of valuing 'loving you for yourself alone', but we need not compulsively add 'and not your yellow hair'. Even your yellow hair is part of your creaturely endowment and is not to be excluded. It is lovable as far as it goes. If it fades or falls out, we shall be no nearer to a being called 'yourself alone', who is not blonde or grey or bald. To hunt such a being, to catch it and try to love it, is a desperate exercise which need not be embarked upon. The people we love are people with innumerable characteristics which develop rather than diminish.

What any kind of valuing does require is recognition. A coin has its 'image and superscription', but it does not matter if we cannot tell one individual coin from another. The kind of valuing which recognizes irreplaceability has to be more specific. What is irreplaceable is the particular person, not the general form of a person. If people are 'special', each one is specially distinguishable. I know who I am by being me: but if other people are to mind about me, they also must know who I am. 'Minding', in other words, needs some content, not to do sums with but to identify people by. We are not interchangeable units of value like coins and nor are we, so to speak, interchangeable units of minding. An irreplaceable self may be good or bad, complex or simple, interesting or dull, normal or abnormal, but it cannot be characterless. We must treat with suspicion any notion that creatures can be valued, by God or man, quite apart from their qualities. The stuff of creation is particular detail, not general form.

❦ 10 ❦

Being and Doing

Why should the particular and appealing detail of what a person is like be lost sight of in the name of love? Why, when we are especially concerned with the value of a person, should we have to struggle with this tendency to shrink real people into characterless entities? People are more than interchangeable units: they are distinctively irreplaceable. People are more than abstract beings: they are actively individual. Yet the battle against formalizing the real person to a mere geometrical point seems to be a recurring one. The onion seems to ask to be peeled away.[1]

The trouble is that we are nervous: nervous that somebody might turn out to matter more than somebody else. This fear is hard to scotch. It is fed by common sense, which tells us it is true: to every one of us some people *do* matter more than others. It is fed by piety, which tells us it is wrong: God is no respecter of persons. So we still keep trying to come to a God's-eye view by the short cut of simply discounting individuality. 'Love me not for comely grace . . . No, nor for my constant heart'[2] sounds almost theological. Undiscriminating regard comes to seem praiseworthy.[3] But the onion is a good image. People are not like nuts with a central kernel we can reach if we are tough enough to crack away the extraneous outer shell. Their real selves are through and through the layers of characteristics which we rashly discount in the name of unconditional love. They may grow and change and they may be loved through their growing and changing. What is to be loved is the whole pattern, not a vanishing point in the midst of it. God's love, we may say, is ready for any amount of growing and changing, to encourage or redeem it. If we aspire to be like Him, we shall not be in too much of a hurry to reduce people to standard shapes and sizes.

Equality in God's sight is important, of course. It is a kind of over-weening half-truth. Our equality as human beings ought to be a relatively dull part of the truth about us. It hardly begins to do justice to what each one of us knows really matters about himself or herself as a unique individual.[4] But since human beings are so prone to get stuck in unjust inequality, we find ourselves obliged to take a great deal of trouble to establish equality before we can dare to relish diversity.

'Unselfishness' is another over-weening half-truth. In saying that people are lovable it is tempting, for fear of selfish partiality, to reduce their specific lovableness to something merely notional that is never expected to make any difference to the world. But unselfishness, likewise, is a dull part of the truth about love, though important when we are stuck in self-interest. In each case we need to go on to say something more, that what matters about people, what is there to be minded about and loved, is their individual uniqueness which has distinct qualities and shows itself in characteristic behaviour.

We still are not to love people *for* their behaviour. To get the emphasis right needs a good deal of care. In particular, the slogan that it is *being* not *doing* that matters about people is too important to be allowed to go by default. It needs both strong affirmation and a little caution in its application. The point is to continue to make sure that the idea of 'being' remains definite.

In many contexts the slogan 'It's not what people *do* but what they *are*' is exactly what we need. It can be constructively said to people (oneself or others) who are anxious to be helpful, torn by ambition, afraid of failure, unable to relax, concerned about the development of their children, wishing they could forget an injury, or wanting to be better Christians. Human beings, even Protestant human beings, need to be reminded again and again that doing is not all that matters. People cannot justify themselves by their works, whether in everyday life or in religion. Salvation is not to be earned. We cannot earn our own and we are not to expect other people to earn theirs. Human effort is liable to let us down, when it has no roots in what people really are. Goodness is a harvest to be cultivated, not a product to be assembled. It means something quite specific, not a platitude, to call virtues 'the fruit of the spirit' (Gal. 5.22–3).

People who mind about goodness need to keep remembering that strenuous application is all very well, but the conquests it wins can be deceptive. Early victory against weakness is apt to be turned into defeat at the next stage by legalism or self-righteousness. We can see this perfectly well in other people if not in ourselves. If we forget it, we expect qualifying achievement and find that Sisyphus' boulder always seems to roll down again. So we get disappointed and angry with ourselves and one another. That is how we are prepared for the refreshment of realizing that New Testament perfection has not much to do with earning. The decisive choices in the gospels, even the most exacting, are not so much a matter of screwing oneself up to make an effort as of taking, or refusing, something that is offered. The recurrent themes are wanting and being satisfied, drinking a cup, harvesting a ripe crop, hungering and thirsting after righteousness, seeing and believing.

But when people are being perfected something definite is expected to happen. So the time comes for pointing out that to be an individual person is not just to be distinct and recognizable, but to be capable of activity. Although the slogan 'It's not what people *do* but what they *are*' has done good service, sooner or later 'doing' will have to be recalled from banishment to take its proper place. Being, as lovable, cannot be permanently divorced from what it does. That is not a selfish statement. Doing need not be for *me*: but when I appreciate kindness or wit or fairmindedness, I really do hope to see these admirable qualities in action. If I am just as happy to see passive neutrality, that merely means that I am passively neutral too. Having rightly insisted that what counts is what people are rather than what they do, I still need to acknowledge that I cannot, selfishly or unselfishly, love of some kind of inert being with no character, that never does anything.

Along these lines we ought to be able to feel less confused about some of the current perplexities over the 'work ethic', its humanity and inhumanity, the ways it can be a support or a tyranny. Can we or can we not detach the 'real person' from his role in life, without going all the way into a sort of flower people ethic which belittles endeavour and makes nothing strenuous worth doing? It would be nice to have our cake and eat it, to comfort the unappreciated and encourage the strugglers both at once, but it is only too easy to discourage and discomfort, in a world where 'what people are' has come to mean chiefly the work they do or once did.

'What people *are*' can be invoked in a tone of voice which would like to be uplifting and manages to be depressing. It can have echoes of 'What do you want to be when you grow up?', a question apt to elicit the response, 'I don't particularly want to be anything', or even, tacitly, 'I shall do my best to resist being made into anything.'[5] Being, in this sense, is no escape from the tyranny of doing. It is a sort of congealed doing, according to which people hope to be able to judge one another and create stereotypes. This is no long step from the world where people are to be characterized adequately as butcher, baker, or candlestick-maker, the world of ambitions fulfilled and unful-filled, of 'callings' of the sort that 'vocational training' prepares for, of qualification and job-satisfaction and round pegs in round holes. This far-sighted, highly-organized, improving kind of being could only ever connect with a limited range of human life. If being is to be reduced to this, it needs only to be stigmatized as 'irrelevant' or even 'classbound' and any human point that might have been made is thoroughly lost.

Appreciation of what people are does not have to be put into this social straitjacket. Anybody who has ever wanted two people to like each other, or considered the question 'What *is* it about her that is so special?' will have sought an answer like 'It's not what she does but what she is', or 'He makes life more worthwhile somehow', or 'There is nobody like her'. We can describe people up to a point and give potted life-stories of them, but in the end there is no substitute for meeting them. People do not have to be heroic or efficient or amusing, or even very good, for there to be 'something about them' that makes us warm to them as the particular people they are. The last thing we want is a kind of smooth level of similar merits. Some people are cool and calm, some passionate, some gentle, some energetic, some reserved, some ebullient. When we love them we want them to go on being themselves, whatever we hope they will do or not do.

The 'harvest' image is still at hand. Just as goodness is the fruit of the spirit, are people's *doings* the fruit of what they *are*? To say this can be misleading. Because this biblical image is so attractive, it is tempting to use it in an all-purpose way which yields diminishing returns. We seem to be talking sense with it, saying for instance that we cannot make people do things, only encourage them by patient cultivation. But suddenly we have missed the point. The harvest, after all, is what matters to the farmer. The ear in the corn is what the whole exercise is for; and that is exactly what we do not want to say about people. What they do may show what they are, but what they do is essentially *not* all that matters about them.

A different simile may help more. People's doings, we might say, are like the tip of an iceberg. They are neither insubstantial, like the froth on beer, nor all that really counts, like the peas in a pod. What someone does is only a small proportion of the person but is continuous with the whole. To try to separate the 'real self' from the way it shows itself in the world is like trying to cut off the ice under the water from the ice above. It is all part of one block; and it behoves us both to take heed of what is there to be seen and to remember that people are much more than they can ever show to each other. What people are, the whole of themselves, is what makes them, as it were, float the way they do.

This image for being and doing can explain a good deal. It can suggest how achievement both does and does not matter. Achievement is that important but limited aspect of the real human being that rises up above the waves and can be seen. It is not imaginary or flimsy or even hollow, though it gives very little idea of how much more there is.

We meet each other first and identify each other by way of our doings. We want our meetings to be propitious, so we mind, sometimes inordinately, about how much we and our friends and our children are positively able to show to the world. Yet we really ought to know that when we regard each other as potential achievers we are at least missing a lot and may be running into perils.

Having said all this, we can come back to the question of the 'work ethic'. To emphasize what people are has not committed us, either to saying that they are what they do, or to belittling what they do. There is no need for people to sink themselves in their roles or to cease to be themselves when they take on roles.

Another simile may help. The roles people fill are much like clothes. There is no reason why they should have to be called 'inauthentic'. They fit us well or badly, keeping us warm and allowing us to meet the world, or constricting our movements and stifling our personalities. Without a role we may bask in the sun or shiver in the wind. To appreciate people for the roles they fill, breadwinner, lame duck, mastermind, darling child, pair of hands, is inadequate, of course; but so is it inadequate to forget that our roles do express positively something of what we are.

With doing partially rehabilitated, we may now dabble in an even more dangerous heresy, that even 'having' is not altogether hopeless. This needs to be explained, not to justify greed and selfishness after all, but to clear up a possible muddle. In emphasizing what people *are* we have seemed at some stages to be travelling alongside Dr Erich Fromm, whose urgent message is that *being* ought to prevail over *having*.[6] One can hardly help warming to his insight that people today are eaten up by having and truly live when they start to be. It is surely true to say that many people in the modern world would be much happier if they could understand this; and every world is a modern world. So we can blithely condemn 'acquisition' all together.

That is the way to lose the chance to say something more that needs saying about human values. Dr Fromm writes finely about sharing and especially the sharing of experiences when people love and admire one another;[7] but he is not able to do full justice to the value of *giving*. His emphasis could eliminate not only grasping possession but grateful acceptance. There is no need to look on all gifts as bribes, corrupting their recipients. If we love people, we want to give them things. We use things as pledges of love. St Augustine understood this, in his analogy of the man who made a ring for his betrothed.[8] 'Certainly let her love his gift', not instead of its giver but for his sake. We could try to say this in Dr Fromm's language, but at the risk of missing something important about the sacramental character of the material world.

Things, even possessions, can be laden with good significance as well as with bad. That belonged to my mother. We must all stir the Christmas pudding. She has a tremendous flair for lovely clothes. They always keep biscuits in that box. Jane Austen lived here. That scent makes me homesick. Do stay for a cup of tea. The full meaning of these innocent statements would be hard to express without bringing in 'having'. As human beings we can enjoy the fact that what people *are* is garnished with what they *have*, but more than that, is expressed in what they have. People are themselves in the midst of patterns of characteristic objects and we do not feel that they would be freer or better if they shed them all. Even St Francis had his brown habit, which is still lovingly shown at Assisi. People meet each other in settings which are partly material, not wholly spiritual. Not all having is acquisitive, any more than all wanting is acquisitive.

To think otherwise would make nonsense, not only of individual style and self-expression, but of the whole ancient and honourable notion of hospitality. Abraham had curds and milk and cakes and veal to set before his unknown guests.[9] To feed five thousand people it is necessary for somebody to have five barley loaves and two small fishes. The bread and wine of the Eucharist are taken before they are blessed and given. A host is someone who makes other people welcome to what he has.

❧ 11 ❧

Mattering

Suppose we define a person as an irreplaceable centre of minding. By this means we do not dispose of the mystery of personality, but point to where the mystery is. There is an evocative passage in the Book of Revelation, to which Archbishop Anthony Bloom is wont to refer: 'To him that overcometh will I give to eat of the hidden manna, and will give him a white stone, and in the stone a new name written, which no man knoweth saving he that receiveth it' (Rev. 2.17).[1] To be given that white stone would be to find one's soul, one's special identity.

In this way talk about souls begins to make sense, without committing us to any theory of 'ghosts in machines'. There is no need to imagine souls as etherial detachable components of human beings, mysteriously indestructible but frustratingly invisible. The soul is the person as irreplaceable and we can affirm this whether or not talk about 'immortal souls' comes naturally to us.[2] If we believed that human beings were essentially perishable, 'soul' would still not be meaningless but we should have to mourn the death of soul and body together. But if we believe in the God of Abraham, Isaac and Jacob, who is not the God of the dead but of the living,[3] we shall be able to have faith that He will maintain or re-create the irreplaceable person for eternal life. Each of us is as important in His eyes as we are to ourselves and one day we shall see ourselves as He sees us.

Can this way of thinking about people really claim to be Christian? There is certainly ample foundation for it in the gospels. The second commandment tells us to love other people, not instead of ourselves, not more than ourselves, but as ourselves. The emphasis on reward, which has embarrassed moralists down the ages,[4] is a reminder that we are wanting, needing, minding beings, who are told to love because love is good for us and will make us happy. 'Give, and it shall be given unto you; good measure, pressed down, and shaken together, and running over shall men give into your bosom' (Luke 6.38). We might think that this way in to Christian morality was just a concession to our frailty, of which we should take as little advantage as possible, were it not that overarching everything else is the essential, inescapable and controversial message that God is our Father. A father is one who minds individually about his children. We have been told often enough that the Father's love is 'unconditional'. We think we know what that means, and it can actually mislead us. It makes us into indistinguishable units again instead of special, lovable, demanding and exasperating children, with unlimited promise and distinctive needs, capable of hurting and of delighting anyone who loves us.

Christian morality, when it takes its foundation in the Fatherhood of God seriously, is both specific and realistic. It starts with human beings as they find themselves from infancy: wholly separate and wholly dependent. Every baby that yells is saying both 'I matter' and 'I need you'. Each human creature is its own world and morality is about the interlocking of our worlds. We find in experience that our worlds can and must interlock, that each individual mattering is not all the mattering there is. People who are lucky enough to grow up surrounded by human love are taught from the outset, not merely to adjust themselves to other people's mattering, but to enter into it.[5] What the gospel adds is the assurance that we are made for this, that the mattering we have experienced is real and is the purpose of creation.

Now we can return to the idea of the 'sacredness' of persons,[6] not as some magic quality conferred upon them by God or man, but as their irreplaceability. We know what this means for ourselves and those very dear to us. It is an act of faith to realize that everybody is irreplaceable, that every human being is a *person* in this special sense. It need not be an act of religious faith: there is no need to try to exclude the unbeliever from this kind of humanism, any more than the unbeliever has the right to exclude the Christian. We can all be personalists here together.

It remains true, though, that it is open to the unbeliever to exclude himself, while it is not open to the Christian to exclude himself, from the conviction that every person matters uniquely. The unbeliever is not being illogical if he casts his moral net widely or narrowly; whereas the Christian is bound to try to cast it as widely as God casts it. Everyone can agree that Michelangelo is irreplaceable; but when God says of a drunken tramp, 'But I loved that one. I did not want him lost', God's other children must try to see the point. We should see it, after all, if the tramp's human mother said it. What the belief in a heavenly Father requires is the exercise of imagination to see each other's irreplaceability.

The story of the prophet Nathan and King David[7] has been much told in pulpits, and 'Thou art the man' made to prove many moral points, but perhaps it can be re-pointed to illustrate the value of a human being. Nathan is the hero of the story because he dares to rebuke the king. Maybe whenever one takes it upon oneself to administer a rebuke or a criticism, a rebuff or a compliment, one is in fact dealing with a royal personage, a son or daughter of God, exalted even as a sinner, responding to deference not to presumption.

This way of understanding the sacredness of persons is more not less practical than insistence on equality. It has more to say both to people who want to go deeper and to people who have no intention of going deeper. At the best, it can help us to enter into God's point of view; but at the lowest, it makes irrelevant the facile arguments about actual inequality with which people stave off their duty to their fellow human beings. 'All men are equal' is too easily despised as a simple falsehood. 'Each of us is irreplaceable' is both truer and more exhilarating. It leads instead of drives, by giving the imagination something to work on. The dead weight of evils such as racism, sex prejudice and class-consciousness, after all, is more negative than positive. It is not depraved so much as thoughtless to fail to see that one's moral ideas are far too narrow. It is only too natural for people to look on their own kind of person as real and the rest as a blurred mass in the background. Emphasis on equality often does not unblur the mass: it only makes it seem threatening. We bludgeon one another with slogans instead of taking heed of one another's significance. Of course 'irreplaceability' could become a slogan too, but until it trips as glibly off our lips as 'equality' it has a chance of saying something we could listen to.

Even if all it does is make disputants more comprehensible to each other, it can be of use. The words at present in use are darkening counsel. 'Sacredness' remains obscure. 'Equality' makes people indignant. Sometimes they take their stand on apparent relevant inequality. Sometimes they are anxious to regard equality but at a loss how to apply it. When we are thinking, say, about abortion, how are we to compare a new innocent life to be snuffed out unaware, or a known human being to be made desperate? How are we to balance extinction against misery? Somehow we must plump for one with apparent insensitivity to the other. But if we ask whether a foetus, undoubtedly a human being, is already irreplaceable at the stage it has now reached, we have begun by talking the same language. The problem is not 'Will it have a good life?' or 'Will it stop other people from having a good life?' but 'Will another one do?' We shall have to ask questions like, 'Irreplaceable to whom?' To itself? Is there anything yet we can call 'itself'? To God? Is there a God and is this already His child? To humanity? Is what we propose to do life-enhancing or life-diminishing? To its mother? What does all this really mean to her whose concern in the matter is fundamental? We may end with less assurance of the rightness of our actions, but we should at least be able to act with our eyes open, seeing how what we do matters.

All this talk of irreplaceability could be just another way of expressing Kant's dictum that people are ends in themselves and are not to be used merely as means.[8]

> In the kingdom of ends everything has either Value or Dignity. Whatever has a value can be replaced by something else which is *equivalent*; whatever, on the other hand, is above all value, and therefore admits of no equivalent, has a dignity.[9]

Need any more be said? It can still be useful to re-state something we have known for a long time. To re-state it, in all diffidence, with qualifications and even modifications, can be a good way of standing on someone else's shoulders.

Two criticisms which have been made of Kant are worth taking up respectfully and using to amplify the account of the value of a person. The simpler criticism is that, entirely innocently, people do often use one another as means, and even merely as means. We send letters, and buy pins and petrol, and live in houses made with hands; and often we never see the people who do things for us, or even know which jobs have been mechanized and which have not. The answer is not to insist that all this using of each other is wrong: it is to accept it and reiterate that it is not what people do which is irreplaceable, but what they are. What people do can properly be a means to all sorts of ends of their own and of one another; but what each of us *is* is something unique which is an end in itself.

But how far does all this have to go? Not all living beings can be irreplaceable persons. Where do we draw the line? The second criticism, rather more complicated to sort out, is that Kant drew it too narrowly. He drew it at what he called rationality,[10] thereby excluding animals, though not angels or Martians. He expressly repudiated the error of setting store by humankind as such, for which the hideous name 'speciesism' has recently been coined by people concerned about animal rights;[11] but it is still rather easy to criticize him, both for drawing the wrong line and for not drawing it consistently. Why, on the one hand, does capacity to reason matter more than capacity to feel?[12] And why, on the other hand, are we so sure that non-rational human beings such as babies and the severely mentally handicapped are still to be treated as ends in themselves?[13] Mary Midgley in her book *Beast and Man* makes both these points, but goes deeper. She recognizes that Kant is 'clearly sensitive to aspects that go far beyond his official view'.[14]

She is able to illustrate from Kant's own writings an attitude towards the animal world which is very near to making all kinds of creatures into ends in themselves: ' "The more we come into contact with animals and observe their behaviour, the more we love them, for we see how great is their care for their young. It is then difficult for us to be cruel in thought even to a wolf." '[15] She goes on: 'Another example goes further. "Leibnitz", says Kant, "used a tiny worm for purposes of observation, and then carefully replaced it with its leaf on the tree, so that it should not come to harm through any act of his." '

By this appreciative route, Mrs Midgley is able to use and extend Kant's own insight that the value of other persons is not any usefulness they may or may not have for us but is simply *because* they are other. They are

> something good we did not invent and do not own, something genuinely outside and over against us, capable of opposing our wishes. The economic metaphors of exchange, from which such words as *value, worth, preciousness*, are devised, must be broken through here. Kant says that while things have value or price, people have something different, called dignity.[16]

Her whole book is an impressive plea that animals too, from Kant's wolf to Leibnitz' worm, Iris Murdoch's hovering kestrel,[17] or the chimpanzees that may or may not be able to use language, are in some sense, ' a sense that can certainly do with study', ends in themselves.[18]

It is here, just where Kant's view thus expanded becomes really appealing, that we must call a halt and make a distinction. The concept of 'dignity' is so congenial that it is tempting to let it conceal a shift in the meaning of 'end in itself'. It is time to point out that something which is truly an end in itself in this attractively extended sense is not necessarily irreplaceable in the sense in which persons are irreplaceable. There are several kinds of preciousness, not just ends and means, in question here. The little worm on the leaf may be a silkworm and have a clear cash value. It may eat greenfly and so be a means to the gardener's ends. I may think it pretty, so that to me it has what Kant called 'fancy value'.[19] But whether I like it or not, it is a beautifully formed creature which I could not invent and have no right arbitrarily to destroy. I am not being sentimental in responding to the idea of its dignity. If it is the last of an endangered species, it is even in one sense irreplaceable. All this we want to affirm and then we must add: it is still not intrinsically irreplaceable. If there happens to be a little worm on nearly every leaf, one is as good as another; or if one is special this is because it is a particularly good specimen. It is not a 'me'.

We may call the little worm an end in itself in Mary Midgley's sense but not in Kant's. It is definitely not a person. Do we have to move all the way up the scale to human beings before we arrive at what it lacks, and is what it lacks something quite clear and specific? Are we looking for rationality, or for self-consciousness, or for individuality, and must these stand or fall together? The debate about the educated chimpanzees gives us an opportunity to sort out what we really believe about people and their value. It can both explain further and apply the notion of irreplaceability.

The argument is not about whether chimpanzees, talking or otherwise, have dignity or are ends in themselves. We may gladly agree that they have and are. It is about whether their apparent capacity to acquire some use of language proves anything about whether we ought after all to start thinking of them as persons. Have they souls? This is not a matter of 'vapour done up like a new-born babe'[20] which will float up to heaven when they die. It is a matter of whether a chimpanzee can be a 'me'. We are pretty sure it has sentience and can feel. We are beginning to wonder if it has more rationality than we had bargained for. But is it inside or outside the world of persons?

There is a technical question here about whether or not the chimpanzees really are *using* language, syntax and all, in anything like the way human beings use language. The answer to this question may very likely be: no, they are not and cannot. But the answer cannot, surely, be no by definition.[21] We cannot derive from the meaning of the words 'human being' and 'animal' the certainty that no animal can enter into real linguistic communication with us or among its own kind. Suppose, one day if not now, we are satisfied that this is really happening? Could learning to talk give an animal a 'soul' or prove that it had a soul all along?

For some religious people these questions are deeply worrying because, by revelation if not by definition, an animal *cannot* have a soul. To suggest that an animal could be or become a person seems almost atheistic, in the sort of way that Darwin seemed atheistic. To try to teach an animal to talk *must* be written off as sentimental folly, because if it is serious it is treating an animal as a child of God, which they think we know it cannot be.

It ought to be a commonplace that faith does not mean sticking to blind assumptions. It means looking at the real world with open eyes in the light of trust in God. If Christians since Darwin have had to learn painfully that a child of God can also be a real animal, they ought not to brush aside unconsidered the converse idea that an animal could be eligible to become something like a child of God. We are speaking figuratively, of course, but so we are with human beings. God adopts us and surely some human beings adopt some animals. This could be a picture not merely a parody of what it is to be made in the image of our Creator. What the facts suggest is that our notion of a person may be too clearcut. It cannot really be an insult to God to suggest that the universe He makes is less simple, and that His creatures have more complicated possibilities, than we have tended to suppose.

Instead of starting with a boundary to fortify, let us hold on to what is more fundamental. There is no need to be defensive about the concept of personality as if we might find out after all that we had lost our grip of it. Each of us knows at least one person who really matters, oneself; and most of us know a good many. Selfishly or unselfishly, we know what irreplaceability means. To lose one's sense of mattering is pathological not truly human. What we do with it is another question. Some people generously give themselves, some meanly cherish themselves, some rigorously reject themselves, some seem absent-mindedly to mislay themselves; but 'self' as irreplaceable 'me' is for each of us a place where we can see what it means to call persons ends in themselves.

We know then at first hand what is the natural claim of a person. But we also know perfectly well that claims can be more than just acknowledged: they can be encouraged and fostered. That, after all, is the most significant role of a parent, to draw out the 'mattering', the irreplaceability of each child, to enable him or her to grow into a person. We all need this nourishment, first from our parents, then from one another, as much as we need physical nourishment. Without it people are impaired and stunted, or even starved.

It is true to say that to a great extent people create one another. So it becomes a reasonable question how far this responsibility can go. No human being can create *ex nihilo*, from nothing. But if mattering, being a 'me', is not simply ready-made but developing, it is time to remember as a plain fact that it is not only human beings who can be regarded as irreplaceable individuals. Can we give a chimpanzee or a dog a white stone with its name written upon it, Washoe or Tray or Fido? People mourn their pets; and although it is only fair to say that they often do actually replace them, they do it with a kind of reverent regret. There is an echo here of the way in which human generations succeed one another. In the love of a human being for an animal we seem to have a gentle model of the doctrine of election. Perhaps a human being can make an animal matter, confer irreplaceability upon it, in something like the way in which God makes us matter.[22] This way of being, or becoming, an end in itself is different from the way in which the little worm or the hovering kestrel is an end in itself by being sheerly *other* than the watching human beings. It could have a wide range of moral consequences: for instance, we might well deplore the incongruity of teaching an animal to communicate by telling it a lie.[23]

The question about the language-using chimpanzees at its most interesting is a sophisticated version of the naive enquiry 'Will my doggie go to heaven?' It is not silly or irreverent to ask whether in this sense an animal could have a sort of soul. It is a way of trying to understand more thoroughly both human and animal nature. If the answer turned out to be no, it would be because there is not enough 'me-ness' in the creature to start with to be the foundation upon which this sort of mattering could be built. A child's teddy bear, presumably, is not really a 'me' at all, and if all goes well the child will gradually and painlessly grow up to understand this. But to assume that there is *no* spark of 'me' in some of the animals with which human beings seem to enter into relation is a harsh, or convenient, assumption which the facts do not appear to support, still less require. It is a less callous defence of fox-hunting to assert, however improbably, 'The fox enjoys it' than 'Animals cannot suffer'. An animal abandoned by its owner cannot express itself in poetry but can surely have the beginnings of feelings analogous to George Herbert's,

> O that thou shouldst give dust a tongue
> To cry to thee
> And then not hear it crying![24]

12

One-way Love

It begins to look as if we have made a gradual but complete reversal of the argument. All this discussion of the value of persons was begun as a way of insisting upon the idea that values are for finding not for our choosing.[1] Yet here we are after all delighting the hearts of prescriptivists by conferring value upon one another and upon our fellow creatures. Are we going to eat our words?

What we need is not to retract our views but to clarify them. The reversal is only apparent. Finding and making are still elaborately interwoven. The world, we may agree with Keats, is a vale of soul-making. People are made by God, by life, by each other, and their value emerges and is there to be found. Value can be elicited; it can be given; it can be neglected and abused; it can be recognized; it can be authenticated. We can set a value on things and people for other people's sake, whether by merely taking it on trust or by full appreciation. In this sort of evaluation we can both confer and discover. 'It belonged to my grandmother.' 'She taught me to enjoy contemporary painting.' 'I am so glad to meet you, having heard so much about you.' 'Any friend of his is welcome here.' 'I cannot lay violent hands upon the Lord's Anointed.'

The foundation of all these ways of thinking is the notion of a person as a particular sort of living claim, the kind of claim which is based on being a 'me'. A person's development may be encouraged or diminished, but his or her central being, or heart, is this 'me-ness' which can be characterized variously as rationality or self-consciousness, but which is fundamentally the capacity to *mind*.² We mind sometimes about important and sometimes about foolish things, but it is our mindings, like Mrs Bennett's, that preserve us from insensibility.

The personal claims that creatures make upon us depend upon the character of their minding, which we ourselves may, or may not, have helped to develop. A dog minds being put into quarantine, but a cow does not mind standing about all day in a muddy field. A worm, we hope, has not the capacity to mind being put on a hook. An animal that cannot 'look before and after' will mind being hurt but may not mind becoming another animal's dinner. Johnny does not seem to mind being teased. Mother does not mind my coming home late; or if she does, she would never admit it. To get to know somebody better is to find out what he or she really minds about. Selfishness and sentimentality in different ways will get this wrong. To love is to be able to identify oneself with someone else's minding. We are still talking about something real outside ourselves which is there to be discovered. The argument has not been reversed by the understanding that this 'me-ness' of other persons can be fostered by ourselves and that we can help to elicit one another's value, thereby getting a glimpse of what creative love might mean.

The argument is not reversed, then; but some people may feel that it is high time that it was. To base love, in anything like its Christian meaning, upon the concept of 'me-ness' sounds like a terrible contradiction. It is the recalcitrant 'me' which is the enemy to everything that Christ stood for. How dare a Christian presume to ignore the demand for self-denial which is the very heart of the gospel? We may get used to Christians who doubt the resurrection and even the incarnation, but surely selfless love is what the Christian faith is about, supreme and sacrosanct? A recent appeal to the nation to put God first, others second and self *last* was not criticized for its doctrine.

The rebuke has truth on its side, but not the whole truth. The trouble is that to learn to put God first, others second and self last is so far from being the answer to our problems that it is itself our problem. If we really knew how to put God first we should be home already. For most of us, the conscious attempt to put self last could make us at best difficult to live with and at worst eaten up with spiritual pride. We cannot forget ourselves on purpose. What we need is something or better still someone to take our minds off ourselves.

That makes the problem of self-love sound purely practical. It is really more fundamental. Self-denial could never be an end in itself. 'We were put into the world to do good to others. But what were the others put here for?' If any creatures are to be loved and cherished, then sooner or later we ourselves are likewise to be loved and cherished. What is sauce for the gander is sauce for the goose. To shut our eyes to this for ever would be inverted pride or faithlessness rather than Christian humility.

The affirmation of the significance of each individual person, including one's own self, is as much part of the authentic Christian tradition as the theme of self-denial. Many worldly accommodations and evasions of the full impact of the gospel have been made down the centuries, but this is not one of them. The way of Christ is to take up a cross, but the end is to glorify God and enjoy Him for ever. In putting God first, what we are to find is not negation but fulfilment. The kingdom of heaven is something we are to want and seek, a pearl of great price we may aspire to gain. In keeping with this, St Paul was not ashamed to hope for a heavenly prize. Throughout Christian history, this notion of fulfilment claims great names, and notably the names of St Augustine and St Thomas Aquinas.

There is nothing soft about this tradition. The Christian beatitudes stand happiness on its head and bless the poor, the mourners and the persecuted. The promise of fulfilment can go with some distinctly austere views about this life: St Augustine at least is generally thought of as world-denying, certainly not as world-affirming. Yet throughout it is happiness that is in question and our faith presents itself to us as a recipe for happiness. 'Thou hast made us for thyself, and our hearts are restless until they find rest in thee'[3] has been quoted many times and so has, 'We shall rest and see; we shall see and we shall love; we shall love and we shall praise. Behold what will be, in the end, without end! For what is our end but to reach that kingdom which has no end?'[4] Aquinas put it more dryly: 'God is the ultimate end for all things without exception.' 'He alone, who fills with all good things thy desire, can satisfy thy will, and therefore in him alone our happiness lies.'[5]

These statements can sound like platitudes. They are more likely to be allowed to sink into dreariness than to be indignantly repudiated. Their apparent conflict with the theme of self-denial is not noticed too much and meanwhile talk of Christian unselfish love also takes on a platitudinous air. Maybe both themes could be refreshed and enlivened by being brought into relation with one another. To organize a sort of clash of platitudes could be constructive not mischievous.

For many Christians the proper result of such a clash appears obvious: fulfilment must give way. Its honourable recurrence in the Christian tradition is taken to be an aberration. Regard for self is just one insidious way in which selfishness, the great enemy, is manifested. What Christianity is really about is *agape*, that totally selfless love for which Christians had to find a name to distinguish it from all our human egoistic loves. It is agape that 'seeketh not her own', that 'never faileth', that abides when prophecies, tongues and knowledge come to an end. Agape, then, is the precise opposite of self-regard. It asks no reward. It does not even ask for a worthy subject to love but chooses out the insignificant and sinful. That is how God loves and so that is the sort of love we are to learn. The cross of Christ represents the 'I' crossed out. How after hearing all this can we possibly hanker after fulfilment?

Yet these true Christian affirmations can slide, I believe have slid, into a lopsided emphasis. To try to correct them is to dare to take issue with a great book to whose influence the present strong prevalence of these ideas is due: Anders Nygren's *Agape and Eros*, first published in England in the 1930s, and reissued since the war.[6] Its ideas have become part of our mental furniture. Though it has been weightily answered, notably by Burnaby in his profound study of Augustine's thought, *Amor Dei*,[7] its influence upon less technical Christian moral thought seems to continue unabated.

Nygren has hit the notion of fulfilment in Christian ethics hard, because he appreciates what he eventually repudiates. For him, it is in the end only agape which is truly Christian: but first he sets out *eros* in a way which makes the whole argument significant. Eros is far more than the erotic. It is the love which is desire, but not necessarily sensual or even earthly desire. It is the love which seeks fulfilment and in the end, for Nygren, it has to be seen as a temptation and a snare; but it certainly does not have to be either trivial or gross. Nygren traces the eros tradition back to Plato and describes its glories positively and even warmly. 'Eros is love for the beautiful and the good.'[8] It is 'the soul's homesickness, its longing for what can give it true satisfaction'.[9] It is the love which strives upwards, so that it can even be man's way to the divine.[10] 'Ladder symbolism is one of the favourite forms of expression of the Eros motif.'[11]

The point is that eros does not come downwards. We may mount towards God, but this God is always at the top of the ladder. He does not condescend. So the description of eros is used to set up a fundamentally adverse comparison with agape, that total love which has nothing to gain but seeks only to give. Nygren's verdict on eros is that, lofty as it may be, it is essentially acquisitive. It is 'motivated by the value of its object'.[12] It has nothing to do with the love which seeks not her own: quite the contrary. Nygren is sure that the Platonic tradition can make no room 'for any spontaneous and unmotivated love'.[13] So he wants Christians to leave eros firmly behind, for they know about a love which seeks to give rather than to possess, a love which does come downwards to search out even the unlovable.

At this point, Christian common sense may find itself bewildered. Why cannot God's love come down to us *and* our need-love mount to Him? Of course we are the takers in relation to God. Why are we not allowed to combine agape and eros in our understanding of what love means, rather than being forced to repudiate the love that aspires upwards? Might it not be actually presumptuous to think that human love could model itself upon agape? Eros as described by Nygren sounds more suitable to the human condition. May it not rise to meet the condescending love of God? On the face of it, that would be the obvious view for a Christian to take. It has been magnificently developed by great Christian thinkers.

It is part of Nygren's strength that he does much more than acknowledge this position. He even expounds it. In particular, his discussion of St Augustine's teaching on love as charity is a better introduction to Augustine's thought than many more neutral accounts.[14] If it misleads, it is by putting St Augustine in a sort of straitjacket, not by underestimating his greatness. He

shows how Augustine brings together as compatible and com-
plementary the inspiration of God's love that comes down and
the longing which is our love trying to find God.

Augustine himself might have been surprised to learn that in
his praise of *Caritas* he was 'synthesizing agape and eros'. His
terminology is not as neatly sorted out as Nygren would lead us
to suppose.[15] He knows that 'God is love' and his concern is to
make love real to his hearers. He asks,

> What outward appearance, what form, what stature, hands or
> feet, has love? None can say; and yet love has feet, which
> takes us to the Church, love has hands which give to the poor,
> love has eyes which give intelligence of him who is in need.[16]

So he is able to declare,

> He that has charity sees the whole at once with the under-
> standing's grasp. Dwell there, and you shall be dwelt in: abide,
> and there shall be abiding in you ... Listen to me, my
> brothers: here is a great treasure, which I would urge you with
> all the power that God gives me to win for yourselves.

This is a fine example of that kind of praise of charity which
stirred Augustine's hearers to 'acclamation and applause'[17] and
which Nygren would see as both his strength and his weakness.
He is aware how much Augustine did 'to deepen the Christian
idea of love'[18] and he is even willing to ascribe this to the
influence of neo-Platonism. Neo-Platonism is dominated by the
thought of love and Augustine is 'gripped by it in a way that is
decisive for his whole life'.[19] Yet this love is eros and is
irrevocably linked with the idea of seeking happiness for
oneself. In Nygren's view, therefore, it will not do: eros hardly
deserves the name of real love at all.

> The entire structure of Platonic Eros is egocentric. Everything
> centres on the individual self and its destiny. All that matters
> from first to last is the soul that is aflame with Eros.[20]

He sees Luther as the real hero who smashed the synthesis, like
re-setting a bone, and went back to pure Christian agape.[21]

Nygren goes so far as to call the Protestant return to
'theocentric love' a Copernican revolution.[22] He is severe about
what he calls the 'egocentric tendency' of Catholic piety, which

extols God as the highest good, the *summum bonum*. Such praise sounds devout, but what is it really but to measure God by the standard of human desire and put ourselves at the centre of the universe? The tendency to do this, Nygren insists, 'must first be rooted out if there is to be room for true fellowship with God, which has its centre in God Himself, God who gives everything and has a right to everything'.[23]

This is where the platitudes clash. Of course God is our true fulfilment; of course we must not seek God for our own sakes. It does pay to be good; but we must never take that into account. We are of infinite value; we are of no value at all. The extreme emphasis on agape has let many Christians lately affirm the second set of platitudes at the expense of the first. It is time to correct the balance. Perhaps the clear distinction of agape and eros is really a kind of teaching aid, like the division of human history into periods, a help at first but misleading if pressed too far. If we take it as absolute we shall find ourselves impoverished. If we concentrate entirely upon agape, worshipping God only as the Redeemer who loves the unlovable, we risk neglecting God the Creator whose works were not made to be unlovable. We forget how 'the morning stars sang together and all the sons of God shouted for joy' (Job 38.7).

Nygren himself has emphasized 'true fellowship with God'.[24] At the risk of being polemical, we must ask him what is to be the point of it, if we have to avert our eyes from all thought of its being finally and triumphantly *satisfying*?[25] Nygren deserves better than polemics; but on recovering from the impressiveness of his analysis, one may well find oneself fundamentally unhappy about his relentless separation of agape and eros. Once they are taken apart, of course a Christian must vote for agape. But do they have to be so radically taken apart? We crave for the synthesis, in spite of all the moralists who assure us that we are only hearing the voice of our unregenerate selfishness. Is our discomfort just because we are not good enough yet to breath the pure air of agape, or is there really something stifling about it?

The doubt grows about whether after all to talk about self-giving entirely separately from fulfilment does justice to the love of God or man. The gospels encourage no such separation. On the contrary, the unselfconscious promises that our heavenly Father is longing to reward us suggest that we may blur the stern contrast between the love that gives and the love whose whole idea is to grasp. Not all wanting is acquisitive. Not all pleasure is possession. Not all happiness has anything to do with ownership. We can enjoy what is never going to belong to us. We can long for enjoyment and delight and even for pleasure, without taking, or even giving, coming into the question at all. Such longings are not greedy. They may happen to be distractions from what we really ought to be doing at a particular moment; but they may be our link with our real home. This was the delight Traherne celebrated:

> Your Enjoyment of the World is never right, till evry Morning you awake in Heaven: see your self in your fathers Palace: and look upon the Skies and the Earth and the Air, as Celestial Joys: having such a Reverend Esteem of all, as if you were among the Angels.[26]

The one-way picture of agape, after all, fits remarkably badly with the Christian image of God as our heavenly Father: badly enough to cast doubt on Nygren's whole system. It is all very well to say that God's love seeks no return. It is quite another thing to define His love in such a way that it would be impossible for it to be reciprocated. Surely our heavenly Father would wish us to love Him, if the image of fatherhood means anything; yet we can hardly have agape, in Nygren's sense, towards God.[27] We can hardly even be allowed to have a thoroughgoing gratitude towards Him, since the idea that we might want His gifts is so deeply suspect. Such is the austerity of the love from which eros is excluded.

As Burnaby points out,[28] it is an odd theory which cannot accept Christ's summary of the law in its most natural meaning. Is the first great commandment, 'Thou shalt love the Lord thy God' to be fulfilled, not by love at all, 'but by something else – namely faith'?[29] It is better human beings, not worse, who have longed to obey it as it stands, whose lives have been governed by 'the love of God' as something human as well as divine. The obstinacy which makes one go on insisting that love is a reciprocal idea is not a selfish obstinacy.

So it is legitimate to look more critically at the one-way picture. The object of this exercise is by no means to knock

down agape and set up eros, but to reunite them in a love that is
not nervous of being made happy. Far from forbidding such an
enquiry, reverence towards God as well as affection towards
mankind encourages us to ask whether Nygren's great key-
words 'unmotivated' and 'unconditional' are now doing more
harm than good.

In one important sense, God's love is unmotivated: He does
not stand to gain by loving us; He has no ulterior motive. But to
press this to the limit makes us begin to think that God's love is
pointless, that creation is a sort of doodling. Anyone who has
ever tried to make anything, even if it is only a piece of tolerable
prose, can see the mistake here. It needs to be said that doodling
is not better than making and that purposeful activity is a good
thing, not unworthy of God. However disinterested He is, we
need not think of Him as uninterested. It is worth keeping on
insisting upon the ancient affirmation that God saw everything
that He had made, and behold, it was very good. Creation is
costly, not idle. Thomas Traherne said,

> It is very strange; Want itself is a Treasure in Heaven: And so
> Great an one, that without it there could be no Treasure. GOD
> did infinitly for us, when He made us to Want like GODS, that
> like GODS we might be satisfied. The Heathen DEITIES wanted
> nothing, and were therefore unhappy; For they had no Being.
> But the LORD GOD of Israel the Living and True GOD, was from
> all Eternity, and from all Eternity Wanted like a God. He
> wanted the Communication of His Divine Essence, and
> Persons to Enjoy it. He wanted Worlds, He wanted Spectators,
> He wanted Joys, He wanted Treasures. He wanted, yet he
> wanted not, for he had them.[30]

These statements are not platitudes. Nor are they proved. But if
we warm to them we can at least realize that there are other
ways of glorifying the Creator than to call His love 'unmotivated'.

Likewise, there is a good sense in which God's love is
unconditional. If we think we can earn it or that we need to earn
it we have missed the whole point. We do not have to bargain
with God about His requirements. He does not love us 'on
conditions'. He loves us, unworthy as we are. But again, this is
not the whole story. The word 'bargain' can remind us of

something we might overlook. It is not quite true to say that we can make no bargains with God. If we know Him at all it is as a God who makes covenants with His people.[31] Too much reiteration of the word unconditional could eventually lead us to think that He does not care whether they keep their side. Perhaps we should say for a change that He loves us, not without conditions, but in spite of our breaking them. This is a way of returning to the idea that we matter and that what we do or fail to do matters.

Of course our evident unworthiness makes us unwilling to presume to think we matter, but that very unwillingess could be part of our trouble. If sin shuts us off from God, consciousness of sin can complicate our disease rather than cure it. Our very remorse can shut Him out more than ever. It can suggest that we ought to repent of being what God made us: creatures that matter because we are creatures that mind, made in God's image because He minds about us. Misdirected as our minding is apt to be, it is the heart of our value. Self-ness is not evil, quickly as it spills over into selfishness. If we refuse to try to draw this fine distinction, we are not playing safe, we are playing into the hands of a new Manicheeism more insidious than the old. The ancient Manichees deplored the physical bodies that God had made and the church has barely shaken off their influence yet. The new version, high-minded enough to distract a new St Augustine, suggests that the very people God has made are a bad sort of thing. If we can manage to reject this sub-Christian notion, we can come to realize that whole human beings are supposed to be temples of the Holy Spirit. Of course, so far we are not fit to be anything of the kind, but it is offered glory, not denigration, which can best encourage us to repent in any worthwhile way of our present selfishness. We shall not be better givers by being worse takers, as George Herbert knew. Far from being cast out from the divine banquet, he was not even to be relegated to a menial role:

> 'You must sit down,' says Love, 'and taste my meat':
> So I did sit and eat.

❧ 13 ❧

Minding

Heaven forbid that in all this Christian agape should seem to be belittled. The notion of love for which a practically new word was needed, the love whose faithfulness is undaunted and unending and depends on no merit in the beloved, the love Christ came to show, is not to be argued into unimportance. The first Christians were able to expand the whole idea of what love meant and it is not to be thought of that their heirs should show themselves insensitive and ungrateful.

But what has expanded can begin to contract again and it is possible for the word agape to begin to be used to diminish, not enlarge, our ideas of what Christian love is meant to be. This is happening when it is thought very important to reject aspects of real human love from Christian understanding. We know of course that there is no craving in agape, no favouritism, no possessiveness, no dependence. Not only passionate eros but partial *philia*, friendship-love, is to be laid aside. But these contrasts, which are propunded in order to set up agape as superior to our unworthy kinds of love, can begin to hem it in. The perfect love of God somehow seems more restricted after all than the love of husbands and wives, parents and friends, when it has to be described in such a careful way.

We understand God's love more positively when we allow ourselves to compare it instead of always contrasting it with every sort of love we know as human beings. When we have emphasized for all we are worth the divine faithfulness of agape, surely we can then enrich our idea of what Christian love properly is by adding, not subtracting, the warmth of eros and the appreciativeness of philia?

The truth that God does not 'need' us has been over-emphasized and has given rise to the notion that the most real and perfect love cannot take any delight in its beloved. If this is what we have to say about the love of God, something has gone wrong. As Burnaby put it, 'If perfect love is spiritual communion, a definition of charity which would restrict its proper activity to a "one-way" relationship, a giving without receiving, seems strangely inadequate.'[1] Surely it is not sentimental to feel sure that love is meant to be returned. It need not be symmetrical, but it ought to be correlative.

It is not impossible to see what has gone wrong. The idea of God as Saviour has been so reverently emphasized as to obscure the prior idea of God as Creator.[2] If we can redress the balance, we can hope to enrich rather than contaminate our understanding. If the Redeemer is first of all the Maker of the world, we can dare to ascribe to Him eros as well as agape. He wants and He minds, not dependently and helplessly of course, but sovereignly and creatively.[3] To say 'God wants' is no more analogical than to say 'God loves'. We can affirm that what He wants matters; and it seems that He wants us. God does not, as it were, have to put all the value into us at the redeeming stage. He lays its foundation from the beginning and He knows what He is doing. Our capacity to want is part of His image in us.

Of course God's image in us is defaced, some would say ruined. The point is that redemption is recovery of something that was meant to be ours. Dame Julian of Norwich begs us to see this:

> [The Lord] wants us to see our wretchedness and meekly to acknowledge it; but he does not want us to remain there, or to be much occupied in self-accusation, nor does he want us to be too full of our own misery. But he wants us quickly to attend to him, for he stands all alone, and he waits for us continually, moaning and mourning until we come. And he hastens to bring us to him, for we are his joy and delight, and he is the remedy of our life.[4]

We are made to be God's children, to take after our Father and to do Him credit: in other words, to glorify Him and enjoy Him for ever. It is not too much to believe that at last the enjoyment is to be mutual. So we can say that eros as well as agape is part of the image of God in us. The wanting, striving character of our love is part of our created goodness, not just part of our sinfulness. Christian redemption is restoration to our proper kind of wanting, not the quenching of want.

It would be no small thing if we could get back the deep longing for the love of God that has made the great saints. 'If you long for that Sabbath', St Augustine told his congregation, 'you are not ceasing to pray . . . You will lapse into silence if you lose your longing'.[5] We may well wonder if that is what is really wrong with the church today. Perhaps we could begin to recover our longing by asking in all reverence why we think God made us. Of course the question is beyond us; but if the only answer we can give is 'in inscrutable love', why do we call it *love*? At least we may believe that we are meant to be glad of it. It is nonsense to worry in this context about valuing God's gifts above Himself. When the gift is God's love, it makes little sense to distinguish the gift from the Giver. St Bernard grasped this nettle:

> You wish, therefore, to hear from me why and how God should be loved? And I: the reason for loving God is God Himself; the way is to love Him beyond measure. There is a twofold reason, I should say, why God should be loved for His own sake: because nothing can be more justly, nothing more profitably, loved. Indeed, when the question is asked why God should be loved it may have one of two meanings: whether it is God's title to our love or our own advantage in loving Him. To be sure, I would give the same answer to both of these questions: I find no other worthy reason for loving Him except Himself.[6]

If we believe that God somehow values our fulfilment, surely we may value it too? 'God shall be all in all' must mean that all His purposes shall be fulfilled. It is hardly 'man-centred' to believe that this includes His purposes for us and that in the end no part of the creation is to be unworthy of its Creator. Dame Julian is surely God-centred enough in affirming that 'still endlessly our courteous Lord regards us, rejoicing in this work'.[7]

Of course we are not to suppose that God's love for His creation is all the love He has. Having said so much to reinstate eros as worthy of God, we may dare to say more: more presumptuously but even more theocentrically. Of course we cannot see behind creation to the love which is within God Himself before the foundation of the world, but we are meant to believe that it is there. That love is assuredly not to be sorted out into human terminology – our minds go blank when we try to think about it – but one thing we must be able to say of it, that it is fully reciprocal. To think about the Trinity is to picture a sort of eternal pattern of giving and responding, an eternal mattering and minding, not needing us but wanting us to join in. Our best hope is not merely to catch some overflow from it, as the strict agape terminology would suggest, but to be caught up into its circle. 'Give and take' is often recommended as a commonsense recipe for getting on reasonably well with our families or neighbours. It could mean more than that.[8] A pattern of giving and taking, united and transfigured, is a good description of our best understanding of love.

But at this point we must come down to earth and ask whether all this, so fine in theory, might not be dangerous in practice? Until we know how to love like saints, we ought to be careful before we let 'taking' have an inch, or we may find that natural selfishness has claimed far more than an ell. Can human beings be trusted with a hope of self-realization, or will it necessarily slide into a reality of self-centredness?

So much has been admirably written about the Christian life as a great crusade against self that it feels like treachery to seem to take the infidel side. But taking a side need not be a militant exercise. It can be a kind of exploration. The words we decide to use, whether literal or metaphorical, align us with a particular and limited point of view. The whole truth is larger and deeper than any of the two-dimensional diagrams we try to make of it can adequately indicate. One sees the whole complicated reality of creation truly but incompletely, correcting distortions and always introducing new distortions of one's own: not because truth is 'only relative' but precisely because it is not. 'Words slip and slide' and give more or less purchase on the surface we are trying to explore. Words about love seem particularly slippery, maybe because they are worn smooth with so much use. So it may be promising to try a fresh track to get a better grip of reality. But then if we stray too far we shall have to be helped back again.

We are not trying to set up selfishness. We are trying to show that we cannot make our selves a special case for bad any more than for good.[9] People are to be loved. This applies to each of us. So instead of choosing self-giving for ourselves and self-realization for others, we ought to be trying to understand how these are related, for us all. They are apt to present themselves as contraries, but the serious attempt to separate them distorts them both. When they are put asunder they lead separate lives, like estranged spouses or Christian denominations, denying each other and falling short of what they could be together.

Self-giving and fulfilment are not, of course, synonyms. They do stand for distinct ideas. The point is that they need each other. On the one hand, self-giving on its own does not make as much sense as Christians are apt to think. One cannot give from emptiness. One cannot give to someone who is too selfless to receive. Relentless competitive unselfishness is a ghastly caricature of Christian love.

Selfish fulfilment, on the other hand, does not make as much sense as unregenerate humanity is apt to think. Macbeth discovered its true destination:

> I have liv'd long enough: my way of life
> Is fall'n into the sere, the yellow leaf;
> And that which should accompany old age,
> As honour, love, obedience, troops of friends,
> I must not look to have.[10]

Macbeth may seem an unfairly extreme example of unregenerate humanity. His trouble was not ordinary selfishness but overstepping the limits of callous ambition. On a less dramatic level people can undoubtedly live selfishly for years in a sort of satisfaction, flourishing like the green bay tree, and it would be naive and priggish to deny that this is possible. What we are saying is that the more selfish they get and the more they approximate to real heartlessness, the more substantial human happiness they are missing. Surely the glimpses most people have had of the pleasures of lovingness are enough to put the onus of proof on anyone who would deny this. Anybody who would set up sustained selfishness as satisfying in the long run is up against the massive witness of the human race. Christians at least do not need to explore that No Through Road.

The point that believers need to take hold of out of this argument is that it does indeed go both ways. If we can love other people as ourselves, we can cope with the fact that they will be apt to love us as themselves; so our fulfilment and theirs need not and should not be separated. We can take the selfishness out of the idea of getting what we want and think of it as part of the fulfilment of the people who love us. Charles Williams had a word for this: he called it 'co-inherence'. There is no need to be nervously scrupulous about the fulfilment each of us has been promised, because it is simply not capable of being enjoyed alone.[11] It is essentially something to be shared. So we need not fret ourselves that it is 'selfish' to want and seek this fulfilment. On the contrary, it would be cold-hearted and even ungrateful to be indifferent to it.

If we can say all this, there is no need to ban eros, the love that wants. There is not even any need to keep it sternly distinct from agape. Even in seeking happiness love seeketh not *her own*. We cannot say where the well-being of one person ends and the well-being of another begins. What people want when they succeed in loving each other is their own happiness and the happiness of the other person as part of the same happiness, neither as complete in itself.[12]

If this makes sense, we shall no longer think tidily of taking as selfish and giving as unselfish. We know it is more blessed to give than to receive, but we do not always know which is which. So the stern opposition of 'myself', 'other people' and 'God' loses a great deal of its point. The last thing we want to do is organize a sort of confrontation between them. If sometimes we take them one at a time, it will merely for clarity. What we can hope for is a refreshed understanding of people, including ourselves; a clearer idea of love between people; and even may be some glimpse of the meaning of the worship of God.

A hopeful approach to human beings as meant to be happy need not be stupidly idealistic about them. Sin and selfishness are real enough, but they have the reality of a bad dream: gripping, haunting, exhausting and eventually incoherent. The right message for selfish people, including oneself, is not 'stop wanting' but *'Wake up*. Come back into the world that has real people in it and join in with them.'

Analogies are incomplete. The nightmare analogy does not apply very well to selfishness as malice: but real malice is rarer than we may think. Goneril and Regan are more monstrous and less real than Macbeth. Generally when people hurt one another it is because they have got into a state where they know not what they do. It is not sentimental or soft to believe this, unless one were to persuade oneself that it is quite all right to be in such a state. It needs to be reiterated that the nightmare *is* a nightmare. Waking from it is not always gentle.

It is not just an idle-day-dream, it is a sort of horror, to be in a condition where one asks about everything, 'What is there in it for me?' Human beings are quite prone to get into such a state, to look even at religious belief in this light. But to punish ourselves, to suppose that only God and other people are eligible for being loved, does not cure this trouble but drags other people and God down too. We can see for ourselves that we are not the only unworthy ones, if unworthiness is the point; and if our unworthiness really is the whole point, it makes a poor thing of our Creator.[13] 'What is man that thou art mindful of him?' is a salutary question provided that it does not stop in hopelessness or bitterness. Mankind has sunk very much lower than the angels through sin, but what we were made for was to be crowned with glory, not to be permanent down-and-outs for celestial patronage.[14] 'What ails men,' asked Traherne, 'that they do not see it?'[15]

It is an insult to God and our fellow human beings to treat *ourselves* as negative. If we are to look on other people as lovable, we cannot opt out of being lovable too. This is a less forbidding way than usual of following the advice to 'see ourselves as others see us'. Generally this exhortation means that we ought to become aware of our glaring or our subtle faults. To set about doing that is quite difficult and not always very productive. Suppose instead we take to heart the fact that some people are really fond of us.[16] Then we may be more encouraged to become what they want and need us to be. It will be easier to overcome our failings for their sakes than to keep trying to improve ourselves on our own. As long as we look on ourselves as poor worms of earth, it is neither surprising nor important if we eat or drink too much or fritter away our time or bore people. If we think of our health and effectiveness as valuable to our neighbours and to the Lord our God the case is altered.

If anyone loves us, and especially if God loves us, we are not to be feeble, blank or dull any more than we are to be grasping, strident or hard-hearted. There is nothing heretical about the hymn that says,

> Let every creature rise and bring
> Peculiar honours to our King.

We can take this in its old sense and sometimes in its modern sense as well. People's peculiarities are not just to be borne with but to be relished, and not always too solemnly. To imagine our heavenly Father laughing gently at our funny little ways could be nearer to real humility than terrible self-abasement. To expunge our individual lovability is to expunge our reality. A generalized love has nothing upon which to get a purchase. It suggests a mirror in an empty room reflecting only another mirror. It is in the predicament of Ogden Nash's shrimp seeking his lady shrimp, who found that

> At times, translucence
> Is rather a nuisance.

This is the answer to the question, 'What were the others put here for?'[17] We were all put into the world to meet each other as real people. Christians will want to say a great deal more than this, but they ought not to say less. Love is not like the pot of gold at the end of the rainbow, never to be located in a specific place. It is not always for the sake of something or someone else. There is a disappointment in the moral tale of St Francis and the leper: that when the saint brought himself to kiss the horror he found nothing there but clothes. It would be a far more satisfying story if he had found a particular human being.

'Particularity' is not always a 'scandal', even when we are talking about love. That is what the 'doctrine of election' says, that God loves His children individually. Much distress at the idea that God 'has favourites' might have been avoided if people had not been so ready to assume that generalized love is more worthwhile than special love. Of course among human beings partiality topples over into exclusiveness; but so does impartiality blur into vagueness. Both are negative when they go wrong and need each other as correctives. With God they do not go wrong.

It is an impoverished human being whose highest hope is to be at the receiving end of a merely accepting love. Tolerance, after all, is not the top virtue. It assumes an enormous importance when we are among intolerance. The whole of human history ought to make us tremble to seem to undervalue it. It can be a difficult and important moral achievement. But even so, its role is to clear the ground for something better: something which we may provisionally and rather inadequately call 'appreciation'.

Any child that has put his or her heart into a task, whether of work or play, and has been told 'very nice, dear' will see the point. What one needs is somebody who will really look, who will positively like the good parts and be sorry about the bad parts. Even a remorseful sinner who has screwed up the courage to apologize is not looking for tolerance. The reply 'never mind' is an anticlimax. The calm acknowledgement that one just is that sort of person may be less alarming than bitter reproaches but is not really sustaining. If acceptance is all people have to offer one another, we are more likely to feel that they do not really care than that they are mediating to us God's overflowing agape. It is mercy we all want and need of each other and of God, the mercy that has been likened to olive oil; and even beyond mercy, the hope of a sort of love that is looking for something positively good, however hard it is going to be to draw it out.

Why should we hesitate to allow the excellence of the love that expects something of us? The trouble is that we are afraid of any such idea because we know how prone human beings are to intolerance. Instead of transcending 'acceptance', we are only too likely simply to fall short of it. So it seems too dangerous to suggest that people can hope to draw out the best in one another, for fear of encouraging ourselves to slip into an aggressive bossiness that wants to improve another person, like mending a machine or altering a frock. It seems too dangerous to say that love can expect a response, for fear of letting ourselves suppose that affection either needs to be or can be earned. We know it is wrong to make conditions for loving other people. We know that if God made conditions we could never meet them. So the whole notion that human beings could ever be worth loving comes to seem the most dangerous of all. It looks much safer to rest in acceptance, God's acceptance of us, ours of other people.

Yet there is something profoundly depressing about Elizabeth Barrett Browning's poem:

> If thou must love me, let it be for naught
> Except for love's sake only. Do not say,
> 'I love her for her smile – her look – her way
> Of speaking gently . . .'
> But love me for love's sake, that evermore
> Thou mayst love on, through love's eternity.

It is worth reiterating the contrary conviction that people want to be loved for their own sakes, which may be a daring but is not a selfish or an unrealistic hope. The condition we have to meet is not merit so much as a kind of uncalculating childlike responsiveness which in fact is not rare in human beings. The love we are asking for, and not always in vain, is something warmer, more partisan, than acceptance. It is a kind of love that looks at what people see in themselves, that positively elicits their own special character and then is glad of it: a love that creates enjoyment and enjoys creation.

It would not be altogether unfair to call this kind of love 'demanding', but to say that needs some explaining. We are not committing ourselves to approval of the exacting old domestic tyrant who 'loves' her unmarried daughter and requires her constant attentions; or the parent whose son has 'failed' because he has not gone to the same university or entered the same profession; or the friend who takes offence when letters remain unwritten; or the child who wants to be played with all the time. There are also good loves that make demands: people who can be hurt by inconsiderateness, who will not be contented with shoddy work, who mind whether one another are still there or not.

Human affections are so corruptible that 'making demands' quickly slides into 'making conditions'. That is why we need to be continually reminded about the divine love for the unlovable that asks no reward and expects no benefit, and does not have to be earned by 'doing'. Because we know how easily love is spoilt by conditions and limitations and requirements, we keep looking for safety in the idea that it would be better to ask for nothing at all. But sometimes there comes a time when we also need to remember that somewhere in all that bath water to be thrown away is a baby; something real to be loved. It is not greedy or selfish to remain aware that what people are, and even what they do, does matter. We need to be allowed to enjoy it. Love, however unconditional, is meant to come to rest somewhere. It does not have to be insensitive, insensible, or even undiscriminating. It takes notice and it minds. We are not supposed to avert our eyes from excellent qualities like gentleness or vivacity or enterprise, or from skills of hand or mind. On the contrary, if we are alert to notice them we may find them in unlikely places. We may even learn how to elicit them.

Christian suspicion of wanting makes us inclined to underestimate the sort of love whose fulfilment is not bestowing but appreciating: admiring, contemplating, rejoicing in the existence of what it loves; or better still, delighting in the company of the beloved. Whatever name best fits this kind of love, it is admittedly not detached or unmotivated. It is based on minding and on mattering: but acquisition is simply not the point. It asks to approach not to appropriate. When people are absorbed by the conversation of their friends or rapt in serious delight before a masterpiece, possession is the last thing they are thinking about. What we truly appreciate does not have to belong to us: quite the contrary, it claims our attention by its upstanding otherness.

Yet in another sense, Traherne's sense, what we appreciate is our very own: not bits of the world but its whole range, which is there to be enjoyed, paid for by the Creator not by us. 'Is it not a Great Thing, that you should be Heir of the World? Is it not a very Enriching Veritie?'[18] There is no need to neglect the cost. Traherne did not: 'Thou wast slain for me: and shall I leave thy Body in the feild O Lord? Shall I go away and be Merry, while the Love of my Soul and my only Lover is Dead upon the Cross.'[19] Such consideration of how the creation has been bought with a price is for giving profundity to appreciative love, not for belittling it.

Admiring love is not greedy and selfish, making conditions and wanting rewards for itself. The fact that it has to do with wanting is an enrichment not an aberration. Enjoyment can be disinterested. Hopes and fears need not be mercenary. Motives need not be ulterior. Asking need not be bargaining. We must accept that there is more to love than acceptance. Love is more vulnerable than tolerance, more capable of delight or disappointment.

But if appreciation is not greedy and selfish, maybe it is idle and selfish, wanting an easy life? It seems to have to do with feeling rather than with effort. How can we enjoy appreciating people when we could be unselfishly serving them? How can we justify gazing at works of art or wonders of nature? In particular, how can we sit still saying we love God when there is His will to be done?

At this point it is worth pausing to appreciate the kind of love that pauses to appreciate. It may seem odd that contemplative love should need defence among religious believers, but it must be admitted that there is even a kind of vested interest in treating it as a form of self-indulgence. If it were to turn out after all that the mystics were right and contemplation was meant to be the true end of our lives, then quite a number of us would be hopelessly on the wrong lines. A good deal of judging and blaming has gone on and compromises seem particularly unsatisfying. So the simplest and most comfortable way of avoiding feelings of guilt at having no vocation for contemplation can readily seem to be to put the whole idea aside and think of it as nothing more than a way of occupying time which is a rival to the things people ought to be engaging themselves with for the love of God or humanity.

If on the contrary we are able to affirm that contemplative love is not a sort of special exercise we decide to spend our time on, but is simply appreciation in its highest form of what is going on outside ourselves, then the judging and blaming can stop. Appreciative love and active love can be parts of one pattern, not conflicting claims upon us. They fit together like warp and weft. We cannot say we are more loving by deciding to be either less or more busy. To get the pattern right is to achieve a harmony, not to engineer a compromise. In a good pattern some threads can be conspicuous or inconspicuous.

If we are at all capable of pausing and being quiet so as to notice what is there to be appreciated, then we are not unspiritual activists missing the point of contemplation. If we are capable of bestirring ourselves to respond to what we have seen, then we are not self-indulgent visionaries cut off from the everyday world. These are real ifs. Most of us will go on falling short on both, in practice. But we need not be at odds over the theory. It is no more nor less than a proper Christian and human understanding that goodness has something to do with attention.

To develop this understanding we need to ring the changes on words. 'Appreciation' can sound patronizing or merely aesthetic, suggesting connoisseurship rather than love. 'Enjoyment' ought to be right, as it encapsulates joy; but in some contexts it seems trivial or egotistic. 'Delight' is excellent, when we can aspire to it. The kinds of satisfaction that love properly wants and often finds can cover the whole range from contentment to enthralment. The upper reaches are worship and devotion; but the lower ranges of liking and pleasure are not to be belittled as unworthy. Far from it: appreciation at any level is able to take us out of ourselves into unselfconscious and innocent happiness, which we may dare to say is not far from the kingdom of heaven. To call this self-indulgent would be to call gratitude self-indulgent.

❧ 14 ❧

Liking

'Appreciative love' is cumbersome and has a self-conscious sound about it. 'Liking' is less pompous and more naturally human. Unfortunately, among Christians it is deeply suspect as arbitrary, trivial and partial. To give importance to what I happen to like looks like the very essence of selfishness, far removed from Christian love and doing the will of God, and not much to do with secular morality.

It is a commonplace that I cannot help my likes and dislikes, so liking is left out of morality. Since love can be commanded, it seems that it must be entirely distinct from mere liking. Kant's axiom that 'I ought' implies 'I can' seems to leave matters of taste firmly outside ethics. Moralists cheerfully grant that there are plenty of people we cannot like; but that is quite in order so long as we set ourselves to will their good for God's sake. Conversely, there are the people we make friends with according to individual preference, but our affection for them is at best permissible and has little to do with our Christian duty to love one another.

Is it any wonder that on these assumptions Christians have been unable to prevent their good word 'charity' from shrinking its meaning to something that people are apt to say they 'don't want'? Human beings may *need* to be helped but what they *want* is to be liked. Instead of turning away dutifully from this obvious fact, let us try to build it into our understanding of Christian love. Maybe the time has come to rehabilitate *liking* as not just respectable but excellent: as a central element in what we ought to mean when we talk about love.

If we begin by defending liking against the charge that it is *arbitrary*, we may find that it is also less *trivial* than we might suppose and that even its *partiality* is capable of defence. It sounds conclusive to say that we are commanded to love but we cannot be commanded to like. We know that our tastes are not in our control. I can no more like this tiresome neighbour of mine than you can like garlic. What I can do is will his good, not retaliate when he tips rubbish into my area, and pray to God to take him to heaven one day. Of course that is a caricature, but it is a powerful caricature which is helping a great many people not to find out how far their dealings with each other are from the 'love' they profess.

Suppose we try the effect of admitting that love is not obviously in our control either, in fact that there is something paradoxical about its being commanded. We may well discover that it is no more difficult after all to try to like than to try to love. People do learn to like things. We talk about acquired tastes. When people refuse even to try to like garlic, we call them faddy. When they are sure they cannot like people, we call them prejudiced. The conviction that one cannot be expected to like, only to love, is defeatist. The belief that likes and dislikes are one's own business and are not to be criticized is inhumane. The separation of loving and liking is not noticeably productive of goodwill of any kind.

When the human warmth and reality of liking is officially left out, it takes a saint to impart a heavenly warmth and reality to the 'love' which is supposed to remain. We are apt to find that the saint has cheated by not leaving out the liking after all. It is all very well for him: he really likes those terrible down-and-outs who come to him for help. It is all very well for her: she is interested in those boring friends of hers and their dull lives. People who 'like people' can stand being at the mercy of their fellow human beings all day without losing their tempers. 'Christian love', for them, is not an extra reserve to bring up to stop themselves from behaving badly, as we sometimes think it is for most of us. If we are inclined to suppose that they are not being 'good' at all, might it not also occur to us that somehow they are living their lives the right way round?

There is a way of meeting the world with a readiness to be pleased, which is at least as much within our power as behaving as if we were pleased when we are not. Loving is not really any more within our own capacity than liking is. Loving without liking, far from being something we can simply decide to do, can readily become a kind of pretence, an inhuman strain which sooner or later breaks down more destructively than if it had never been attempted. 'Lilies that fester smell far worse than weeds.'[1] Christians have no need to be surprised at this. Did they think they could keep God's commands in their own strength? Here as elsewhere what they can do is put themselves in the way of keeping them, with trust and a good deal of patience. They are not being let off from making an effort. Learning to enjoy and appreciate demands as much effort as other kinds of learning; but the effort required is a direction of attention rather than a prodding of the will.[2] So there is no reason why liking should not be a practicable way in to loving and every reason why it should. Especially for people who believe that God saw that His creation was good,[3] it seems a reasonable beginning to hope to find something endearing about His Creatures, if only one is willing to look. 'Seek and ye shall find' is a promise of wide application.

That is all very well, but there are plenty of things and people I simply cannot like. Am I to be deprived of the reassurance that Christian love is still within my scope? I cannot like aniseed and surely that is not a moral defect. I cannot like dreary people nearly as much as lively people, but surely God expects me to love them just as much. And how can I like my enemies: surely loving them is enough to ask? Some dislikes are solidly based, but Christians are forbidden to let their love keep step with their preferences.

This is not one objection, but needs sorting out. First, some people like aniseed and some detest it, and if anything is a clear example of a 'matter of taste', this is one. Morality does not come into it: until I have to decide how far it is polite or kind to show my dislike. I really cannot learn to like it and there seems no good reason why I should. We do not identify with the Queen of Heart's conviction that

> He can thoroughly enjoy
> The pepper when he pleases.[4]

Human beings however are not simple like aniseed or pepper, to be liked or disliked just like that. I might be able to learn to like something complicated in which aniseed played a part and find this effort worthwhile. So somebody's gushing manner, which jars on me though other people warm to it, might fit into place in my picture of this human being as part of a likeable whole.

Secondly, the point about the dreary and dismal people is that a great deal of what passes for loving them is as dreary and dismal as they are. It is no good loving people officially. Something has to be done to make it come alive and what better than to find out what there is to be seen in them after all. Where Christian faith comes in is not an obstinate refusal to believe that dullness matters in the sight of God, but a rational conviction that dullness cannot be the whole truth about a child of God. 'A little encouragement, and putting her hair in papers, does wonders for her.'[5] The kind of love that does not feel called upon to like may by-pass the encouragement and connive at the dullness. Boredom, and even repulsion, are better overcome than tolerated.

But thirdly, suppose repulsion is well founded? It may be true that dreary people, and even fretful, mean, self-centred or bossy people, could be liked into lovability; but what about the hostile and the unscrupulous? Some people actively repel our regard and to suggest that we could possibly set about liking them seems not only unrealistic but outrageous. Enough harm has been done to the idea of Christian 'meekness' by allowing it to be identified with softness towards plain evil. Many would-be Christian attempts to make excuses for villains are neither very honest nor very kind to their victims. That is quite true: in fact, it is exactly the point. The false meekness comes from the very idea that there is a sort of 'love of enemies' which we can choose to go in for which shuts its eyes to what the hostile human being is really like. The idea that loving is something easier than liking dangerously underrates the sheer hardness and paradox of real Christian forgiveness.

In trying to redress the balance, there is no need to overstate the case. Of course we are hardly touching the edges of the problem of what it is God is asking of us when He commands us to forgive. If we have the sincerity to admit how hard this commandment is, and how unsuccessful many Christian struggles with it have been, we may be grateful for a way of getting a purchase even on part of it. If we happen to discover that although love seems humanly impossible we can *like* our enemies, or some of them, more than we think, we may as well make a start here. Some foes we can respect for their courage, or even half admire for their cunning. At least these are qualities they really have, which well-meaningness is not. Even to say 'What cheek!' is more in the spirit of the teller of the story of the unjust steward than the hollow-sounding 'Of course he didn't mean any harm.' Perhaps we can harness the natural human admiration for bad characters like Don Giovanni and Milton's Satan in the worthy cause of loving our enemies. It is more wholesome and honest to tell stories about engaging rogues or doughty foes, Shakespeare's Richard III wooing Lady Anne, or Dick Turpin, than to tell stories in which everyone is wrapped in a kind of blanket of good intentions. So we shall not underestimate the power of evil or infuriate our contemporaries by our unrealistic weak-mindedness. Whatever real forgiveness of our enemies turns out to be, it will surely have more to do with magnanimity than with petty self-abasement. And in the meantime, it will surely do no harm to remember that many of the people we think of as enemies are really no more than opponents or rivals, who are not candidates for our forgiveness. For these, the courtesy and goodwill which belong to liking are more suitable than the pious forbearance which sometimes passes for love. It is not trivial that variegated human beings often seem to like each other so little, in public and private life. We are a long way from Dante's paradise where St Bonaventura the Franciscan praises St Dominic, and St Thomas Aquinas the Dominican praises St Francis.

All this is all very well when the right advice is 'Don't take yourself too seriously.' By all means let us have a policy of liking political opponents, romantic rebels and even people who tease us or pilfer from us, if we can; but none of these are real malevolent enemies. Some evils are to be taken seriously, particularly evils directed against other people. It is an insult to our fellow human beings to think it is all right to like oppressors, terrorists, Nazis, gangsters. Liking for such as these is not an achievement but a sin, maybe a temptation to be overcome. If they seem to have a heady glamour (and it is an alarming fact that they often do), people ought to avert their eyes from it. In particular, the young and inexperienced ought not to be encouraged to think that cameraderie or hero-worship are self-justifying or an excuse for evil. 'Only disconnect' seems a wiser motto than 'only connect' where wickedness is in question.

The point to be reiterated is that 'love' is under the same shadow here as 'liking'. Loving other people's enemies is dangerous, not just difficult like loving our own. We may find a poignant meaning in 'Who but God can forgive sins?' It looks as if only God can securely hate the sin and love the sinner. When we try, we walk gently into corruption, or more probably into the sort of feeble condoning of evil that makes Christians seem spineless and indifferent friends. It only remains to add conventionally 'and of course we are all sinners' to invite a charge of hypocrisy as well. We are indeed: but we are not all every kind of sinner. To excuse the malicious and violent by accusing ourselves of malice and violence, when we are more probably guilty of complacency and sentimentality, is to fail to reckon with real malice and violence. A balanced indignation on behalf of people who are being made to suffer is a more promising exercise of Christian compassion than a good deal of talk about love.

Yet, when all this is said, as Christians we are still under orders both to love and to forgive. Can the idea of liking serve us any further? We have defended it against charges of arbitrariness; and we have found its seeming triviality not unhelpful. The very unpretentiousness of liking has commended itself as a kind of passport through the perilous frontier of self-esteem. But when we come up against real moral baseness, especially when it hurts other people, liking does begin to look entirely inept. Can it be of any more use to us, maybe in a different way?

The moment when we really have to dispense with liking is the moment to consider seriously where we stand without it. We knew that it could not solve the whole problem of forgiveness. Now we must have a look at the unresolved part. The time has come, not just for a dogged reaffirmation of love, but for a more thoroughgoing admission of human defeat, if we want to know what love is and what it is not. When we have given liking every chance, we are in a position to ask what kind of love this can be which remains unreachable by this route.

What can it mean to say that there are people we are expected to 'love' but forbidden to 'like' for fear of treachery?

If we keep asking this question, we may at least become constructively dissatisfied with the counterfeit 'love' with which it is all too easy to fob ourselves off. If we are really discounting people instead of loving them at all, it is better to realize what we are doing. Each of us has his or her own candidates for a place beyond the pale: the racist, the spy, the fascist, the kidnapper, the enemy we have never seen who wants to destroy what we hold dear, the person who has hurt someone we love. Suppose we try admitting that if we dare not like these people we ought not to talk yet about loving them. The most we can do may be to refrain somehow from hating them, and if this is real as far as it goes it is better than a pretence of loving. What this means is that we leave them in God's hands, knowing that His love can encompass them where ours at present cannot. We leave the way open and if one day we come to love them, it will be by seeing them with different eyes. A real forgiveness to come is better than a sham forgiveness imagined. Even the conquest of bitterness is a beginning. Our behaviour can be pacific for God's sake and we may hope that in the end He will help us bring our feelings into line. If our enemies were truly sorry, we should be happy not disappointed.

The advantage of acknowledging defeat is that we shall know that all is not well yet. As long as we suppose that we can love people without liking them, whether they are our enemies or not, we shall be apt to let dislike and even contempt creep up upon us under cover of honorary love. The converse of sentimental goodwill is the equally human tendency to make scapegoats and stereotypes and this too can shelter under the umbrella of 'hating the sin and loving the sinner'. It feels quite moral to look on people with distinct ill-will, provided that we can label them as oppressors or thugs, skinflints or adulterers or cheats. 'Hating the sin', we acknowledge realistically that there is such a thing as plain evil. 'Loving the sinner', we accept this fact more comprehensively than we need. We assume that we are in some way 'willing their good' and so we acquiesce in the stereotypes, bypassing the sharp recollection that these are real human beings who have developed into these sorts of sinners. To try to appreciate the particular point of view of people we do not naturally understand is exhausting and open to misinterpretation: how much easier to claim to love them with an unconditional love! The admission that we are *not* either liking or loving them would force us to try to keep this category small. So we could be on the lookout to discover that real wickedness is rarer than we may have thought. Generally the truth under the label is quite complicated. Few people answer completely to their stereotypes. They are selfish and lacking in imagination rather than malignant or corrupt; or, more sadly, the hero has his weaknesses. If we are on someone's side, ready to see things from his point of view, we relate his failings to the whole person in quite a different way from any easy labelling. If we are not on somebody's side, to talk of loving him is a well-meaning but not very reliable short cut.

What would real love be then? The point of this whole argument has been to suggest that what love needs to make it complete, dangerous as it seems, is an element of partiality: and this is what liking can bring in if we dare admit it. 'Partiality' ought not to scare us. It is no more and no less than the acknowledgment of individual mattering, the love that appreciates and minds about particular people for their own sakes. It is the love that is *pro* someone, on someone's side, without needing to be paid or urged or bargained with to do what is needed. Partiality would rather do more than can be expected of it, not on principle but precisely because it wants to. What is wrong with 'taking sides' is not the good we do one side but the hurt we may do the other. For that reason, human beings dare not be as partial as God. 'Impartiality' is not a divine virtue, but a human expedient to make up for the limits of our concern on the one hand and the corruptibility of our affections on the other. If we find ourselves neglecting, or spoiling, or abusing, we need to be more even-handed and partiality becomes a vice; but the august partiality of God is a taking hold of the special character of each creature as uniquely significant. To insist that liking is a strand even in God's love sounds odd but is meant to point to something about it which is demanding, gentle and in a way light-hearted.

✣ 15 ✣

Attending

To talk about liking as a sort of real love is to arrive at the idea of friendship. But here so many warning bells ring that we shall have to listen to them. To make friendship morally important seems to be blatantly against the teaching of the New Testament. It looks as if we are particularly warned against supposing that friendship is a fair substitute for the kind of love the Lord is interested in: 'If you love those that love you, what reward have you? Do not even the tax collectors do the same?' (Matt. 5.46). In St Luke's Gospel he is fiercer still: 'When you give a dinner or a banquet, do not invite your friends or your brothers or your kinsmen or rich neighbours, lest they also invite you in return, and you be repaid. But when you give a feast, invite the poor, the maimed, the lame, the blind, and you will be blessed, because they cannot repay you' (Luke 14.12).

There are easy ways of evading this challenge. Of course, we are not to suppose that the gospels give the very words of the Lord. Of course, first-century Middle Eastern customs of hospitality were different from ours. Of course, this teaching was always hyperbole. So, of course, we are not forbidden to give dinner parties for our friends and naturally we go on doing so; though perhaps we indulge in a little guilty feeling that we are settling for a soft option, which is no encouragement either to our friends or to down-and-outs. But when a challenge like this is evaded easily instead of properly reckoned with, it is apt to hit us harder in the end. Although, or maybe because, we readily put the teaching on one side in *practice*, it has tended to find expression in a stern *theory* about human affections which Christians adopt with alacrity and are not apt to criticize.

Brunner has put the theory in its standard form:

From the point of view of faith friendship is a natural fact which can only become ethical through the love of our neighbour . . . Friendship does not say: I love you because you are *there*, but it says merely: I love you because you are like this! Thus it is not unconditional but conditional, exclusive and not universal. A person who claims friendship with everyone has not begun to understand the meaning of friendship.[1]

He goes on to allow an attractive subsidiary place for friendship as a form of human refreshment granted us by a kind Creator, alongside the refreshment of love between the sexes and of art. What more can we ask?

What we can ask is that we should have a further look at friendship in relation to neighbour-love, not for the sake of justifying unregenerate human exclusiveness, but in the name of real relationship. There is a kind of Christian slide away from friendship which is supposed to be a progression in love,[2] but which humanly speaking is apt to be a progression in shallow-ness or even self-deception: a slide to the sort of 'fellowship' which is no more than camaraderie or civility; to the kind of 'love of neighbour' which has no enjoyment in it; to the assumption that a stranger is more valuable than an old acquaintance; and eventually to the tacit belief that the love of people who are relentlessly hostile is more 'Christian' and therefore more worthwhile than any of our other affections. The last of these has been well answered by Burnaby, that love of enemies may be a test of love but is not a better kind of love;[3] but the slide remains slippery.

The way down the slide allures us because it is meant to be a flight from smugness undertaken in loyalty to the Lord; but it is apt to end in insincerity or a worse smugness or both. So it is worth making a fresh start. Perhaps it is *not* particularly Christian after all to belittle friendship. It is fair to point out that friendship is under no more condemnation than brotherhood. If the Lord called people to reject their friends, it was in the same sense as he called them to reject their own families:[4] a sense which still does not forbid us to use human love as a picture of divine love. If God is our Father and we are all brethren,[5] may He not also be our Friend and make us friends with one another? The stern saying about the feast, which we dare not reject either as uncharacteristic or as inapplicable to our times, is no more *about* friendship than it is about brotherly love as a good or bad model for Christian love. It is about our ordinary agreeable reciprocal social lives with their conventions and their expectations, in which it is unhappily easy to get stuck. It asks us to broaden our likings and not to fossilize them. So it is open, even to a literally-minded believer, to refuse to belittle friendship in the name of the kingdom. The love of friends is on a footing with the love of siblings: a picture of the love we are to develop not diminish.

If we can allow ourselves to take friendship alongside brotherhood as another promising model of Christian love, we shall be commending partiality; but partiality is not the same thing as exclusiveness. Exclusiveness is not properly a characteristic of friendship at all. There *are* exclusive loves, particularly the love of husband and wife; and some exclusive loves are good loves, even serving as pictures of the divine jealousy of God; but friendship at its best is essentially sharable. What it requires is not that we should 'forsake all other' but that we should seriously attend to what *this* person is like.

Far from putting exclusiveness into friendship, what we need is to put friendship firmly into the exclusive loves. For one thing we know about the exclusive loves is that even at their noble best they are not eternal. What we may hope to find is that what is durable about them in the end is a special kind of friendship. We can see for ourselves that this is true of the love of parent and child when it has outlived its original singularity. Let us hope that something analogous is true of marriage. This would be an encouraging way to understand the hard saying that in the resurrection people neither marry nor are given in marriage but are like angels in heaven.[6] It would be defeatist to suppose that the unique quality of true lovers' attention to one another is either doomed to perish or a second-best.

None of this need be unrealistic about the corruptibility of all human loves. C. S. Lewis, in an influential book,[7] made much of the distinctiveness of affection, friendship and eros in order to stress how each of them in turn may and indeed must become demonic unless they undergo death and resurrection. One can disagree with him at some stages along the way, but his main point remains. No human love can stand being made absolute. If the praise of friendship were to lead to some kind of cult of personal relationships as intrinsically holy and self-justifying, we should indeed be on a slippery slope. But the present argument is not really going that way at all. The opponent is not someone who reminds us of our weakness and corruptibility. Friendship is neither to be identified with Christian charity, nor set up in rivalry to it. What the argument is trying to do is pick out whatever aspects in human love as it *is* are already pointing to what love is meant to be; and especially to dare to suggest that *partiality*,[8] strange as it may seem, can be such a pointer. The 'enemy' is that recurring fashion in Christian thinking which denigrates the particular and the specific in favour of the general and the abstract.

The characteristic partiality of friendship, which makes it after all a promising rather than an unworthy model of Christian love, is a matter of *attentiveness* not exclusiveness. We can love people who are like ourselves with whom we have plenty in common. We can love people who are unlike ourselves and give us a fresh slant on the world. We can love people who are good to us and we can love people with all their failings. Certainly we do not love our friends in proportion to their moral goodness, any more than we love them in order to do them good. These have rightly been called 'over-moralized' views of friendship.[9] But still partiality is related to what people really are, the characteristics they actually have. We cannot love people we have never really noticed.

Even holy love is able to say 'I love you because you are like this!'[10] and there need be no 'merely' about it. Partiality is a matter of looking to see what the special individuality of the other person really is and attending positively to it. God can have this kind of special love for each of His creatures. We, of course, cannot, but the limit is our finitude, not something essentially restrictive about particular love. What Brunner says is true, that 'a person who claims friendship with everyone has not begun to understand the meaning of friendship';[11] but not because friendship in its nature has to be exclusive, but rather because real friendship takes time and energy which human beings have in limited amounts. We cannot have too many friends for the same reason as we cannot do too much work. We cannot spread ourselves too thin. But our limits may be much less narrow than we suppose. We may take our natural likings as a lead, but it is a shame to take them as a governor. Karl Barth said 'the friend is a model of the *neighbor*':[12] model, not rival. It can be more Christian to say this than to treat friendship as an unworthy distraction or an optional extra for our leisure hours.

Of course Christian love transcends natural liking just as it transcends natural compassion, but it need not repudiate its lowly origins in human feelings. Surely the good Samaritan was not a better Samaritan if he looked on the man who fell among thieves with repulsion? Friendliness and willingness to like are only a small start towards any kind of love, but they are a start and a better start than dogged dutifulness. With many of our human neighbours we shall never, in this world, get further than the start, but at least we can look around us in hopeful expectation.

But does all this underestimate friendship in a different way, by assimilating it too closely to love in general? Surely friends have a special relationship with its own character, distinct from the most attentive goodwill to the world at large? The way to acknowledge this is not by emphasizing the distinctiveness of friendship as a different *kind* of love. The point about friendship is that it is reciprocal. It is a symmetrical relationship. Friends attend to one another and do so on equal terms. That is what constitutes a friendship. To have friends is to love those who love you. We can call it 'conditional' if we must, but all we mean is that asymmetrical love, however good and genuine, is not called friendship. We are not smuggling exclusiveness back in.

Have we in characterizing friendship in this way destroyed the analogy with God's love instead of commending it? If friendship is symmetrical, we can never claim to be friends with God. But so does the analogy with fatherhood fail at what might seem the crucial point. God does not beget us. We must always 'compare and contrast', never think we have encapsulated our relationship with our Maker in human language. We must keep changing our analogies to do justice to His transcendence,

while continuing to hold on to the point the analogy was
designed to illustrate: in this case, the attentive partiality of
love.

There is no need then to apologize for the fact that Christ at a
solemn moment calls his disciples friends:[13] still less for the
saying 'Greater love hath no man than this, that a man lay
down his life for his friends.' Certainly in the Fourth Gospel
Christian love is evidently losing its unmotivated one-way
character, embarrassing as this tendency may be to those who
would set agape in opposition to eros.[14] Nygren has to suggest
that the Fourth Gospel is at the beginning of a decline: but is it?
On the contrary, it is worth insisting that specific love for
specific people is not remote from the imitation of Christ.

The Fourth Gospel is not idiosyncratic in building particular
affection into the very foundations of the good news. We know
that Christ was called the friend of publicans and sinners, but
we may have learnt to understand by this that he had an
unmotivated love for outcasts. It need not be tendentious for a
change to give this tradition its setting: which, far from
approval, was the accusation of worldliness.[15] 'A gluttonous
man and a winebibber' was a taunt which seems to have stuck.
It would be false reverence to underestimate the fact that the
Lord liked disreputable people and they liked him, enough to
welcome him at their gatherings. Worldly people are not
inclined to respond to condescension, however divine. It is not
unmotivated acceptance but friendly appreciation that warms
hard hearts and makes people want to be less selfish and more
human. There is nothing trivial, petty or 'unspiritual' about the
attentive care by which this process of entering into relationship is made possible.

People suppose that if the highest love is a partial love then
there can be no hope for sinners, or the wrong kind of hope.
Quite the contrary can be true. What partiality does is look at
sinfulness differently. It does not see it as something intrinsic,
but as woefully impeding or damaging the real person. Partiality
does not have to be indulgent or unrealistic, though there may
be a refusal to be indignant which looks unrealistic to those
outside. Sometimes when we really look, we dislike intensely
what we see; but what partiality tells us is, That is not the whole
story.

These considerations are not offered as a way of evading the implications of that triumphant reaffirmation of God's love for the humble and the weak which goes by the name of 'liberation theology'. On the contrary, the divine 'option for the poor' is precisely a preferential love. It looks attentively at seemingly insignificant people as what they really are, children of God capable of entering into their heritage. But it is much to be hoped that if this kind of Christian partiality were better understood, it would not merely become a way of demolishing inhuman stereotypes in one direction only to set them up in another. The more politically conscious Christians become, the more important it is for attentiveness to people, looking, listening, appreciating and trying to understand, to characterize the whole of their thinking, not only selected aspects of it.

But if this is a good model of Christian love, it is too high for us, not too low. The more loftily we understand partiality, the more unreasonable it looks to demand it in our dealings with one another. It asks a lot more of us than the settled goodwill which is generally recommended as the sum of our Christian duty. Surely in loving my neighbour as myself I cannot be expected to find him endearing or congenial? It may after all be true that I have very little in common with him.

I cannot, of course, be required to find; but I can be asked to keep looking. The answer to the question 'Who is my neighbour?' was not actually the comparatively easy answer of the person you can help, who draws out your sympathy, but, more surprisingly, the alien Samaritan, the person with whom I am *out* of sympathy.[16] The parable, of course, is just a story, and many people who are alien to us in real life are extremely unlikely, humanly speaking, to act in any way to invite our regard. This is where Christian faith comes in, that I do as a matter of fact have reason to believe that there is something worth loving about any human creature.

'Say he is a stranger,' said Calvin. 'The Lord has given him a mark which ought to be familiar to you. Say he is mean and of no consideration. The Lord points him out as one whom he has distinguished by the lustre of his own image.'[17] Traherne makes the same point more picturesquely:

[Human beings] lov a Creature for Sparkling Eys and Curled Hair, Lillie Brests and Ruddy Cheeks; which they should love moreover for being GODS Image, Queen of the Univers, Beloved by Angels, redeemed by Jesus Christ, an Heires of Heaven, and Temple of the H. Ghost: a Mine and fountain of all Vertues, a Treasurie of Graces, and a Child of GOD. But these Excellencies are unknown.[18]

People whose faith is that these descriptions are well-founded have every right to adopt as a kind of rule of thumb the ancient maxim 'Nothing human can be alien to me.'[19] The world being what it is, they will still have plenty of negative relationships, neutral or even unpleasant. But there will always be the awareness that to look upon a fellow-creature without appreciation is to miss something. There *is* something there, if only one had the sensitivity, or humility, or even just the time, to see it.

❧ 16 ❧

Worshipping

Now we can suggest what is wrong with the tendency among some Christians to underestimate friendship as an inferior kind of love, good for us within due limits but essentially secular. To honour friendship so little is to miss a good chance to take heed of those aspects of love which are appreciation, attention and delight in somebody's company. If friendship is a way of learning to attend and enjoy by being taken out of ourselves, it is teaching something we do not have to unlearn.

This kind of personalism, far from turning its back on the glory of God, is finding us a way to approach it. The worship of God is, for many of us, something difficult, both practically and intellectually: so difficult that we are easily distracted from even attempting it. So if we discover that our human affections are after all not just another distraction but a true small-scale model of what worshipping is supposed to be, we can hope to do more justice both to the human and to the divine.

Human thinkers have been so afraid of making God in their own image that they have emphasized at all costs the discontinuity between God and man. The cost is heavy, if it means neglecting available analogies and actually impoverishing one's notions of the God one aspires to worship. The God of our tradition did make men and women to be like Himself; and when they had gone astray, 'He was made man,' as Athanasius dared to put it, 'that we might be made God.'[1] To assume after all that He is Wholly Other than us, and also that He wants us continually to tell Him so in abject terms, is no more Christian than it is properly human.

Yet we believe that worship *is* required of us. Somehow we must find out what it is meant to be. The fact that so many sincere Christians find prayer difficult shows that there is a serious question here. There are some to whom it seems to come quite naturally to adore; but others want to know *how* and *why*; and some believe they see reasons *not* to adore. These are good human beings to whom the idea of constant praise seems repugnant, pointless, empty, even unworthy, and unless we shut our minds we can see what they mean. How can we show that worship need not involve a wrong abrogation of our autonomy? We need an answer to Richard Robinson in *An Atheist's Values*: 'One cannot abase oneself before a perfectly moral person, because a perfectly moral person treats one as an equal and as having a right to one's way of life.'[2] We ought to take heed of the simple fact that many people find prayer boring; for if it is rootedly boring one must wonder if it is unworthy, not just of mankind but of the Deity Himself who demands it. 'You are God: we praise you.' The bald modern words emphasize the oddness of the activity.

When Christians sympathize with these difficulties, let alone feel them, it is not much use trying to batter our consciousness with emphasis upon our unworthiness and our duty. A gentler approach is in order, by way of the analogies between mankind and God which are embedded, indeed authorized, in the fundamental teachings of our religion. We can allow ourselves to look at our actual relationships with one another for illumination of this mysterious obligation we seem to owe to God.

To worship, we know, is to ascribe worth. Properly understood, this should be neither a self-conscious debasement of oneself nor a cold giving of due, but a combination of reverence and joy in someone's presence. Keith Ward has admirably linked the earthly and the divine here. Worship 'is not to say "How good and marvellous you are", like a sycophantic courtier. It is not to say anything in particular. It is just to contemplate with appreciation the worth of what lies before one ... To worship is to allow the mind to rest in the loving contemplation of what is really good and valuable', whether that is people, scenery, or even the crown jewels.[3] So we can hope to reach the worship of God 'by first of all learning to worship beautiful and valuable things and persons'.[4] As H. A. Williams put it, 'worship surely is concerned exclusively with the simple but profound matter of response to perceived value'.[5] If we believe we have learnt anything about God, we let our minds dwell upon it and then praise should take care of itself.

To this two points need to be added. First, that worship is not always better for being silent. It can be celebration as well as contemplation. It may be excellently uttered, in words or music or paint or stone. When one hears a work like Bach's B Minor Mass it dawns upon one that praising is an important human activity. Maybe this understanding could spill over into our dealings with one another and we could get over thinking that 'praise to the face' has to be 'open disgrace'.

Second, what counts here is not an attempt to make our worship proportional to the estimated worth of its object, a notion which could slip in and spoil the whole idea. That is why friendship is a good model. Unless we are Aristotelians, we attend to the particular characters of our friends, their value as individuals rather than their value as deserving. The relevant point is the attention and not the degree of moral esteem. Austin Farrer stressed the significance of really looking, of 'the appreciation of things which we have when we love them and fill our minds and senses with them, and feel something of the silent force and great mystery of their existence'.[6] One is reminded of Iris Murdoch's hovering kestrel;[7] and if this loving attention is a good attitude even to things, it can be much more so to people. So there could after all be a sort of ladder of contemplation leading towards the understanding of divine worship rather than away from it.

It is not a debating point to recall the human use of the word 'worship', which is by no means peculiar to the 1662 marriage service. His Worship the Mayor is no demigod, but a human being filling an honourable role. In several places, according to the old translations, St Matthew's Gospel tells us that people 'worshipped' Christ,[8] whereas the new versions avoid the theological implications by giving us 'knelt' or 'fell at his feet' or even just 'bowed low'. In showing proper reverence to one another human beings have until recently used the same terminology, symbols and gestures as they have found it apt to use for their gods. By losing this continuity we have lost an important range of analogies. People who kneel only to God are inclined to become stiff in their knees. It is too late now to revive what has become an archaism and to think in terms of worshipping one another. It is to be hoped that it is not too late to build our worship of God, not only on unique awe, but on a kind of extrapolation of human reverence to which appreciative attentiveness gives the best clue.

But surely it is a sin, the dire sin of idolatry, to worship God's creatures when we ought to worship only God? Is it not at best dangerously irresponsible, at worst treacherous, to try to make 'personal relationships' continuous in this kind of way? The martyrs died for the sake of the discontinuity between God and Caesar. How dare a twentieth-century personalist smooth over the great gap which cost them their lives?

Since Austin Farrer has been quoted on the theme of appreciation, it is only fair to hear his voice again putting a check on taking the argument too far: 'There is indeed a worship of God in which no human object can have a share.'[9] M. C. Darcy in *The Mind and Heart of Love* asserted that 'Worship and adoration are unlike any other human act or response.'[10] With characteristically sweeping eloquence Teilhard de Chardin declared, 'What I cry out for, like every other creature, with my whole being, and even with all my passionate earthly longings, is something very different from an equal to cherish: it is a God to adore.'[11] In comparison with these reminders, talk of continuity and appreciation sounds sociable rather than reverent, like an image of heaven sketched out with more poetic sparkle than theological orthodoxy in a poem by Kipling:

And oft-times cometh our wise Lord God, master of every trade,
And tells them tales of His daily toil, of Edens newly made;
And they rise to their feet as He passes by, gentlemen unafraid.[12]

It will not do to ignore the classic distinction, authoritatively explained by Augustine in *The City of God*, between the kind of worship we owe to the Deity, for which he uses the Greek word *Latreia*, and the service of earthly masters which is *Dulia*. He acknowledges:

There are in fact many ingredients in the worship of God which are also to be found in the honour paid to human beings

. . . but even when men are said to be worthy of homage and veneration, and even, in extreme cases, of adoration [and it is agreeable to reflect that Augustine himself is now a canonized saint], it is to be remembered that they are still human beings. But who has ever thought it right to offer sacrifice, except to a being known, or supposed, or imagined to be God?[13]

The point is that the unworthiness of the creature to be put on a level with God is not just that the creature in fact happens to be sinful and God happens not to be, as we might say that someone's fiancée is not good enough for him; but that it is part of the meaning of holiness that abasement is fitting, that we have a contrast not an analogy.

Of course the discontinuity between God and mankind is to be emphasized, not ignored. Of course personalism, which attempts to describe God in human categories, leads to an inadequate understanding: how could it not? The difference between God and His creatures is a difference of kind not just a difference of degree. But let us still intransigently affirm that analogy is a good way of leading up to contrast.[14] It can bring us to the point of crossing a threshold. As Professor Ninian Smart has put it, to speak of continuity 'is not, incidentally, to deny that there may be a "critical point"'[15] where 'a difference of degree will look *intense*'.[16] In other words, the distinction between a difference in degree and a difference in kind is itself not absolute. It is by first making comparisons, giving them every chance and then finding that our comparisons have suddenly become wholly inadequate, that we best come to appreciate contrast. To refuse comparison is to produce, not worship, but incomprehensible technicality.

For example, it is true that sacrifice in the technical sense is, essentially, only for God; but the technical sense of sacrifice is for us a notoriously obscure idea. What sacrifice most simply means, the bringing of oneself or the bringing of what one most values as an offering, in willingness to give it up and lose it for someone else's sake: this people do for one another all the time. It is when we understand this humanly, even if we are not very good at doing it, that we are in a position to push the idea to its limit and find ourselves at the brink of what it ought to mean to offer sacrifice to God. Instead of trying to appease a capricious deity, we imagine what it could be like to offer total unhindered attention and reverence to the origin of all worshipfulness. First we assert a likeness, then a difference of degree so great as to amount to a difference in kind. Comparison brings us to the threshold of contrast. There is no demeaning abasement of people, but a discovery of the immensity of God. This is what I. T. Ramsey used to call a 'disclosure situation'.

Human beings, we may agree, are not 'numinous'. They are not mysterious as God is mysterious. But they are wonderful; and in their way they are rightly called 'transcendent'.[17] Their value transcends numerical price.[18] Their claims transcend legal demands. There is something about them which can truly be said to go *beyond* the level of plain fact. They are not totally unworthy to illuminate God's claim upon us. What this kind of analogy is doing is using the *derived* to interpret the *original*. We need not take fright at saying that people are fit for worship because in their way they are holy; but we make it plain that their holiness is no more their very own than the light of the moon is its own. Are sunlight and moonlight different in kind or in degree? Certainly the moon really is bright and we can see by its light. There is nothing sham or fictitious about reflected glory.

Protestant Christians have been anxious, with some reason, about the human tendency to confuse the derived with the original and to offer to human saints that absolute adoration which only God can claim. But the present argument is not mainly about saints with haloes. The great saints are right to refuse worship[19] and in a way we are right to heed them when they insist that they are *not* holy and to redirect our reverence to God. Their actual moral achievement could be enough to confuse the issue, so they and we need to be especially careful.

But what 'holiness' means in this argument is not something saintly people have in greater degree than sinners. It means something more like 'claimingness', 'love-worthiness', 'per-sonalness', 'importance'. Then we say that what is potential and finite (and, we must admit, spoilt) in creatures is actual and infinite in God.[20] So we have our analogical path from the human to the divine, and ordinary friendship, which attends to the particular importance of an individual person, is a gateway to it. It is not that we first bow down before an idol and then somehow learn to bow down before the true God. It is rather that we attend to what a person is really like and get into practice for attending to what God is really like.

Often when one really attends to a human person one will have glimpses of what we rightly call 'goodness', as well as, and mixed up in, 'lovableness'. For all the sincere protestations of this potential saint, one can cherish the conviction that what one is finding oneself in a position to acknowledge are miniature but real facets reflecting the glory of God.

❧ 17 ❧

Images and Idols

The trouble with this argument is not that it makes us complacent about idolatry by allowing us to worship unworthy objects, but that it makes us complacent about idolatry by suggesting that there is no such thing. According to the present view, worship is for persons. It means reverence, love, the offering of oneself. Divine worship is the limiting case of this: or rather, beyond all limits, the transcendent case. But if finite persons have their finite worshipfulness, what has happened to our tradition which has always taught that the worship of creatures is one of the gravest sins?

On the usual view, worship is a special activity belonging to God, but people persistently offer it to unworthy objects. On the present view, worship is the activity of reverently appreciating a person; and divine worship is the activity of reverently appreciating God. If we can begin to learn how to worship God by attending to one another, so that God is not so to say in fundamental competition with His creation, what is it that is so very apt to go wrong? We can and do worship inadequately: but what is this terrible misdirection to which we are supposed to be so prone?

On the face of it there are only three positive ways in which worship can go wrong; and none of them seems to meet the case. First, devil worship could be very wicked indeed, but is surely humanly too rare to account for the persistent conviction that idolatry is a prevalent temptation. Formally to take sides with wickedness and say 'Evil be thou my good' is more dramatically defiant than most bad people aspire to; and even that is not quite to say 'Evil be thou my God', to give the devil something like the disinterested adoration we owe to a deity.

Secondly, there is of course the error called 'inordinate affection': a disproportionate devotion to a finite being. Some people seem to idolize their lovers, or their teachers, or their children, or their pets, and discover in gentle or bitter disillusionment that all creatures have feet of clay; or never discover it and live their lives in systematic unfairness to the people they neglect for their idol's sake. The Epistle to the Colossians says that covetousness is idolatry.[1] Preachers exhort us not to idolize wealth, or social status, or our own selves; but surely all these ways of talking about idolatry are metaphorical? These gods that allure us are false enough; but we know, even when we worship them, that they are not literally gods.

But thirdly, people have thought they knew what idolatry really means. It was summed up in the line, 'The heathen in his blindness bows down to wood and stone.'[2] The trouble with this view of idolatry is obvious: we shudder at its condescension. We can no longer enjoy gloating with the Psalmist: 'As for the images of the heathen, they are but silver and gold' (Ps. 135.15) or 'They have ears and hear not: noses have they and smell not' (Ps. 115.6). So in the name of tolerance it is still tempting to explain idolatry away.

Tolerance is not enough as a substitute for thinking the question of false worship out, if we want our ideas about true worship to be coherent. We cannot smuggle personalism into the centre of the argument by muzzling tradition like an old watchdog. Even if we could, the question of idolatry deserves attention in its own right. It might fairly be described as a muddle. Is there really such a person as an idolator and what is he supposed to think he is doing?

On the one hand, there is our easy conviction that the 'heathen' is simply doing his best to worship God and that as long as he truly is sincere in his faith, the only true God will assuredly accept his devotion as meant for Himself, like a misdirected letter. We may have agreeably ecumenical thoughts, not only in a mosque where there are no idols and Allah is another name for our own God, but in an ancient pagan holy place, a Greek temple, an *asklepieion*, where there once came religious men with whose strivings we have something in

common. We may notice that sermons preached about the
carpenter in the book of Isaiah,[3] who used half his wood to light
a fire for cooking and the other half for making an idol, have
changed their tune. Once he used to be blamed for supposing
that something he had made could be God; now he is reproached
for not offering everything he has to the God he worships. At
worst, idolatry becomes a forgivable error. At best, God will
deign to be present in even the most inadequate image, as we
hope He is in our own inadequate ideas of Him. But then what
has become of the ancient grave sin of going after strange gods?
And does this approach not have a potentially arrogant condescension of its own, that the images which are good enough for
'them', the ignorant heathen, are not good enough for 'us' who
know better? Is it not treating somebody with more respect to
tell him we believe he is mistaken than to humour him in what
we take to be his error? Or do we suppose that no religion is ever
really erroneous after all?

So, on the other hand, we are obliged to reckon with the
uniqueness of true worship. Professor Peter Geach in a fierce
article called 'On Worshipping the Right God'[4] has set about
rehabilitating the notion that idolatry can exist and is not
harmless but serious and dangerous. He is against inter-faith
ecumenism. In all the scriptures, he insists, 'There is not a hint
that *bona fide* worship of a heathen god does the worshipper the
least good':[5] rather it alienates. It is worshipping a *nothing*. He
declares sternly:

> The upshot is that we dare not be complacent about confused
> and erroneous thinking about God, in ourselves or in others. If
> anybody's thoughts about God are sufficiently confused and
> erroneous, then he will fail to be thinking about the true and
> living God at all; and just because God alone can draw the
> line, none of us is in a position to say that a given error is not
> serious enough to be harmful.[6]

In a way, he is echoing Luther:

> It is not enough to say or think: 'I am doing it to God's glory: I
> mean it for the true God; I will serve only the true God.' All
> idolators say and intend that. Intentions and thoughts do not
> count, or those who martyred the apostles and the Christians
> would also have been God's servants.[7]

We have here rather a strong warning against trying to set up merely facile continuities between true and misdirected worship.

Yet the last word is far from having been pronounced. As Professor Ninian Smart has well said, 'We owe it to human beings at least to try to understand them.'[8] Professor Geach's definition of idolatry, 'divine worship paid to a human artefact',[9] seems to make it too stupid to be wicked. It is surely attractive, if possible, to take one's stand not on the imprecations of the old covenant but on the Inasmuch saying.[10] If the Lord is willing to accept for himself practical service offered to creatures, will He not likewise accept 'divine service' offered to the best God the worshipper knew?

Is it adequate to say that all that matters is to 'do our best'? C. C. J. Webb defined idolatry long ago as 'the worship as God of that which, at the moral and intellectual level occupied by the worshipper, is less than the Highest'.[11] That at least sounds like a real sin than a mistake, while allowing room for an ecumenical humility. Its trouble is that instead of making idolatry seem impossible, this definition inclines a little, with the Idealism of its day, towards making it ubiquitous. All human aspirations are less than the 'highest'. The specific error of idolatry is not so easy to catch. Yet it does need to be identified as a real aberration, if personalism is to defend itself from the charge of straying too far from the tradition.

It is worth pointing out here that there is no need to belabour our own selves always with every sin. Whatever we say about the logical and psychological possibility of the worship of false gods, it may not be a particularly characteristic error of modern Western man. It may be true that we should need to hunt long and hard to find much of it among our immediate contemporaries. It looks as if our besetting sin is *not* worshipping rather than worshipping in the wrong places. On the whole it is reverence itself that we lack. Irreligion and superstition go off in contrary directions. To blame ourselves for superstition could be to bark rather pointlessly up the wrong tree.

Professor H. D. Lewis has insisted in *Our Experience of God* that idolatry is 'an essentially religious phenomenon, possible only where there is at least a spark of genuine religion'.[12] It is the attempt of human beings, terrified of God yet also drawn to Him and needing Him, 'to limit or restrict their own consciousness of God by containing it' within its images,[13] in other words, 'to incapsulate the divine within its finite symbol'.[14] 'The symbol draws into itself the glory it should only be transmitting.'[15]

This is interesting because it puts the emphasis on symbols of the divine as capable of use as well as of misuse. Idolatry is not an activity in its own right but a perversion of true worship. An image does not have to be an idol; and if we want to arrive at some clarity about what idolatry is and what it is not, it is worth looking first at the notion of an image. 'Image' is a more neutral word than 'idol'. It moves along a scale. At one end, it can be practically synonymous with 'idol': a pejorative sense is not ruled out. But 'image' can be used without blame for someone else's holy thing; and it is not wise, Professor Smart points out, 'to look upon the image as a simple object'.[16] More positively still, 'image' can be used in our own tradition with the good meaning of 'ikon'. It can suggest the 'image of God' and all the cluster of ideas for which that phrase can stand. There is a great deal of theology here, especially belonging to the Eastern churches, which is more constructive than plain condemnation of idols. Iconoclasm seems extremely far from being obviously right.

The gist of a theology of images is that a true ikon neither usurps the place of the holy, nor merely serves as a reminder of it. In some way it *mediates* the holy. With this role the material image itself has its holiness; and veneration, properly understood, is not out of place. Neither is it out of place to say, ecumenically, that most images of the divine which human beings have made are capable of being ikons. They are possible means of grace. The physical can convey the spiritual. There is no need to overspiritualize our ideas of the Creator by putting Him out of all relation to the material world. It is not images as such that constitute idolatrous religion. How then are we to stop ourselves from proving too much and making all worship apparently true worship? At least we need to ask what images are properly *appointed* images. Maybe idolatry is a matter of wilfully choosing out images of our own. Though an image does not have to be an idol, human beings can make it into one.

The worship of idols seems to have something to do with enthralment, with letting oneself be captivated. An idol is something one goes after, turning one's back on real claims. What a personalist ought to say about idolatry is that it is fundamentally a failure of attention. An idol is not false because it is an image: some images focus our minds upon the truth. An idol must be an image that distracts, that takes attention away from the truth. Idolatry needs to be explained as a sin of unfaithfulness, not a sin of faith.

Now we can reconsider the three ways in which worship might go wrong[17] and see that as failures of attention they can indeed account for the sin of idolatry. First, the idea that idol worship is really devil worship need not be so far wrong after all. Some human beings easily devote themselves to the thrills of religion, to the numinous and even the merely spooky, letting the workaday moral claims that are bound up in the full concept of holiness go by default. Second, 'inordinate affection', considered as idolatry, would not be pathetic uncritical fondness but an obsessive attention to such limited objects as to impoverish one's capacity to appreciate and enjoy the world at large and God as its Creator.

Third and most to the point, to bow down to a man-made image, to give one's attention to a god one has made for oneself, may not be as naively innocent as it sounds. Why after all should human beings ever want to make idols for themselves? The idea makes sense as a way of staving off consideration of what the true and living God is really like. It seems much better if possible to have a god one can manage, even maybe use for one's own purposes. Augustine gave a description of idolatry that is not altogether out of date:

> There is a god for you! See what a god he is! Let him draw nigh, let him cast his spell on you. Listen, here is this or that high priest on the mountain. Perhaps you are poor because that god is not helping you: supplicate him and he will help you. Perhaps you are ill just because you do not pray to him: pray to him and you will recover. Perhaps you have no children for the same reason: make supplication to him and you will have them.[18]

Idolatry makes petitionary prayer commercial or diplomatic.

So it is not making images and bowing down before them, even when the images are inadequate, that is to be blamed as idolatry. It is avoiding paying attention to complete reality in favour of something one prefers instead. The most characteristic form of idolatry, the really dire error about God, is to treat Him as manageable, to think one has Him under control. A real idol would not be just any image that represents divinity to mankind. It would be an image of God shaped in presumption.

We can explain now how idolatry as a sin can happen: how what looks like a mistake can be morally wrong. The idolater cannot be merely silly. He must be beginning to be corrupt. He sells his worship. He gives his allegiance for the sake of favours. The prayer he cannot make is 'Thy will be done'.

We can even explain how Christ himself could have been tempted so. To worship the devil, to give oneself over to Satan, not so to speak out of 'devilment' but for the sake of what the evil power could offer, is not too peculiar to be a genuinely human temptation nor too crude to tempt God's Messiah.

Now we can sort out our attitudes towards apparently idolatrous religions, not feeling in duty bound to disapprove. Sometimes they shock us ethically. 'Who could fail to realize what kind of spirits they are which could enjoy such obscenities?' asked Augustine in the *City of God*.[19] Sometimes they seem to be an evident decline from something better. But whenever it looks as if sincere worship is being offered, we find it impossible to believe that the true God will not accept it for Himself.

But most happily for our present purpose, with this view of idolatry we can know what to think of the reverence we owe to one another. There is no need at all to call human honour or even human devotion by the name of idolatry. It is an entirely proper finite worship. Even if it seems to get out of proportion, what is 'inordinate' about it is not the affection but its blinding and deafening effect upon one. In general, the more we reverence one another the better. To fail to reverence other people is nearer to the sin of idolatry than over-fondness could ever be. To manage people or humour them or categorize them instead of attending to them and appreciating them for what they are is the equivalent for creatures of what idolatry is for God. Personalism, properly understood, is miles away from idolatry.

It would be agreeable if that could be the whole story: but unfortunately a difficulty remains. The material aspect of the sin of idolatry has been brushed aside a little too easily. The second commandment says 'Thou shalt not make to thyself any graven image'; so Professor Geach's definition of idolatry, 'divine worship paid to a human artefact',[20] must be allowed still to have weight. Professor Smart asked whether it is 'just a coincidence that three, or rather two and a half, major religions have stressed that one should not make images of God'?[21] Plainly, one must be very careful in talking about ikons and allowing images to be vehicles of God's presence.

To resolve this resurgent objection, we can take a clue from an article by Ian Crombie as long ago as 1957. In the midst of an argument he says somewhat incidentally 'It was the ban on idolatry which taught the Jews what God is.'[22] This can be taken in conjunction with an observation of Professor Smart's: 'One reason for not wishing to portray God is that the absence of visible representation symbolizes both the invisible transcend- ence of God and the fact that he is not to be thought of anthropomorphically.'[23] One might say that the very lack of outward symbol makes itself into a symbol. The empty Holy of Holies is the best image of God.

Or rather, it is the second best image. The best, 'the brightness of his glory and the express image of his person' (Heb. 1.3), is a perfect man. It is significant that the ban on material images should happen so notably in one particular context. From a Christian point of view the old covenant between God and His people can be characterized as 'pre-incarnational'. The absence of visible symbols is essentially not to be permanent. There is to be an overwhelmingly visible symbol of God in a human life. We could go so far as to say that in the Old Testament there seems to be a positive *withdrawal* from potentially excellent vehicles of God's presence. A critic of Hebrew religion might well ask whether things, beautifully made, could not convey God's presence to us; whether the ban on images may not be an impoverishment of religious practice? But if Christians are right that the New Testament is the fulfilment of the Old, the sacramental principle has been thoroughly vindicated in God's good time. Its absence was educative not perpetual. Images, however carefully fashioned, were to be put aside, the Holy of Holies was to be empty, only until the purposed coming in human flesh.

So we may say that in general idolatry makes sense not as a unique activity but as a captivating distraction. It makes especially clear sense as an attempt to set up a god one can manage; and on top of this in one special context it was a rebellion against a given commandment. Both these are coherent concepts, substantial enough taken together to bear the weight of what the Judaeo-Christian tradition has wanted to say about idolatry. Neither of them forbids a personalistic approach to the idea of worship, stressing its continuity with our relationships to one another as well as its transcendence of them.

❧ 18 ❧

The End of Man

Christians are allowed to call God Father. We have been taught that He has always dealt with us in a way that allows us to use human analogies and stress continuities as well as discontinuities. Believing that we are made in His image, we cannot be obliged to think of Him as Wholly Other. The worship of God need not be simply distinct from human love. The personalist way of trying to approach God has no notice on it saying No Through Road or Broad Way to Destruction. It is promising to explore it to see whether it will bring us where we need to be. It may not be a short cut: it could still be a good route. Can the value of persons be a signpost pointing towards the vision of God?

Our destination is supposed to be 'to glorify God and to enjoy Him for ever'.[1] It is time to take this classic statement of the 'end of man' and consider it, critically but hopefully, from the point of view of Christian personalism. One can warm to it without finding it transparently clear. Anyone who is able to take it for granted could be a saint or could be not looking at it carefully enough. The vision of God seems to be the kind of idea that we cannot either do with or do without. Evidently it cannot as it were settle down to be one human goal among many. It is supposed to be able to satisfy us entirely. Can it do so only by swallowing up all our variegated aims and suppressing at last the humanity we have been trying to build upon? Can the 'chief end of man' either be, or not be, our sole end?

The kind of answer personalism offers to give to this question has been more than hinted at already. The hope is to be able to build upon the bonded brickwork of appreciation, attention and mutual delight, as ideas which are both firmly founded in ordinary human life and are also capable of sustaining the magnificent structure of transcendent reality. But castles in the air are easy to build. Have we any right to think that these upper storeys could ever be a house for us to live in?

Both parts of the traditional statement of our goal can be made to seem dubious when they are taken in what seems the most straightforward way. To 'glorify God' undeniably means to worship Him, but a gap still opens up between the worship of God and our relationship with other people. Granted that worship, understood as contemplative attention, has its place in human life: does it after all topple over into idolatry precisely when it aspires to move on to the worship of God? Let us have human honour and reverence by all means, but be aware of the possibility that the ultimate glory they seek to converge upon could be a vanishing point on the horizon.

If that seems a somewhat sophisticated difficulty, the problems of 'enjoy Him for ever', taken in its plain meaning, are only too simple. What this part of the classic affirmation evidently means is that God's good children are to be *rewarded*;[2] and human self-concern, banished only for a moment from disinterested worship, seems to come rushing back in a way we are inclined to call positively unethical. Are we to make use of God in the end by loving Him for the sake of enjoyment?

These two sorts of problems about the vision of God are not as separate as they seem. They claim that there is something *unworthy* both about the idea itself and about the pursuit of it. The intellectual difficulties were posed particularly sharply by Professor J. N. Findlay, who propounded what he somewhat mischievously called an 'Ontological *Dis*proof' of the existence of God.[3] He maintained that no real object could be the true Absolute. To exist is to be limited in one way or another; so, as he put it, the throne of God must be untenanted.[4] There is no great point in discussing whether any idol could really represent the true God, if one is seized of the idea that any God must really be an idol.

In other words, for Professor Findlay the empty Holy of Holies is more than a potent image of God: it is the very truth. As he put it historically:

When the sacrilegious Titus stepped into the Holy of Holies at Jerusalem, hoping to see the Most High seated among the Cherubim, how much more shocking would it have been had he actually encountered some particular object, rather than the mystical void that stretched before him? And when some sacred congregation meets to debate an issue central of faith and morals . . . how shocking and how suspect it would be were the issue to be resolved by some fluttering dove-like appearance, perhaps making announcements at variance with the wisdom and experience of the members.[5]

Here is the refusal of idolatry made into a positive principle. 'I am,' said Professor Findlay, 'by temperament a Protestant, and I tend towards atheism as the purest form of Protestantism.'[6] This may sound less shocking if we try it the other way round. One could be by temperament a Catholic, like Browning's Bishop Blougram, and tend towards superstition as the strongest form of Catholicism. There is a slippery slope here and it may well be difficult, though we must hope not impossible, to find foothold in the middle. Professor Findlay himself stayed on the slope at its atheistic end and gloried in the paradox. 'We give ourselves over unconditionally and gladly to the task of indefinite approach towards a certain imaginary focus where nothing actually is.'[7] He would find a way out of his religious impasse by 'accepting the non-existence of God and seeking to make of this a majestic and glorious thing'.[8]

For Christians this must be too austere, but unless they can feel the argument bite they have maybe not understood what a strenuous concept worship can be. In the end the only answer must be somehow to reach the limit and find for oneself that there can be and is something, or rather Someone, there; or at least to listen to those others further ahead of oneself, who have certainly not found the limit a vanishing point as they advanced nearer towards it. Yet, even when one is at an early stage, one can respect Professor Findlay's argument without succumbing to it. The personalism that proceeds from analogy to contrast[9] has more to say for itself than Professor Findlay can allow. Personalism takes what we know about relationships among human beings and applies this as far as possible to our relationship with God until it becomes wholly inadequate.

Professor Findlay, on the contrary, seems first to assume a unique relationship with God and then find that he cannot think about it except in human terms, which by definition will not do. So his ontological disproof of God's existence, like the ancient ontological proof, works by assuming its own conclusion; and is tantalizingly unsatisfactory to those who are not convinced by it before they begin.

A finally inconclusive argument can still deserve respect. It can make us notice what we might overlook and speak with more circumspection about what must in the end be beyond us. Professor Findlay's argument picks out the intransigence in the idea of worship, the difficulty in saying that any real being could be worthy of it. So it is a suitable background to the moral problems which cluster round the idea of pursuing the vision of God.

If 'glorifying God' is readily presented as questionable, 'enjoying Him for ever' can be hard to present as anything else. On to this problematical sort of obeisance we are supposed to attach the notion that if we do it properly we shall be rewarded: and that is bound to raise indignation. We seem to have plunged, open-eyed, into a mercenary faith.

Part of the answer has often been pointed out. The reward is not something other than God Himself. To seek a reward in the sense of seeking a goal is not in the least dubious. To marry for love is not mercenary. To marry for money is, precisely because marrying for money is seeking the wrong goal. To love and seek after God is no more mercenary than to love and seek after a chosen human being. It is not corrupt to hope that such devotion will have its reward, the reward of finding what it seeks. Those who hunger and thirst after righteousness are promised that they shall be filled. Those who pursue the vision of God as the 'one thing needful' have a quest that, for them, is simply self-justifying. It is a matter of logic, not of pious obstinacy, that a real saint is not mercenary. St Augustine is a good example, with his longing for God and glimpse of its fulfilment: 'Late have I loved thee, thou beauty so old yet ever new.'[10] To call that kind of religion self-seeking is woefully to miss the point.

But piety achieved by some creates rather than solves problems for others, not just practical problems but moral obstacles. Single-mindedness can be as unlovely in its way as double-mindedness. When someone relentlessly pursues his own goals, it is true that we do not generally call him 'mercenary'. He may still be hard-hearted, one-sided and even obsessional. The history of religion has examples of all these unattractive characteristics. It must sadly be admitted that Augustine himself is not clear of them. The question is whether these are aberrations or whether they are intrinsic to the idea of enjoying God for ever.

To compare the vision of God with marrying for love rather than marrying for money sorts out the questions about motivation a little too easily. Not to be mercenary is not enough. A goal can be entirely suitable in itself without being comprehensively self-justifying. If we say that marrying for love is right and marrying for money is wrong, we have not ruled out every possibility of human effort but marrying for love. It is perfectly in order to *trade* for money. That too is a proper goal, though not an all-embracing one. Because we do not generally see trading as a glorious quest, we know perfectly well that it is only one eligible pursuit among many. We reasonably prefer people who do not pursue it to the detriment of all else. Even marrying for love is not a comprehensive goal. It may be self-justifying; it may be totally demanding; but it does not really invalidate all other aspirations. For some it has not even been a proper goal, when the well-being of millions depended upon their political alliances, or when the beloved was committed to somebody else. So although this analogy of human devotion may defend religious devotion against charges of hypocrisy and self-seeking, it is of no use against charges of obsessiveness. If the vision of God has to be all-consuming, may it not after all be humanly diminishing? This is not quite the same as the fear that true religion is fundamentally mercenary, and is more difficult to answer.

In practice, the two sorts of accusations interact with each other in a more complicated way. We are still asking whether the true God turns out to be an idol after all. He sometimes seems to have the captivating distracting effect of an idol upon those who follow Him wholeheartedly. The vision of God seems splendid, as long as it is optional. But when it is taken seriously it seems to involve the notion of a final consumma-

tion that will make all the hopes and struggles of our earthly life
into foolishness, like a dream we wake from. We seem to be
required to believe in a single heaven in store for us which is
bound to satisfy everyone except perhaps the damned. The
multifarious aims and excellencies of variegated humanity are
discounted even if not condemned. Surely the devoted few who
sincerely take this line are excellent only because they are few?
In general, good human beings ought to have a wider scope. It is
no wonder that many people never let themselves in for this
problem at all and remain 'humanists' in a secular sense. They
avoid all these difficulties by thinking little of the vision of God,
letting it hardly even attain to being one goal among many in
their scheme of things. Far from being mercenary about heaven,
they do not seem to want it at all. Is God to thrust Himself upon
them?

As usual it is the people in the middle for whom all the
difficulties remain alive. They are not able to throw themselves
wholeheartedly into the quest for the 'one thing needful',
disinterested even if they are obsessive. Yet they cannot be so
defeatist as to abandon it. Heaven cannot be allowed to go by
default. Somehow we must be able to qualify to 'enjoy God' in
the end. So, without aspiring to spiritual heights, what one does
is somehow tack on to everyday life the idea of the vision of God
as an ultimate goal, somewhat awkwardly unrelated to most of
one's present endeavours. So the obsessiveness of religion is
simply left out: but suddenly its integrity has to be called into
question again.

Unless we have the good fortune to be wholehearted already,
seeking the 'one thing needful', we ought to ask about the
honesty of trying to include the vision of God as our final but not
our immediate end. Unless it is all we want, do we truly want it
at all? Are we really just acting on the assumption that when
earthly happiness fails us, heaven will be better than nothing? If,
in search of salvation, people fix their eyes on a heaven they do
not fully want, they will become time-serving and essentially
shallow human beings.

This is not a sermon-like complaint about worldliness. It is a
worry that *un*worldliness, unless complete, is ethical neither in
its own terms nor in terms of the world: in other words, that
attempted unworldliness is no substitute for real heavenliness.

Sanctity is not mercenary; but in a complicated way the aspiration of the ordinary Christian is; and it gets worse as it goes on, as he tries more and more to tailor his wants to his hopes. We can see this best for other people: they would not be morally better if they devalued their present admirably assorted goals for the sake of another world because they thought they should. It could be ethically inadequate to pray for them the Collect for the Tenth Sunday after Trinity: 'that they may obtain their petitions, make them to ask such things as shall please thee'.

The worldly run their race, said St Paul, 'to obtain a corruptible crown, but *we* an incorruptible' (I Cor. 9.25). The question is whether the ordinary Christian with one eye on heaven and the other eye on earth is after all *less* ethical than his neighbour who has both eyes on the corruptible but real world around him. It seems more creditable to throw ourselves thoroughly into our human concerns, putting off as long as possible the day when the white radiance of eternity will come crashing through our dome of many-coloured glass;[11] and at least not cheating our contemporaries who believe that this world is where we really belong and should be looking for proper rewards.

It is right for Christians to be conscious of these problems but not to be oppressed by them. A personalist faith will hope to find answers to them, not by removing the vision of God from real human existence, but by persistently putting the emphasis back upon continuity again. If 'to glorify God and enjoy Him for ever' seems inhuman, something has gone wrong; and what has gone wrong could be really quite simple.

The trouble has been that the *worship* of God leading to heavenly *rewards* has seemed both obvious and unsatisfactory as a way of explaining what glorifying and enjoying means. The obviousness and the unsatisfactoriness can both be accounted for if we say that we need these explanations but we need them the *other way round*. If we take worship with *enjoying* and reward with *glorifying* we can relate the 'end of man' more coherently to earthly realities.

At first sight the proposed 'solution' looks irritatingly paradoxical. It is just our human difficulty, that worshipping is apt *not* to go with enjoying. Worship has to be our final fulfilment but

seems depressingly unrelated to normal human enjoyments. To
offer it as the ultimate hope seems literally impertinent. This is
where the humanist obstinacy abut continuity comes into its
own.[12] We have all along been refusing to separate out worship as
a special kind of activity belonging only to God, which people
must try to do on earth as a dress rehearsal for heaven where every
other activity will have ceased. We have been naive enough to say
that to worship is, at heart, to enjoy somebody's company.[13] To
worship God, after all, is no more and no less than to 'come before
his presence with thanksgiving', to be glad that He is there and
that we are allowed to approach Him. There are likely to be at
least as many different ways of approaching God as there are of
approaching our fellow creatures, but we are not trying to do
something either superhuman or subhuman. It is entirely true
that if we have not acquired a taste for worship on earth we shall
be lost in heaven; but what this means is that now is the time to
grow as human beings in relationship. The proper meaning of
'worship' is not something either legalistic on the one hand or
spooky on the other, but appreciation, reverence and delight.
To 'enjoy God' by worshipping Him is no more paradoxical
than the happy acknowledgment of other human beings is
paradoxical.

There is no need to be ashamed of the fact that words like
'enjoy' and 'delight' are value words for us without being
apparently religious or even moral in content. On the contrary,
these words are particularly well suited to illuminate the idea of
the fulfilment of persons. Part of our difficulty in believing in a
heaven that could fulfil us as human creatures is a tendency to
separate off 'aesthetic' from 'moral' value, to the impoverishment of both. Personal relationships are supposed to be moral or
indeed immoral. Pleasures of all kinds are supposed to be merely
aesthetic. But what a word like delight can do if we will let it is
bring everything we mind about into relation with our Creator's
purposes. We take delight in sounds and tastes and lovely things
of all kinds, in natural objects and works of art, in comfort and
fun and wit and company; and in virtuous qualities like
kindness or courage only in so far as they please ourselves. But
because delight is a strong word, stronger than pleasure and
more important, it begins to bring this world of aesthetic value
into relation with moral value. To put it rather pompously, the

beautiful and the good can meet here. When the delights people enjoy are important, which they often are, the full response they claim is akin to contemplation, even *is* contemplation; so we are talking about a kind of moral claim.

That sounds fairly obvious: of course contemplation is supposed to be edifying. Less grandly, we may say that delight is not altogether different from love and is therefore much nearer the heart of morality than we might have supposed. Even if we jib at saying that we were made for enjoyment, we shall hardly jib at saying that we were made for love.

The point is that this enjoyment is not selfish. So we can safely bring 'reward' back into the picture, not as a doubtfully ethical prize for doing our duty, but as the ultimate worthwhileness of creation. The difficult idea of 'glorifying God' (difficult, that is, once one has become self-conscious about it) can begin to come to life. God is glorified, not by endless adulation but by the life of creatures made for fulfilment. He can be glorified by contentment or sacrifice, by skill or effort, by an adventure or a joke,[14] by play or high seriousness. Just as to magnify is not merely to call great but to show as great, so to glorify is not just to call glorious but to show as glorious; and this is the final reward, God's and ours. Then praise, the traditional glorification, comes in as delight expressed.

The vision of God does not have to be a private obsessive ecstasy removing the saint from human life. It could be a glimpse, which we hope one day will be more than a glimpse, of God the Creator in action making and working upon a world of people in action. We are not required to attend to an abstract static focus where nothing really is, but to a wanting, loving Energy looking for a reward of His labours in giving us the reward of ours. Creatures are made to 'be a credit' to their Maker, to delight Him by delighting one another. Along these lines, we can interpret the Pauline idea of the fulfilment of the whole creation[15] as a vast multiplicity of creatures glorifying God by their ability to delight and receive delight in interrelationship. When we realize acutely that human beings are not delighting one another but making each other suffer, neglecting and misunderstanding and even hating each other, hurting and killing each other by accident and on purpose, we may realize with shuddering how far we are from fulfilment. Creation is anything but painless.[16] Human beings are apt to exact the full price of their Maker and their fellow creatures. A great deal of the time we are miles from home; but lost as we are, we have not completely forgotten what 'home' is like. It may be platitudinous but it is not unrealistic to reiterate that if indeed we are made for loving, then the satisfactions of loving are intrinsic satisfactions belonging to human nature not extraneous trophies to be earned. The 'rewardingness' of creation, however hardly-won, is ultimately natural.

So we have made a large circle and returned to answer a plain yes to the question 'Does it pay to be good?' We have come back to Bishop Butler's assurance that 'goodness', properly understood, is good *for* us, because it is deeply in accord with our nature.[17] But the circle is really a spiral and the question is not quite the same. It certainly is not a matter of choosing between a selfish, man-centred ethic of happiness and an unselfish, God-centred ethic of obedience. What we are aspiring to do is bring benefit and duty into focus and maybe to dare to say that we can transcend both, so that benefit appears as delight and duty as devotion. Our old friend 'the greatest happiness of the greatest number' is to be enriched by being characterized in terms of fulfilment. 'They who participate', said Augustine, 'in the beauty of God's house, in whom God's glory dwells, they form the abiding place of God's glory. In whom does God's glory abide, I ask, if not in those who so glory as to make the Lord their glory, not themselves?'[18]

We have to go beyond utilitarianism, not because utilitarianism in the last resort is wrong but because it is apt to be pedestrian. As Father Thomas Gilby put it, editing Aquinas, St Thomas himself has 'a certain utilatarian temper', but 'there is a difference of tone'.[19] This is not a matter of St Thomas's ethical theory being 'more improving' than utilarianism, but that he 'allows for more of a fling, an extravagance, a rapture. There is God, and he is to be loved just because he is God, and sometimes with a recklessness a somewhat pursy moralist may find it hard to approve.'[20]

This enthusiasm comes from further back in our tradition even than Augustine and Aquinas. It runs right through the gospels, as both required of us and offered to us. In the New Testament duty and pleasure do not seem to go out of focus. The

Lord does not ask his followers to give up delight for service but to find delight in service. Even the rich young man does not choose happiness instead of choosing virtue.[21] He has both, in one fashion, and is offered and rejects happiness and virtue in a more demanding mode.

This transcendent morality is the properly natural morality without which human nature becomes a poor reduced thing. To turn one's back on it may be superficially to affirm one's rights, but is really to miss the point of being human. We *need* to go beyond what we barely *ought* even to flourish in a human way, still more to attain an ultimate fulfilment.[22]

Translated into the sober style of an eighteenth-century divine, quietened indeed but not reversed, this message is there to be found reaffirmed in Bishop Butler's Sermons.[23] He approaches the subject of the love of God reluctantly and shyly for fear of being 'thought enthusiastical';[24] but this only underlines his concern to make apparent at last 'a possibility of somewhat, which may fill up all our capacities of happiness'.[25] His exposition of a natural law morality of what is *good* for us leads him with awe to the promise 'that God himself will be an object to our faculties, that he himself will be our happiness';[26] and, like St Augustine, he goes to the Psalms[27] to expatiate upon this theme and refresh his and his hearers' Christian understanding. We may be less afraid of enthusiasm and just as willing to talk about the vision of God and human happiness in one breath.

Hoping

Does it matter that we cannot imagine heaven? Can we say, so much the better for our faith? We may well take to heart warnings against trying to construct for ourselves our own heaven. For instance, Burnaby, in a somewhat austere passage,[1] suggested that attempts to speculate about the quality of eternal life are really 'prescribing to God the kind of heaven he must provide for us if we are to welcome the prospect of it', and so 'betraying our unfitness for the only possible heaven, which is a life of which God and not ourselves will be the centre'.

Christian humanists[2] may well see self-interest as a dragon lying in wait for them all along the way. But the quest for disinterestedness can itself be selfish; and meanwhile defeatism is as threatening a dragon as self-interest.[3] If having come so far we yield very readily to agnosticism about our ultimate destination, we do our contemporaries an ill service. Today's uncertainty about heaven seems often both to reflect and to aggravate a profound agnosticism about God Himself. Far from turning towards the vision of God when we refuse to picture a heaven for ourselves, we seem to get lost in a fog of negatives, apprized only of what heaven is *not*. From childhood we have learnt that it is 'not a place but a state'. There will be no teddy bears there, no pets, no books to read, no sex. This well-meant negative way is too likely to lead to the sad cry,

> Your chilly stars I can forgo,
> This warm kind world is all I know.[4]

The answer cannot be to specify harps or houris; nor to

pretend to be more 'spiritual' than we really are. No earthly happiness within people's imaginations now is fit to be projected straight into heaven; but if we make fulfilment entirely other-worldly, we have cut our hopes away from human reality and made our earthly strivings pointless in God's eyes. What we need to say, surely, is that the vision of God at last will not dazzle but illuminate. A personalist in this discussion will keep suggesting that in its light we may hope to see a whole complex world of creatures in relation to one another. The safest dream of heaven is a dream of fulfilled relationships, a sort of solar system with God as the sun. If, for the present, relationship with God seems the least real not the most, even that need not show us to be on the wrong lines: for *inasmuch* as we attend to one another we are assured that we are not after all turning our backs upon the vision of God.

A personalist can engage in the 'active' versus 'contemplative' argument without becoming hopelessly embroiled in it, heeding the warnings that to put our whole hearts into mystical experience *or* into housing is to take up a one-sided gospel. Of course there is a real problem here. On the one hand, we cannot suppose our ultimate fulfilment to be less than the most sublime experience of which the most sensitive soul is capable; which makes the mystic, or more unlikely still the aesthete, the sole model of a good human being. On the other hand, if we devalue the contemplative life, we pull off the head of one flowering of humanity like an overblown rose. If instead we can develop a kind of personalism in which the end of man is appreciative relationship, there is at least elbow room for fulfilment to be both active and contemplative, without the snobbery of rejecting activism or the shallowness of neglecting contemplation. Appreciation deepening into reverence can express itself quietly or strenuously. It can be exercised through the whole range of creatures for the building of a structure of relationships planted upon earth but reaching up towards heaven.

It is not wrong to nourish this dream of heaven with pictures. 'If we try,' said Austin Farrer, 'we shall fail: and yet we will try, and if what we say is no better, at least it will be different.'[5] So, like a new St Augustine, he attempted to evoke some images of eternal life in his hearer's minds. The blessed ones will explore

God's mind, 'as we may explore the beautiful variety of a mountainous country. We cannot explore all of it, but we can go where we like.'[6] We 'shall share his love for a thousand other happy creatures.'[7] We 'shall not be able, even, to delight in God himself, without calling in our friends to share our delight, while we also delight in their delighting'.[8]

There need be nothing selfish or shallow about such imaginings: they depict something we are meant to long for. They feed our Christian happiness, if we are so disposed. And yet that 'if' does not tuck itself quietly away in the argument. It brings us abruptly to a halt, demanding attention. We may be disposed to Christian happiness, but suppose we are not? What is a Christian who has come as far as this to say to a fellow human being who is doubtful about our whole notion of a fulfilment in store for us? Austin Farrer cannot be to everyone's taste, any more than Augustine can. Not even Dante or Fra Angelico are to everyone's taste, heavenly though their heavens are; and all of them would in the last resort have given the answer, 'If it doesn't suit you, you can go to hell.'

Our dreams of eternal life may not be selfish dreams in the sight of God, nor unworthy to voice before our Creator; but yet our contemporaries who do not believe in a creator may on their own behalf see us as shallow and selfish after all, because we propound as compulsory a fulfilment which they see as inept. Christians can easily make their God sound like a mythical mother at the seaside: 'I brought you here to enjoy yourselves, and enjoy yourselves you shall.' Such a promise of heaven is not so much a 'grand option' in the style of Teilhard de Chardin[9] as a piece of benevolent blackmail.

A personalist faith can make a good start towards resolving this trouble by asking, in the spirit of much modern philosophy, whether we have sufficiently thought out what it would mean to be dissatisfied with the Christian heaven. To refuse to delight in one another, and at last in God if He exists, is not to choose an alternative satisfaction but to turn one's back on reality: in fact, to starve oneself of humanity.[10] Christians are bound to accept the conclusion that love is what matters. They do not have to take this as a sort of ready-made arrangement which might have been otherwise. They may understand it to mean that love is what philosophers call a 'conceptual requirement' for real personality. If love eventually involves delight they may affirm it the more gladly. They will deny that they are making a mere unsupported allegation. It is more like an axiom: the sort of foundation statement which cannot be proved, only propounded to see if it will indeed do what it claims.

But there remains a residue of dissatisfaction, summed up in the words, 'It's all very well for you'. Christians may have outgrown 'pie in the sky when you die'[11] for its naive science, without noticing that what is wrong with it after all is its ethics. How dare believers allow themselves to be happy now and content with the way the world ultimately is, just because they are able to postulate a God to take care of them and their friends at last? The real world does not look much like 'a system of personal relationships crowned by the love of God'.[12] Is Christian happiness no more than euphoria, a conscious or unconscious attempt to escape from harsh reality? The 'pie in the sky' attitude appears to assume that nothing really matters because it will all come right; that troubles are to be brushed aside not endured or conquered.

People who preach a felicity which outsoars the agonies of humanity can appear worse than shallow. They can look heartless and insensitive because they seem to have nothing to say to the real distresses of other people. Misery is somehow to be made light of and even suicide has to be patronized. The Christian tradition has not been at its most sustaining here. Someone who wanted to end his life had to be very sinful; or, if not, perhaps he was just out of his mind? Despair of that order has been a concept Christians have been unable to cope with except superficially; as Job's comforters could not cope with the misery and the integrity of Job.

There is a kind of pious thankfulness which gives an impression of 'a steadfast peace that might not be betrayed', a confidence and contentment that has not looked carefully enough either at its own foundations or at the situation of other people. The quotation is from Wordsworth, and one has to ask from the same poem whether all that this kind of happiness does is

> . . . add the gleam
> The light *that never was*, on sea or land,
> The consecration, and the Poet's dream.[13]

When preachers find themselves unappreciated, especially in their own country, it is not always because they are prophets upsetting easy cheerfulness. Sometimes they preach a cheerfulness they cannot validate, with an inadequacy which their own friends and neighbours are in a good position to notice. This weakness unhappily besets a good deal of the everyday moral teaching that is urged upon the church and the world, especially in the name of Christian family life and Christian marriage.

The problem is not merely tactical, a matter of how we can communicate the Christian hope. It is intellectual and moral. Does the Christian hope undercut itself? How can people who have this hope not be weakened by it? Have we any right to say things like, 'Thou shalt show me the path of life; in thy presence is the fulness of joy: and at thy right hand there is pleasure for evermore' (Ps. 16.12)?

It would be easy to be sidetracked into the question of survival, which of course requires and deserves discussion of its own but is not the point here. The immediate problem is the elusive idea of what we are to survive *for* and what we may responsibly say to one another about our hopes of fulfilment, about flourishing, satisfaction and blessedness. Have Christians any right to assure miserable people that their sufferings are somehow taken care of in God's whole scheme of things; to tell happy people that their valid joy is associated with God's love; and to say to both, that eternal delight is offered to them?

Another huge problem looms but is not the immediate point. This is not the place to try to 'justify the ways of God to man'. It is not a theodicy, an explanation of evil, we are asking for here and now, but as it were the converse: an account of Christian happiness. We need an understanding which will not be merely insulting to those whose experience of life differs bitterly from the psalmist's: 'I have been young, and now am old: and yet saw I never the righteous forsaken, nor his seed begging their bread' (Ps. 37.25).

We need not suppose ourselves to be the first to find these words worrying. St Augustine found this psalm no comfort but a real scandal. He went so far as to complain, 'The Scriptures play us false.'[14] The answer he gave was a resort to straightforward otherworldliness. The bread that God's people need not fear their children will lack is not material bread. 'You must conjure up no crude visions',[15] he told his flock, of earthly prosperity. 'There will be another land, then, where we shall dwell for evermore.'[16] 'You are seeking for good days,' he said to them: 'let us seek them together, but not here.'[17]

Indeed, there need be nothing wishy-washy nor escapist about such otherworldliness and Augustine is a particularly satisfying exponent of it;[18] but his inspiring excursions towards the glory awaiting us, taken too soon, could actually constitute the problem not the answer when people are too ready to be convinced. In so far as they have faith, Christians know that they are, in some sense, authorized to be happy. They can adopt the certainty of Julian of Norwich: 'All shall be well and all manner of thing shall be well.'[19] Christians believe this intellectually and may feel it emotionally, but such assurance when it is a premise rather than a conclusion can be a dangerous gift. People who know that there is happiness to be had may not draw it deep enough. They may seem, and indeed they may really be, both shallow and complacent.

Iris Murdoch has gone so far as to say that 'almost anything that consoles us is a fake'.[20] This indeed is the real problem of the Book of Job. We do need to ask whether one kind of religion consists of taking, even snatching, a comfort to which one has no right and trying to pass it off on other people. It may be that Christian happiness is essentially incommunicable, because as soon as anyone reaches serenity at a particular level he or she is thereby incapacitated from talking acceptably to those who have not reached it.

To call this an intellectual difficulty does not make it 'academic'. It can be picked out with a real human example already touched upon: William Wordworth's inconsolable grief at the death of his beloved brother John at sea. The poem with the lines about the 'steadfast peace that might not be betrayed' is called 'Elegiac Stanzas suggested by a Picture of Peele Castle, in a Storm, painted by Sir George Beaumont'. Wordsworth sets in juxtaposition the image of the castle in perfect weather as he had seen it in happier days and the passionate stress under which it appears now in his friend's painting. It had looked as if the sea 'could not cease to smile', and the castle had 'seemed a treasure-house divine / Of peaceful years; a chronicle of heaven.' 'Ah! THEN' the bereaved poet cries out 'if mine had been the Painter's hand, / To express what then I saw', *then* he could have depicted 'the light that never was'. Instead he faces reality:

> So would it once have been, – 'tis so no more;
> I have submitted to a new control:
> A power is gone, which nothing can restore;
> A deep distress hath humanized my Soul.
>
> Not for a moment could I now behold
> A smiling sea, and be what I have been:
> The feeling of my loss will ne'er be old;
> This, which I know, I speak with mind serene.

So he comes to commend 'this sea in anger and that dismal shore'.

These are not conventional poetic sentiments: by no means. The family's letters show the profound and lasting impact of shock and misery.[21] Yet the point of the poem is neither gloom nor comfort, but what distress had done for him. 'Humanised' is a keyword, the more telling because Wordsworth with his warm sympathies and romantic affections, whose youthful imagination had kindled at the French Revolution, could hardly be justly called 'inhuman' to begin with. Yet he had become sharply aware that it was suffering rather than hope which had given him a bond with other people and made him more real as a human being. So he tried to bid farewell to 'the heart that lives alone',

> Housed in a dream, at distance from the kind!
> Such happiness, wherever it be known,
> Is to be pitied; for 'tis surely blind.

Instead he welcomed

> . . . fortitude, and patient cheer,
> And frequent sights of what is to be borne,

and at last was able to conclude,

> Not without hope we suffer and we mourn.

What needs to be said is that the poem as a whole seems to succeed better than its ending, though the ending is what a Christian eventually has to affirm. So it must be asked whether any attempt to fill out the conclusion in a more definitely Christian way, to put in 'with hope' instead of 'not without hope', would only invalidate it? Can I never speak about happiness to other people unless I first cease to 'be what I have been'? Is most contentment to be accounted 'blind', or anyway immature? In particular, is any happiness which is supposed to be rooted in another world dubious and maybe frivolous in the light of the profound and real sufferings people have to undergo here and now? Is taking up a cross the whole story, to the extent of forgetting about resurrection?

The thought that Christian joy is really only euphoria, once it has occurred, is hard to banish. It is easy enough to settle down, even religiously, in a kind of creeping gloom and let happiness get lost. It seems better not to expect too much and at least not be heartless about the troubles of the world. This condition has a name. It is the ancient and modern sin of *accedia*, inadequately translated as 'sloth'. It is easier to name it than to uproot it. It is not to be cured by taking people and shaking them, however much we may be tempted to try. The condition is accurately characterized in Browning's 'Childe Roland to the Dark Tower Came'.[22] The knight's quest had gone on so long and so many had been defeated by it that excitement had entirely yielded to endurance.

> For, what with my whole world-wide wandering,
> What with my search drawn out thro' years, my hope
> Dwindled into a ghost not fit to cope
> With that obstreperous joy success would bring, –
> I hardly tried now to rebuke the spring
> My heart made, finding failure in its scope.

Christians may well look through the description of a knight-at-arms in a romantic predicament and see themselves and their contemporaries in a recognizable state of mind. They need to ask whether this sort of desolation is where the *Christian* quest leads.

> . . . All the day
> Had been a dreary one at best, and dim
> Was settling to its close, yet shot one grim
> Red leer to see the plain catch its estray.

It cannot be a quick or easy enterprise to reclaim the Christian expectation of a real light after our real shadows and be legitimately assured that 'heaviness may endure for a night, but joy cometh in the morning' (Ps. 30.5). At least to have stated some of the difficulties, indeed laboured them, may have helped, by setting up warning notices against certain kinds of insensitivity.

Glibness, Gloom and Glory

If human beings matter, their happiness matters. Humanism affirms so much; Christianity adds a confidence of ultimate vindication. The difficulty is to seize upon this hope in such a way as not to destroy it. But there is no need to be altogether on the defensive about our tradition. If there is a building standing up already, it may not need an elaborate scaffold of argument to support it. Very old houses are not always the first to fall down, nor the most uncomfortable to live in. To shut oneself out is no way to welcome other people in. We might do better to walk about and see what is there so that we may tell them that come after.[1]

Unless we are too much afraid of our faith being written off as childish we ought to be able to find resources to draw upon for dealing with happiness and unhappiness which are ancient without being stale and fresh without being flimsy. Christians for many generations have found such resources in the Bible, both Old and New Testaments. It would be a harsh irony, like another expulsion from Eden, if the energetic and patient work of Christian scholars in our century had made such nourishment *less* available to Christian people who are not experts than it used to be. So maybe it is still in order to be naively Protestant enough to look for oneself, in all humility, to see whether there is a kind of biblical understanding of happiness offered to us which is something more than euphoria, that is capable of standing up in the face of the troubles of the world. The result would be a sketch, a sort of artist's impression of our hope, not a fully-formed creation. If no such picture took shape at all, it would be time to enquire sternly whether whatever Christian encouragement one was trying to offer was only a flower in a glass of water, cut off from its roots.

A non-expert, looking right back first to the Old Testament, is not obliged to explain what these documents meant to the ancient Hebrews who wrote them and read them and listened to them. To chase identity of understanding would be to chase a will-o'-the-wisp. Yet evidently there has been continuity. Enough meaning, diluted and boiled up again of course, comes filtering through the medium of English worship and teaching for us to presume to think and feel ourselves to belong to the God of Abraham, Isaac and Jacob, as we do not belong to Zeus, father of gods and men.

Among many themes and emphases there is one picture of what the covenant means that certainly looks childish to our eyes. Happiness is for God's people if they are loyal to Him. He will reward their fidelity with prosperity and sooner or later punish their unfaithfulness with tribulation. The time-scale may be uncertain, but not the fact. Sometimes the present success of the ungodly is noticed more and God's vindication of His patient poor deferred for longer; but wrong-doers and oppressors are not going to flourish for ever. We are familiar with such confidence from the psalms. The righteous man 'shall be like a tree planted by the waterside: that will bring forth his fruit in due season. His leaf also shall not wither: and look, whatsoever he doeth, it shall prosper' (Ps. 1.3–4).[2] 'The lions do lack and suffer hunger: but they who seek the Lord shall want no manner of thing that is good' (Ps. 34.10).

Modern believers may go on worrying about the naivety of all this, but it is not to be despised. It is still important to reaffirm something specific and not necessarily unsophisticated about human flourishing:[3] that there is a rightness about it in God's sight; that well-being is not something God allows reluctantly, but something He purposes to give; that to be happy is what we are made for. Whatever happiness we find on earth is somehow a token of the happiness we are meant to have. If that belief is what our hedonistic forbears were feeling after, it misses the point to call their hopes euphoria and their faith smug and self-interested. Instead of repudiating their primitive morality, perhaps we can make it the foundation of something more sustaining.

If Christians are going to be able to say something neither shallow nor heartless about what is 'good' for mankind, they need to insist again and again upon holding together the *moral* and the *pleasing* aspects of 'good'.[4] Of course 'pleasing' must be allowed to mean a good deal more than a toffee for an obedient child who has done his sums right. We are allowing for deep delight as well as casual enjoyment. If our God is what we have been encouraged to believe He is, the 'true good' of human beings is going to be neither the platitudinously moral nor the trivially pleasant, but will be more comprehensively satisfying to us and our Maker in something like the way that a work of art is satisfying.

People who believe in a Creator should not find it too strange an idea that God looks upon the universe with the eye of an artist as well as a lawgiver. 'God saw that it was good' does not mean 'God saw that it was behaving itself'.[5] It is paradoxical but appropriate to find this notion emerging from the history of the children of Israel, portrayed as a people much more concerned with morality than with art. Since this idea of the 'satisfying' as richer than the narrowly 'ethical' can help to put to flight some of our religious anxieties, it is worth attempting to develop it a little further.

There is no need to desert our ancient scriptures in pursuit of this development. In their very insistence on giving priority to human obedience, not to human achievement, there is one art they conspicuously practice and that is the art of words. In this context, where the Almighty is not to be painted or sculpted, poetry is allowed to depict His character and moralism simply takes flight. 'They shall be satisfied with the plenteousness of thy house; and thou shalt give them drink of thy pleasures, as out of the river. For with thee is the well of life: and in thy light shall we see light' (Ps. 36.8–9). At moments we may feel that we are even being bewitched by words, our powers of reason succumbing to the creative power of prophet or psalmist, magically conveyed to us through the inspiration of English translators. Perhaps we feel a kind of duty to hold back and resist the enchantment, to remember that 'I know that my redeemer liveth' (Job 19.25) never was a guarantee or even an assurance of resurrection. Nor will 'God is our hope and strength, a very present help in trouble' (Ps. 46.1) compel Him to our side today.

Yet provided that we can be believers at all, we can allow that
this sort of incantation may be, as it were, white magic; that
what we have to do with here is what Austin Farrer called a
'Rebirth of Images', a creative way of reviving and refreshing
something old but not obsolete.[6]

The artistry would be misused if it were made into a
substitute for argument. What it is doing is showing us
something. It is indicating a depth in the simplicity of the
sentiments: putting it in, we should say if we were sceptical,
exhibiting it and exploring it if we still belong to this tradition.
Is it only Wordsworth's 'gleam'?[7] Maybe he spoke too soon
when he repudiated it in his grief. If the artist is able to show us
something we might not have picked out for ourselves but are
capable of recognizing, then it is more than 'the light that never
was' and may indeed be called a 'consecration'.

The thought that people who seek the Lord have a sure
promise of prosperity one day may seem to belong to a crude
religion, much too elementary for us; but when it is wrapped in
heavenly language, it may offer us, not a proof of course, but
what I. T. Ramsey used to call a 'disclosure', a glimpse of
possible meaning.[8] The simplest and most earthly sort of
flourishing can take on a kind of depth.[9] 'Thou waterest her
furrows, thou sendest rain into the little valleys thereof: thou
makest it soft with the drops of rain, and blessest the increase of
it. Thou crownest the year with thy goodness: and thy clouds
drop fatness' (Ps. 65.11–12). When the promise is ambiguous
between heaven and earth, the ambiguity can present itself not
as a trick but as an extra dimension. 'When I awake up after thy
likeness, I shall be satisfied with it' (Ps. 17.16). 'The Lord is my
shepherd: therefore can I lack nothing' (Ps. 23.1).

If the idea of 'prosperity' can be so deepened, still more can the
notion of 'seeking the Lord' seem less remotely primitive if we
can find in poetic speech a manifestation of God's glory. To
borrow a philosophical distinction, we cannot *say* what He is
like; but maybe our language can begin to *show* it in a form we
can receive.

> He bowed the heavens also, and came down:
>   and it was dark under His feet.
> He rode upon the cherubims, and did fly:

he came flying upon the wings of the wind
(Ps, 18.9–10).

'Hear, O my people', He says, 'and I will
   speak . . .
I will take no bullock out of thine house:
   nor he-goat out of thy folds.
For all the beasts of the forest are mine:
   and the cattle upon a thousand hills.
I know all the fowls upon the mountains:
   and the wild beasts of the field are in my sight'
(Ps. 50.7,9–11).

The classic example of this kind of theophany is the climax of
the Book of Job.[10] Job is brought to his knees at last by the poetry
of creation.[11] Some have seen in his repentance an ignoble
defeat for his long-maintained integrity. More profoundly, one
could say that the reward he has won by his arduous struggles is
a revelation, a disclosure, of glory. The poetry seems to feed, not
swamp, the imagination, as if indeed there were some kind of
reality coming through. Of course it can be called imaginary:
but not sham in the sense of shoddy.

The artistry of words is not all that the Old Testament has to
offer for a continuing understanding of human fulfilment under
God. The content matters, of course, as well as the style in
which it is presented. One's attention is drawn to a particular
notion of valid human happiness. The keyword is the idea of
blessing.[12] It can be approached by way of an unsophisticated
belief in prosperity as reward, but there is more to it than that.
What makes it significant is the subtle and curious, and
sometimes paradoxical, way in which the moral and the
satisfying are linked. Blessing seems to have a lot to do with
vitality and energy. Pedersen in his magisterial book *Israel*
defines it as 'the inner strength of the soul and the happiness it
creates'.[13] Sometimes the concept of a good blessing parts
company entirely from commonsense morality, yet the effect is
enrichment not collapse. Blessing is an idea akin to grace, with
the same morally odd character of being evidently undeserved
and yet not out of all relation to desert.

There is a solidity about this way of thinking, primitive no
doubt but impressive. The almost magical importance of the *act*

of blessing could be impatiently written off as superstitious: or
is there after all something sacramental about it? It would be
false not only insensitive to say to Esau 'Never mind' when
Jacob has tricked him and he is left imploring 'Bless me, even me
also, O my father' (Gen. 27.34). Jacob is outrageous by any
standards; but the story of his adventures, culminating in his
wrestling with God (Gen. 32.24–32) has meant a great deal in
our tradition. His saga is evidently not a plain moral tale of
goodness rewarded, but nor is it a plain immoral tale of
cleverness rewarded. What wins the prize is a sort of vigorous
pursuit of vocation. One could call it humanist but more. Again
one has a glimpse, maybe a disclosure, of the glory of God
revealed to the persistent struggles of man. It ought to be
heartening not alarming to find this in the foundations of our
faith.

A more tragic yet more satisfying example of this way of
paradoxically shedding light upon the meaning of fulfilment is
the story of David. It might well be called a myth, not to cast
doubt on its historical truth but in appreciation of its evocative
power.

The story of Saul is essentially a tragedy, distressing and
pleasing both at once. Our satisfaction, which we need the ugly
word 'aesthetic' to indicate, does not invalidate our plain moral
reactions of approval or disapproval but in a way transforms
them. It is itself a more subtle kind of approval. It would be inept
to take Saul and David as a hero and a villain, either way, just as
it would be inept to take Shakespeare's Richard II and Boling-
broke as a hero and a villain. Saul is blessed and unblessed,
David is deserving and undeserving. Then, superimposed upon
the history of the king that God chooses and rejects is the
history of the happy and mournful friendship of the king's son
and the new king. In an obvious sense it is shockingly unfair
that Jonathan is passed over, but in the light of the whole story
there is a tragic rightness that David must have the blessing and
voice the lament (II Sam. 1.17–27). The chosen people are given
a chosen king, who is not chosen for his own benefit. It would be
trivial to complain of favouritism. To say that it is David who is
chosen is not out of all relation to morality. The plain story-
with-a-moral of David and Bathsheba is not going to be at odds
with the rest of the picture (II Sam. 11–12). So it is for the chosen

people themselves: election, freedom, obedience, disobedience, being blessed and being a blessing form a complex pattern not a crude one. The Christian notion of fulfilment which eventually grows out of all this has intricate not simple roots.

The teaching in the gospels develops the complexity of what God's people are meant to hope for. The idea of reward is very much still there and is by no means so spiritual as to be etherial.[14] Human values are turned upside down by the beatitudes, but human fulfilment is still characterized in very definite terms: flourishing and well-being, feasting and making merry, ruling over kingdoms. The parables seem more business-like and less poetical than the psalms.

Across this, and seemingly quite contrary to it, there cuts the overwhelming theme of *dying* to live, of the sacrifice which is self-sacrifice, of suffering that saves. This way of thinking is not alien to the Old Testament but now becomes far more conspicuous. Indeed the cross can seem to dwarf everything else in human life. With this emphasis realism is approved instead of euphoria and compassion instead of complacency; and, more surprisingly, this-worldliness instead of other-worldliness. Although to contemplate the passion of Christ is traditionally an ascetic kind of piety, it sorts well with putting heavenly promises aside and contemplating the sufferings of the world and becomes a characteristically twentieth-century kind of piety too. People for whom another life has become rather a faint dream are glad to find encouragement, especially in the Fourth Gospel, for seeing Christ's glory *in* his sufferings not apart from them. They discover a saviour who is alongside us in tribulation, not coming in the clouds but catching up with his friends as they walk along the road to Emmaus, telling them what they half knew already (Luke 24.13–35).

It is easy enough to point out that there is a further glory which such a this-worldly faith leaves out: the glory towards which the whole creation groaneth and travailleth, not indefinitely but for the sake of a new birth. The Christ who walks to Emmaus is the risen Christ. The two disciples do not just go on with their lives. They rush back to Jerusalem for confirmation of their hopes that something particular has happened. Somehow or other God has specifically prevailed. The victory is given a date: the 'third day' after the despair of the cross.[15] It is a

Christian platitude to affirm that the resurrection makes all the difference.[16] That is how our hope of ultimate fulfilment is founded. Yet if the hope is not to be euphoria after all, the portrait to be drawn still has to be complex.

There is a delicate balance to be kept here or the accusation of glibness will stand. The story of the resurrection can be told in such a way as to look like a facile happy ending superimposed upon a tragedy too alarming to be faced. It often is so told to children, who are supposed not to be able to cope with grief and are therefore left at its mercy when it comes their way. The gentle Jesus who suffers on the cross knows very well that everything is going to be all right very soon. Yet even a child can feel inarticulately that in that case 'it is all very well for him'. Death that is only falling asleep for a while is not real death.

Unless the story of Christ is somewhat different from the story of a martyrdom, it is not the redemption Christians have believed it to be. A martyr's ordeal has a distinct meaning. Sufferings are undergone with heroism to witness to a greater good, more real than this transitory trouble.[17] Some martyrs have been renowned for the peace and joy in which they met their fate. But if Christ died and triumphed simply as a martyr, his suffering and its vindication would touch only one area of human misery, much of which is nothing like martyrdom.

That is why the most profound saying in the New Testament is the one that children are apt to be spared: the cry of dereliction. To say anything about it is intolerably presumptuous, but to say nothing would be to let Christian answers to human hopelessness go by default. Here, if anywhere, the very words of the Lord seem to be given to us. This hero is not Daniel whose God came and shut the lion's mouth, nor Stephen who saw the heavens opened and the Lord ready to receive him. No answer comes: death has to be experienced in failure and defeat.[18] The message about the kingdom has not been understood.[19] There is no point and no pattern. Human beings can bear a good deal if they can make patterns. Then they say, 'No time for lamentation now nor much more cause.'[20] This time there is every cause to lament the waste of a young life and the extinction of hope. What at any given moment is seen as the worst is not bound to be averted.

But there is the hope of resurrection and presently, quite soon in fact, we have to start saying as Christians that it makes all the difference. Insist as we must that the worst may not be avoided or averted, we have to affirm and want to affirm that contrary to all expectation it is to be reversed and redeemed. The rising of Christ, for those who believe in it, is the pledge that the dereliction which is at the very heart of Christianity is not the last word.

What we have here is a foundation for a doctrine of atonement for people who are seized by the problem of evil. Other problems will call for differently balanced answers, but at least there is something here to be said. Bertrand Russell once propounded a picture of the world in which its Creator sat enjoying it like an excellent tragedy and eventually called for it to be performed again.[21] The only thing that stands between a Christian admiration for creation and this horrible parody is the belief that, however suffering began and however bad it can be, God entered into it.[22] Whatever the doctrine of the 'impassibility' of God involves, it must be compatible with this belief. A Christian imagination may be led, in some sense, beyond morality, or anyway beyond a legalistic morality, towards a sort of aesthetic understanding of the way things are, in which the presence of darker elements gives a profundity mere cheerfulness and contentment could never give.

> Evil and good stand thick around
> In the fields of charity and sin
> Where we shall lead our harvest in . . .
> Strange blessings never in Paradise
> Fall from these beclouded skies.[23]

It is imperative for a Christian to add that the God who artistically created such a world was willing to pay for it. It could not be paid for by anything less than the experience of dereliction.

The truth about the world, provided that Christianity itself is true, may give rise to contentment or to desolation. Either of these attitudes may be proper and realistic: but not euphoria or despair. Euphoria shows itself in a certain kind of tidiness, making patterns in life because we cannot bear not to have a pattern: and suffering tears it apart, like the face of the grief-stricken woman painted by Picasso. Many an insubstantial 'special providence' has been seized upon too fast by people who desperately wish for something to happen in good time to 'set all to rights'. Just so Childe Roland approaching the Dark Tower remembered his old companions in momentary hopefulness, but was quickly overtaken by the memory of their disgrace: 'Out went my heart's new fire and left it cold.'

But although euphoria is hopeless and disaster is possible, despair does not become compulsory. There is a kind of courage even more solid than the triumphant courage of the martyr. In the face of silent heavens, human beings can still say things like 'Better this present than a past like that.' Desolation may make them panic or cheat, but it may not. The last but one line of 'Childe Roland to the Dark Tower Came' is 'Dauntless the slughorn to my lips I set'. If we take the poem as a myth of the human situation, we need not find more than a little touch of irony in the word 'dauntless'.

Myths have their place, but we need facts too. The cross is *the* example, the crucial example indeed, of how desolation is to be faced. Before the vindication, in the midst of the dereliction, there is a gleam, not of hope or even of the martyr's courage, either of which could make someone want to say 'It is all very well', but of a solidity, a steadfastness which does not give way. 'My God, my God, why hast thou forsaken me?' comes from a psalm, and from a psalm which ends 'and the heavens shall declare his righteousness: unto a people that shall be born, whom the Lord hath made' (Ps. 22). This is not quoted. It does not cancel the dereliction; but it does flavour it. The God who makes no move to help is still 'Thou'. The victim still belongs to the chosen people. He is in a live tradition. We know now that he was founding one. So we have a pointer away from pointlessness. Today, reverently though presumptuously, we can build patterns around that lack of pattern.

In the face of the troubles of the world, this difficult combination of dereliction without a ready way out and glory which is eventually to prevail seems to offer the possibility of believing in God. Short cuts are obviously inviting. If we cannot bear the dereliction, we try to bring in the 'prevailing' too soon, with a facile glibness which is no real answer. If we can bear it only too well, we stress the glory in the tragedy, with a heartless glibness that is a cruel answer. Dereliction is not to be appreciated aesthetically but may have to be taken as fact: taken like medicine, that may mean, not with pleasure but as something given and unavoidable. To welcome it for oneself or anyone else is masochism or even sadism, not faith. To drink the cup when necessary, to go through the tunnel looking for the light at the end, is the proper Christian attitude.

It needs to be explained why the Christian gospel does not invalidate all subsequent derelictions. It may well be asked of Christians whether, since they are supposed to know the end of the story, they are faithless when they suffer themselves and facile when they attempt to enter into the sufferings of others. The risk remains, as a practical risk. In theory it ought to be able to be answered. To reply that a good story does not become trite when one knows the ending would be something of a debating point. It is more serious to answer that the ending can be lost from view and sometimes is lost from view. In reverence we may suppose that Christ himself could have predicted his own vindication yet come to lose sight of the light at the end of the tunnel. What we say about all subsequent derelictions is not that they are unreal, but that someone has been here before. Such a Christian as George Herbert could endure this experience:

> All day long
> My heart was in my knee
> But no hearing.[24]

Yet, like the Psalmist and the Lord Himself, he is still able to say Thou to the God who has disappeared from view.

So Christian peace can be portrayed, not as a cheap substitute for prosperity, but as something possible though mysterious, a solidity or steadfastness which somehow underlies actual turmoil and distress. One must face the possibility that it really may not be a communicable gift. Like the manna in the wilderness, perhaps it cannot be stored up. A Christian believes that this 'non-despair', this hidden foundation for resurrection, is available but not necessarily to be passed from hand to hand. It may be findable by an individual only when it is needed there and then. One may sometimes have to admit 'No man can deliver his brother: nor make agreement unto God for him. For it cost more to redeem their souls: so that he must let that alone for ever' (Ps. 49.7–8). To offer someone else a ready-made

comfort is usually only a way of cheering up oneself. It is a
platitude, though not an empty one, that unhappiness is more
easily shared than dispelled. But conversely and not too surprisingly, when peace *can* be imparted, the traffic may turn out to go
in the wrong direction. It is sometimes the person who was
supposed to have a tranquil life already who is heartened and
encouraged by the troubled one.

But happiness is real as well as trouble and we can say things
about it too. First, earthly happiness characteristically comes in
pockets. We may say it is valid but vulnerable. In the lives of
individuals, as of countries, there are golden ages when everything goes well. The stretches of happiness that people experience are reminders that well-being *is* healthy,[25] that delight is
according to God's will, that He would not have people cold and
hungry and lonely for the good of their souls rather than warm
and replete and sociable. It is worth insisting that some not rare
aspects of human life are fit to be called foretastes of heaven.
The most solid and heavenly sort of human happiness is the
happiness of appreciation and especially the appreciation of
other people. But then it has to be added that none of this gives
earthly happiness any guarantee. It is a mistake to think that
because something is thoroughly in accordance with God's will
one surely has a right to it, or anyway a right to count on its
continuance. It is not so. Everything human is vulnerable. The
worst can always happen, even to good people. But if the worst
happens, then it is somehow provided for in God's providence.
Beyond it, at the end of the tunnel, there is to be a heaven in
which something better still will be brought to birth.

Secondly, then, fulfilment is rooted in tragedy, God's if not
ours. A 'puritan' ethic is supposed to allege that only what is
nasty can be good for us. That is not the point at all. There is no
need to insist upon desolation. But happy Christians ought to
keep in mind, 'Is it nothing to you, all ye that pass by?' To
understand that happiness has been dearly bought does not make
happiness wrong or false: on the contrary, it invites appreciation.

Nobody expresses this better than Julian of Norwich. Her
vision of the passion of Christ could have been masochistic, but
instead has a serious and joyful balance:

Wherefore we are his, not only through our redemption but

also by his Father's courteous gift. We are his bliss, we are his reward, we are his honour, we are his crown. And this was a singular wonder and a most delectable contemplation, that we are his crown. What I am describing now is so great a joy to Jesus that he counts as nothing his labour and his sufferings and his cruel and shameful death.[26]

So she adds the words she heard, 'See how I loved you. Our Lord revealed this', not to harrow our feelings but 'to make us glad and joyful'.[27] There is a total contrast here with Bertrand Russell's terrible Deity: neither heartless aestheticism enjoying the tragedy of His creatures, nor an almost equally heartless moralism requiring everything to be just and requited, but goodness and a sort of 'satisfyingness' deepening each other.

Thirdly, there remains something else that a Christian must try to say about happiness, with care not to read into the world what theory suggests ought to be there. If Christianity is the truth, one would expect there to be a kind of felicity which has a characteristic that is hard to pin down and easy to caricature, which might be called 'beyondness'. If this is just 'pie in the sky' after all, it will be no more than an unworthy projection of earthly satisfactions. Rather, it needs to be a happiness dependent upon death and resurrection. To die is to surrender oneself, whether willingly or otherwise. What is promised is that on the other side of such a surrender, not instead of it, there is to be a rising again. Christians can expect to find blessing, satisfaction, fulfilment on the other side of whatever there may be to face and undergo, including death itself. Of course, when we start 'expecting', we are taking a short cut. We had better behave like Alice in Looking Glass Land, when to reach the garden of live flowers she had to walk the other way.[28] Yet of course we cannot really help expecting, unless we are to pretend not to have a gospel.

Without Christian faith these arguments are bound to look like complicated wishful thinking, excuses for the absence of fulfilment. Heads I win: I can greet final attainment with an 'I told you so'. Tails you lose: if the satisfaction fails to arrive, it was wrong to demand it. This is a caricature too. It is fairer to say that we are talking about a happiness that is to be achieved but cannot be ordered or organized.

To speak of beyondness is to try to identify a specific characteristic. It could be quite misleading if it meant just saying 'hurrah' for something 'out of this world', or 'boo' to something vague and etherial. What we are talking about is happiness of the kind that comes unsought and arrives when one is looking for something else or even when one has given up hope. Like God Himself, it cannot be trapped into a confrontation. There is a convincingness about the paradox that what one most wants steals up on one from behind and can look almost like a by-product.

The point is not just that one ruins what one grabs, though that can be true as well. It is rather that when vindication and joy appear in such a fashion, as seemingly they did on 'the third day', they commend themselves as authentic and solid. Maybe for any particular individual this kind of dawning of fulfilment will not happen until after actual death. It is worth waiting for, for those who are able to stand in the Christian tradition and assert that Christ is risen. There is room for heaven in this scheme of things. There is no essential falsity or inadequacy in believing that delight is offered to us and that we do well to hope for it. It still needs to be shown rather than argued, recognized eventually rather than proved. Edwin Muir evoked it, suggesting a completion that Childe Roland does not hint at:

> Will you, sometime, who have sought so long and seek
> Still in the slowly darkening hunting ground,
> Catch sight some ordinary month or week
> Of that strange quarry you scarcely thought you sought –
> Yourself, the gatherer gathered, the finder found,
> The buyer, who would buy all, in bounty bought –
> And perch in pride on the princely hand, at home,
> And there, the long hunt over, rest and roam?[29]

NOTES

Chapter 1 Does Happiness Matter?

1. Gabriel Marcel, 'Some Remarks on the Irreligion of Today', lecture delivered in 1930, published in *Being and Having*, Dacre Press 1949, p. 200.
2. St Augustine, *On the Psalms*, Second Discourse on Ps. 26, A Select Library of the Nicene and Post-Nicene Fathers of the Christian Church, Vol. VIII.
3. St Augustine, *Homilies on the First Epistle General of St. John*, IV. A Select Library of the Nicene and Post-Nicene Fathers of the Christian Church, Vol. VII.
4. Cf. Andrew Elphinstone, *Freedom, Suffering and Love*, ed. G. R. Dunstan, SCM Press 1976; W. H. Vanstone, *Love's Endeavour, Love's Expense*, Darton, Longman & Todd 1977.
5. St Augustine, *On the Psalms*, Second Discourse on Ps. 32.
6. The Shorter Catechism. See below, chapter 18.
7. Ps. 8; Heb. 2.6–8.
8. H. J. Blackham, *Religion in a Modern Society*, Constable 1966, p. 113.

Chapter 2 Does it Pay to be Good?

1. William Wordsworth, 'I Grieved for Buonaparté'.
2. Cf. D. Z. Phillips and H. O. Mounce, 'On Morality's Having a Point', *Philosophy* XL, 1965, p. 308.
3. John Stuart Mill, *Utilitarianism*, Everyman Dent 1910, p. 20.
4. J. J. C. Smart and Bernard Williams, *Utilitarianism For and Against*, Cambridge University Press 1973, pp. 98–9.
5. Butler, *Dissertation of the Nature of Virtue*, paragraph 13, *Works* Vol. I, ed. Gladstone, Clarendon Press 1896, p. 408. Also Sermon XV, 'Upon the Ignorance of Man', ibid., Vol. II, p. 259.
6. *Dissertation of the Nature of Virtue*, paragraph 13.
7. Preface to *Sermons*, paragraph 7, *Works*, Vol. II, p. 6.
8. E.g. Sermon I, 'Upon the Social Nature of Man', paragraph 6, pp. 38–41.
9. Preface to *Sermons*, paragraph 29, p. 21.
10. Ibid., paragraph 35, p. 26.

11. Sermon III, 'Upon the Natural Supremacy of Conscience', paragraph 6, p. 71.
12. J. J. C. Smart and Bernard Williams, *Utilitarianism For and Against*, pp. 116–17.
13. Butler, Sermon VII, 'Upon the Character of Balaam', paragraph 16, pp. 134–5.
14. Sermon II, 'Upon the Natural Supremacy of Conscience', paragraph 19, p. 64.

Chapter 3 According to Human Nature

1. Cf. Advisory Council for the Church's Ministry (ACCM), *Teaching Christian Ethics*, SCM Press 1974, pp. 46–55 (including bibliography); Keith Ward, *Ethics and Christianity*, Allen and Unwin 1970, p. 84; James M. Gustafson, *Protestant and Roman Catholic Ethics*, SCM Press 1979, pp. 37–8.
2. G. F. Woods, 'Natural Law and Christian Ethics', *Theology* LXVIII, June 1965, reprinted in *Duty and Discernment*, ed. G. R. Dunstan, SCM Press 1975, p. 36.
3. Cf. ACCM, *Teaching Christian Ethics*, p. 51.
4. Cf. Helen Oppenheimer, *The Character of Christian Morality*, 1965, second ed. Mowbray 1974, p. 96.
5. Cf. C. S. Lewis, 'Illustrations of the Tao', *The Abolition of Man*, Bles 1947, p. 56; A. Macbeath, *Experiments in Living*, Macmillan 1952; H. L. A. Hart, *The Concept of Law*, Clarendon Press 1961, p. 176; G. F. Woods, 'Natural Law and Christian Ethics', *Duty and Discernment*, pp. 41–2; Dorothy Emmet, *Rules, Roles and Relations*, Macmillan 1966, chapter V.
6. C. S. Lewis, *Out of the Silent Planet*, Bodley Head 1938, pp. 64–5.
7. E.g. D. Z. Phillips and H. O. Mounce 'On Morality's Having a Point', *Philosophy* XL, 1965, pp. 309f.; Jonathan Harrison, 'When is a Principle a Moral Principle?', *Proceedings of the Aristotelian Society*, Supplementary Volume XXVIII, 1954, p. 113.
8. E.g. Philippa Foot, 'When is a Principle a Moral Principle?', ibid., p. 104; 'Moral Beliefs', *Proceedings of the Aristotelian Society* 1958–9.
9. Cf. I. M. Crombie, 'Moral Principles', *Christian Ethics and Contemporary Philosophy*, ed. I. T. Ramsey, SCM Press 1966, p. 256; Helen Oppenheimer, 'Ought and Is', *Duty and Discernment*.
10. E.g. the Papal Encyclical Letter of Paul VI, *Humanae Vitae*, 1968.
11. See above, p. 14.
12. Butler, Sermon II, 'Upon the Natural Supremacy of Conscience', paragraph 10, p. 59.
13. Butler, Sermon III, 'Upon the Natural Supremacy of Conscience', paragraph 3, p. 69.
14. Oman, *Grace and Personality*, 1917, Fontana Edition 1960, p. 54.

Chapter 4 Who Chooses?

1. Cf. Helen Oppenheimer, 'Moral Choice and Divine Authority', *Christian Ethics and Contemporary Philosophy*, SCM Press 1966, p. 222; and 'Moral Choice', *Change and Choice: Women and Middle Age*, ed. Beatrice Musgrave and Zoë Menell, Peter Owen 1980, p. 120.
2. Ronald W. Hepburn, *Christianity and Paradox*, Watts 1958, p. 153.
3. See above, p. 18.
4. David Hume, *A Treatise of Human Nature*, 1739, III, i, i.
5. John Stuart Mill, *Utilitarianism*, chapter IV, p. 32.
6. G. E. Moore, *Principia Ethica*, Cambridge University Press 1929.
7. E.g. The 'new naturalists' of the late 1950s, especially Philippa Foot and G. E. M. Anscombe; and more recently Renford Bambrough, *Moral Scepticism and Moral Knowledge*, Routledge & Kegan Paul 1979.
8. E.g. A. J. Ayer, *Language Truth and Logic*, Gollancz 1936, chapter VI; C. L. Stevenson *Ethics and Language*, Yale 1945.

Chapter 5 Autonomy and Authority

1. R. M. Hare, *Freedom and Reason*, Clarendon Press 1963, p.2.
2. But cf. Helen Oppenheimer, *Incarnation and Immanence*, Hodder 1973.
3. R. M. Hare, 'Contrasting Methods of Environmental Planning', *Nature and Conduct*, Royal Institute of Philosophy Lectures, Vol. 8, ed. R. S. Peters, Macmillan 1975.
4. S. I. Benn, 'Freedom, Autonomy and the Concept of a Person', *Proceedings of the Aristotelian Society*, 1975–6, p. 127.
5. Ibid.
6. Jonathan Bennett, 'The Conscience of Huckleberry Finn', *Philosophy* XLIX, 1974, p. 132.
7. R. M. Hare, *Essays on Philosophical Method*, Macmillan 1971, chapter 6.
8. Ibid., p. 113.
9. R. M. Hare, *Moral Thinking: Its Levels, Methods and Point*, Clarendon Press 1981.
10. Ibid., p. 227.
11. Ibid., pp. 186–7.
12. Ibid., p. 228.
13. John Wilson, 'Moral Training in a Pluralist Society', *The Franciscan*, June 1972, p. 129; cf. John Wilson, Norman Williams and Barry Sugarman, *An Introduction to Moral Education*, Pelican 1967, e.g. pp. 27f.; B. Cohen, 'Principles and Situations: the Liberal Dilemma and Moral Education', *Proceedings of the Aristotelian Society*, 1975–6, p. 80.
14. R. S. Lee, *Your Growing Child and Religion*, Pelican 1965, p. 148; Wilson, Williams, and Sugarman, op. cit., p. 52.

15. Wilson, Williams and Sugarman, op. cit., p. 27; but cf. W. K. Frankena, 'Obligation and Motivation in Recent Moral Philosophy', *Essays in Moral Philosophy*, ed. A. I. Melden, University of Washington Press 1958, p. 64; Basil Mitchell, *The Justification of Religious Belief*, Macmillan 1973, p. 130.
16. Derek Wright, *The Psychology of Moral Behaviour*, Pelican 1971, p. 222.
17. Ibid., p. 243.
18. Ibid., p. 247.
19. S. W. N. Watkins, 'Negative Utilitarianism', *Proceedings of the Aristotelian Society*, Supplementary Volume XXXVII, 1963, p. 99.
20. Renford Bambrough, *Moral Scepticism and Moral Knowledge*, Routledge & Kegan Paul 1979, p. 77.
21. H. L. A. Hart, 'Freedom versus Reason', *Philosophical Quarterly* 24, 1974, p. 248.
22. Cf. Hare, *Freedom and Reason*, p. 192.
23. For some examples, see *Duty and Discernment*, note 18, p. 131.
24. Bernard Williams, *Morality*, Cambridge 1972, p. 50.
25. Ibid., p. 93.
26. B. Cohen, 'Principles and Situations: the Liberal Dilemma and Moral Education', *Proceedings of the Aristotelian Society*, 1975–6, p. 85.
27. S. I. Benn, 'Freedom, Autonomy and the Concept of a Person', *Proceedings of the Aristotelian Society*, 1976, pp. 129–30.
28. Paul Halmos, *The Faith of the Counsellors*, Constable 1965.
29. D. M. Emmet, *Rules, Roles and Relations*.
30. R. F. Stalley, 'The Role of the Doctor: Technician or Statesman?', *Journal of Medical Ethics*, March 1980, p. 21.

Chapter 6 Choosing and Finding

1. Cf. Helen Oppenheimer, 'Moral Choice', *Change and Choice: Women and Middle Age*, pp. 117–18.
2. E.g. P. F. Strawson, 'Social Morality and Individual Ideal', *Philosophy XXXVI*, 1961, pp. 1–4, 16–17. (Also in *Freedom and Resentment and Other Essays*, Methuen 1974, pp. 26–44.)
3. See above, pp. 41–2.
4. E.g. R. M. Hare, *Freedom and Reason*, p. 2.
5. R. M. Hare, *The Language of Morals*, Clarendon Press 1952, p. 69.
6. Cf. George C. Kerner, *The Revolution in Ethical Theory*, Clarendon Press 1966, e.g. pp. 177, 194; N. H. G. Robinson, *The Groundwork of Christian Ethics*, Collins 1971, pp. 64–5.
7. P. F. Strawson, 'Social Morality and Individual Ideal', p. 4 (And *Freedom and Resentment*, p. 29.)
8. See above, p. 43.

9. Cf. R. F. Holland, 'Moral Scepticism', *Proceedings of the Aristotelian Society*, Supplementary Vol. 1967, p. 191.
10. Cf. D. M. Mackinnon, *The Problem of Metaphysics*, Cambridge University Press 1974.
11. Cf. Ronald W. Hepburn, *Christianity and Paradox*, Watts 1958, p. 135.
12. Cf. R. M. Hare, *Applications of Moral Philosophy*, Macmillan 1972, p. 53.
13. Edwin Muir, 'One Foot in Eden'.
14. A. M. Farrer, *Said or Sung*, Faith Press 1960, p. 176; cf. John Hick, *Death and Eternal Life*, Collins 1976, p. 252; Helen Oppenheimer, *The Character of Christian Ethics*, Athlone Press 1978, p. 17.

Chapter 7 Valuing

1. See above, p. 48. R. M. Hare, *The Language of Morals*, p. 69.
2. R. M. Hare, *Freedom and Reason*, p. 2. See above, p. 36.
3. Renford Bambrough, *Moral Scepticism and Moral Knowledge*, p. 42; cf. R. G. Swinburne, 'The Objectivity of Morality', *Philosophy* LI, 1976. See above, p. 42.
4. A. M. Farrer, *Said or Sung*, p. 176.
5. Cf. K. Baier, *The Moral Point of View*, Cornell 1958, chapter 2.
6. Cf. K. Baier, 'Decisions and Descriptions', *Mind* LX, 1950, e.g. p. 191.
7. H. L. A. Hart, 'On the Ascription of Responsibility and Rights', *Essays on Logic and Language*, ed. Antony Flew, Blackwell 1951, pp. 146–7.
8. See above, p. 44.
9. Cf. Keith Ward, *Ethics and Christianity*, Allen and Unwin 1970, p. 132.
10. Ibid., p. 156.
11. Cf. Iris Murdoch, *The Sovereignty of Good*, Routledge & Kegan Paul 1970, p. 91.
12. Ibid., p. 34.
13. Ibid., p. 84.
14. Ibid., p. 85.
15. Cf. C. S. Lewis, *Perelandra*, Bodley Head 1943, pp. 208, 209.

Chapter 8 Claims

1. See above, pp. 54–5.
2. I. T. Ramsey, 'Moral Judgments and God's Commands', *Christian Ethics and Contemporary Philosophy*, ed. I. T. Ramsey, SCM Press 1966, p. 164.
3. R. M. Hare, *Applications of Moral Philosophy*, p. 39.
4. Ibid., pp. 37–8.
5. Cf. Austin Farrer, 'Signs of God in the Conscience of Man', *God and the Universe*, Pusey House Sermons, Mowbray 1960, p. 33:

'What pulls My Conscience is My Fellow-being'; David Jenkins,
The Glory of Man, SCM Press 1967, e.g. pp. 2–3f., 9; Helen
Oppenheimer, *Incarnation and Immanence*, pp. 141–2f.; 'Life
after Death', *Theology*, September 1979, p. 332.
6. Cf. Macbeath, *Experiments in Living*, Macmillan 1952.
7. Cf. Mary Midgley, *Beast and Man: the Roots of Human Nature*,
Harvester 1979.
8. Cf. Helen Oppenheimer, *The Character of Christian Morality*,
p. 91.
9. Cf. Helen Oppenheimer, *The Character of Christian Ethics*, p. 16;
Matthew Arnold, 'Dover Beach'.

Chapter 9 People

1. Luke 15.8.
2. Cf. Elizabeth Newson, 'Unreasonable Care: The Establishment of
Selfhood', *Human Values*, Royal Institute of Philosophy Lectures,
Vol. 11, ed. Godfrey Vesey, Harvester Press 1978.
3. Cf. John Locke, *Enquiry concerning the Human Understanding* II,
XXVII, 25; David Jenkins, *What is Man?* SCM Press 1970, p. 13;
Helen Oppenheimer, 'Life after Death', p. 332.

Chapter 10 Being and Doing

1. See above, p. 77.
2. From a madrigal by Wilbye, quoted by R. M. Hare, 'Descriptivism',
Annual Philosophical Lecture, Henriette Hertz Trust, British
Academy 1963, p. 126.
3. Cf. MacTaggart, *The Nature of Existence*, Cambridge University
Press 1927, Vol. ii, p. 152, quoted and discussed by Basil Mitchell,
Morality, Religious and Secular, Clarendon Press 1980, p. 125.
4. See above p. 82.
5. Cf. Graham Markall, 'The Best Years of their Lives', The William
Temple Foundation, Occasional papers No. 3, 1980, pp. 21–2.
6. Erich Fromm, *To Have or to Be?*, Cape 1978.
7. Ibid., p. 115.
8. St Augustine, *Homilies on the First Epistle General of St. John*,
1.11.
9. Gen. 18.

Chapter 11 Mattering

1. Anthony Bloom, *God and Man*, Darton, Longman & Todd 1971,
pp. 88–9; *Courage to Pray*, Darton, Longman & Todd 1973, p. 9.
2. Cf. David Jenkins, *The Glory of Man*, e.g. pp. 7, 51–2, 81; Helen
Oppenheimer, 'Life after Death'.
3. Mark 12.27.
4. Cf. K. E. Kirk, *The Vision of God*, Bampton Lectures 1928, Long-

mans 1931, pp. 140–6 (or abridged ed., Clarke 1976, pp. 69–76).

5. Cf. Helen Oppenheimer, *Incarnation and Immanence*, pp. 141–3, 160–3.
6. See above, pp. 78ff.
7. II Sam. 12.1–15.
8. Immanuel Kant, *Fundamental Principles of the Metaphysic of Ethics*, Longman 1965, p. 56.
9. Ibid., p. 63.
10. Ibid., p. 51.
11. E.g. *Philosophy* LIII, October 1978, has a set of articles on this subject.
12. Bentham, *Introduction to Principles of Morals and Legislation*, quoted by Mary Midgley, *Beast and Man*, Harvester Press 1979, pp. 221–2.
13. Mary Midgley, *Beast and Man*, p. 46.
14. Ibid., p. 218.
15. Kant 'Duties towards Animals and Spirits', *Lectures in Ethics*, quoted in Mary Midgley, *Beast and Man*, p. 241.
16. Ibid., p. 354; cf. E. Maclaren, 'Dignity', *Journal of Medical Ethics*, March 1977.
17. See above, p. 66.
18. Mary Midgley, *Beast and Man*, e.g. pp. 359, 215, etc.; cf. C. Diamond, 'Eating Meat and Eating People', *Philosophy* LIII, 1978, e.g. pp. 474–5.
19. Kant, *Fundamental Principles of the Metaphysic of Ethics*, p. 63.
20. Browning, 'Fra Lippo Lippi'.
21. Cf. Mary Midgley, *Beast and Man*, pp. 216–17.
22. Cf. E. Maclaren, 'Dignity', p. 41.
23. Cf. Eugene Linden, *Apes, Men, and Language*, Penguin 1976, pp. 53–4.
24. George Herbert, 'Denial'.

Chapter 12 One-way Love

1. See above chapter 6 and e.g. p. 71.
2. See above, p. 82; cf. Helen Oppenheimer, *Incarnation and Immanence*, pp. 141ff.
3. Augustine, *Confessions* I, 1.
4. Augustine, *City of God*, XXII, 30.
5. Aquinas, *Summa Theologiae*, Vol. 16, 1a 2ae 48, Eyre and Spottiswoode 1968.
6. Nygren, *Agape and Eros*, Harper Torchbooks 1953.
7. Burnaby, *Amor Dei*, Hodder 1938.
8. Nygren, *Agape and Eros*, p. 175.
9. Ibid., p. 235.
10. Ibid., pp. 177f.
11. Ibid., p. 221 (and Index).
12. Ibid., p. 176.

13. Ibid.
14. Cf. ACCM, *Teaching Christian Ethics*, p. 44.
15. I owe this point to Professor Oliver O'Donovan.
16. Augustine, *Homilies on the First Epistle General of St. John*, VII, 10.
17. Ibid.
18. Nygren, *Agape and Eros*, p. 459.
19. Ibid., pp. 460, 476–7.
20. Ibid., p. 179.
21. Ibid., chapter VI.
22. Ibid., p. 681.
23. Ibid., p. 682.
24. Ibid., p. 682, and cf. p. 45.
25. Cf. Burnaby, 'Amor in St. Augustine', *The Philosophy and Theology of Anders Nygren*, ed. Charles W. Kegley, Southern Illinois University Press 1970, p. 180 (and *Amor Dei*, p. 19); E. L. Mascall, *Grace and Glory*, Faith Press 1961, p. 53.
26. Thomas Traherne, *Centuries*, No. 28.
27. Cf. Burnaby, *Amor Dei*, pp. 18–19, 307.
28. Ibid., pp. 6–7.
29. Ibid., p. 13.
30. Traherne, *Centuries*, No. 41.
31. Cf. G. R. Dunstan, *The Marriage Covenant* (Cambridge University Sermon), Church Army Press 1961, p. 9.
32. George Herbert, 'Love'.

Chapter 13 Minding

1. John Burnaby, *Amor Dei*, p. 307.
2. See above, p. 107.
3. See above, p. 109.
4. Julian of Norwich, *Showings*, ed. Edmund Colledge, OSA and James Walsh, SJ, Classics of Western Spirituality, Paulist Press 1978, chapter 79 (p. 334 in this edition).
5. St Augustine, *On the Psalms*, Discourse on Ps. 37.14.
6. St Bernard, *On the Love of God*, chapter I, in Beach and Niebuhr, *Christian Ethics: Sources of the Living Tradition*, Ronald Press 1955, p. 183.
7. Julian of Norwich, *Showings*, chapter 85 (p. 341 in Classics of Western Spirituality edition).
8. Cf. Helen Oppenheimer, 'Temperance', *Traditional Virtues Reassessed*, ed. A. R. Vidler, SPCK 1964, pp. 33–4.
9. Cf. Elizabeth Telfer, *Happiness*, Macmillan 1980, p. 120.
10. *Macbeth*, Act V, Scene 3.
11. Cf. John Burnaby, *Amor Dei*, p. 127; C. H. Dodd, 'The Communion of Saints' and 'Eternal Life', *New Testament Studies*, Manchester University Press 1953.

12. Cf. Helen Oppenheimer, 'Moral Choice', *Change and Choice: Women and Middle Age*, p. 123.
13. Cf. Anthony Bloom, *Meditations on a Theme*, Mowbrays 1971, p. 67; W. G. Maclagan, *The Theological Frontier of Ethics*, Allen and Unwin 1961, p. 27 note.
14. See above, p. 110.
15. Traherne, *Centuries*, Fourth Century No. 56.
16. Cf. Helen Oppenheimer, 'Moral Choice', *Change and Choice*, p. 122.
17. See above, p. 103.
18. Traherne, *Centuries*, First Century No. 3.
19. Traherne, *Centuries*, First Century No. 89.

Chapter 14 Liking

1. Shakespeare, Sonnet No. 94.
2. See above, pp. 66, 121.
3. See above, pp. 107, 109.
4. Lewis Carroll, *Alice in Wonderland*, chapter VI.
5. Lewis Carroll, *Through the Looking Glass*, chapter IX.

Chapter 15 Attending

1. Emil Brunner, *The Divine Imperative*, Lutterworth 1937, p. 518.
2. Cf. Helen Oppenheimer, 'Head and Members', *The Sacred Ministry*, ed. G. R. Dunstan, SPCK 1970.
3. John Burnaby, *Amor Dei*, pp. 307–8.
4. E.g. Luke 14.26.
5. Matt. 23.8–9.
6. Mark 12.25.
7. C. S. Lewis, *The Four Loves*, Fontana 1963.
8. Cf. Helen Oppenheimer, *Incarnation and Immanence*, chapter 12.
9. Laurence A. Blum, *Friendship, Altruism and Morality*, Routledge & Kegan Paul 1980, p. 82.
10. Brunner, quoted above p. 133.
11. Ibid.
12. Karl Barth, *Ethics* I, 1928, T. & T. Clark 1981, p. 189.
13. John 15.12–15.
14. E.g. Nygren, *Agape and Eros*, pp. 153ff.; cf. Burnaby, *Amor Dei*, p. 18.
15. Matt. 11.19.
16. Luke 10.36–37.
17. John Calvin, *Institutes of the Christian Religion*, Bk. III, chapter vii, paras. 4–6, quoted in Beach and Niebuhr, *Christian Ethics*, p. 286.
18. Traherne, *Centuries*, Second Century No. 68.
19. Terence, *Heauton Timorumenos*, 1.1.25.

Chapter 16 Worshipping

1. St Athanasius, *On the Incarnation of the Word*, SCM 1964, p. 107. Translated by Archibald Robertson who adds in a footnote that the literal translation is 'He was humanized that we might be deified'.
2. Richard Robinson, *An Atheist's Values*, Oxford University Press 1964, p. 138.
3. Keith Ward, *The Christian Way*, SPCK 1976, p. 29.
4. Ibid., p. 30.
5. H. A. Williams, *The True Wilderness*, Constable 1965, p. 155.
6. Austin Farrer, *Reflective Faith*, SPCK 1972, p. 38.
7. See above, p. 66.
8. Mat. 8.2; 9.18; 15.25; 20.20.
9. Austin Farrer, *Said or Sung*, p. 182.
10. M. C. Darcy, *The Mind and Heart of Love*, Faber 1945, p. 251.
11. Pierre Teilhard de Chardin, *Hymn of the Universe*, Collins 1965, p. 190.
12. Dedication to *Barrack Room Ballads*. Reprinted by permission of The National Trust and Macmillan, London Ltd.
13. St Augustine, *The City of God*, Book X, chapter 4, p. 377.
14. Cf. Helen Oppenheimer, *Incarnation and Immanence*, pp. 192ff.
15. Ninian Smart, *Reason and Faiths*, Routledge & Kegan Paul 1958, p. 27 and p. 76 n. 1.
16. Ibid., p. 44.
17. Cf. Helen Oppenheimer, *The Character of Christian Morality*, chapter IV.
18. See above, chapter 9.
19. Cf. Acts 14.14–15.
20. Cf. Helen Oppenheimer, *The Character of Christian Morality*, p. 91.

Chapter 17 Images and Idols

1. Col. 3.5; cf. Eph. 5.5.
2. Bishop Heber, 'From Greenland's icy mountains'. (According to the *Oxford Dictionary of Quotations*, he originally wrote 'The savage in his blindness'.)
3. Isa. 44.13–17.
4. Peter Geach, *God and the Soul*, Routledge & Kegan Paul 1969.
5. Ibid., p. 100.
6. Ibid., p. 112.
7. Luther, *Works* VI, 402, quoted in Philip S. Watson, *Let God be God!*, Epworth 1947, p. 91.
8. Ninian Smart, *The Concept of Worship*, Macmillan 1972, p. 10.
9. Peter Geach, *God and the Soul*, p. 103.
10. Matt. 25.40.
11. C. C. J. Webb, *God and Personality*, Allen and Unwin 1918, p. 263.
12. H. D. Lewis, *Our Experience of God*, Allen and Unwin 1959, p. 69.

Also in 'Worship and Idolatry' *Contemporary British Philosophy*, ed. H. D. Lewis, Allen and Unwin, p. 270.

13. Ibid., *Our Experience of God*, p. 89; and 'Worship and Idolatry', p. 278.
14. H. D. Lewis, 'The Cognitive Factor in Religious Experience', *Proceedings of the Aristotelian Society*, Supplementary Vol. XXIX, 1955, p. 65.
15. H. D. Lewis, *Our Experience of God*, p. 70: and 'Worship and Idolatry', p. 272.
16. Ninian Smart, *The Concept of Worship*, p. 20.
17. See above, pp. 147–8.
18. St Augustine, *On the Psalms*, 1st Discourse on Ps. 34.
19. St Augustine, *City of God*, Book II, chapter 4.
20. Peter Geach, *God and the Soul*, p. 103.
21. Ninian Smart, *The Concept of Worship*, p. 36.
22. Ian Crombie, 'The Possibility of Theological Statements', *Faith and Logic*, ed. Basil Mitchell, Allen and Unwin 1957, p. 65.
23. Ninian Smart, *The Religious Experience of Mankind*, Collins (Fontana) 1969, p. 463; cf. W. K. Guthrie, *The Greeks and Their Gods*, Methuen 1950, p. 34; D. M. G. Stalker, Exodus, *Peake's Commentary*, Nelson 1962, paras. 192f.

Chapter 18 The End of Man

1. See above, pp. 6, 30.
2. See above, p. 3.
3. J. N. Findlay, 'Can God's Existence be Disproved?' *New Essays in Philosophical Theology*, ed. Antony Flew and Alasdair MacIntyre, SCM Press 1955; and *Values and Intentions*, Allen and Unwin 1961, chapter IX, 'Epilogue on Religion'.
4. Findlay, *Values and Intentions*, p. 403.
5. Ibid., pp. 411–12.
6. 'Can God's Existence be Disproved?', p. 74.
7. Ibid., p. 56.
8. *Values and Intentions*, p. 405.
9. See above, p. 144.
10. St Augustine, *Confessions*, X.27.
11. Shelley, 'Adonais'.
12. See above, pp. 140, 142–3, 147.
13. See above, pp. 141–2.
14. See above, p. 118.
15. E.g. Rom. 8.19–23.
16. Cf. W. H. Vanstone, *Love's Endeavour, Love's Expense*, Darton, Longman & Todd 1977.
17. See above, chapters II and III.
18. St Augustine, *On the Psalms*, 2nd Discourse on Ps. 25.
19. St Thomas Aquinas, *Summa Theologiae*, Vol. 16.

20. Ibid.
21. Mark 10.17–22.
22. Cf. Helen Oppenheimer, *The Character of Christian Morality*, chapter VIII.
23. Butler, Sermons XIII and XIV, 'Upon the Love of God'.
24. Sermon XIII, paragraph 14 (*Works*, p. 240).
25. Sermon XIV, paragraph 12 (*Works*, p. 250).
26. Ibid., paragraph 19 (*Works*, p. 256).
27. Ibid., paragraph 20 (*Works*, p. 257).

Chapter 19 Hoping

1. John Burnaby, *The Belief of Christendom*, SPCK 1959, p. 194.
2. See above, p. 8.
3. See above, p. 6.
4. William Cory, 'You Promise Heavens Free From Strife'.
5. Austin Farrer, *A Celebration of Faith*, Hodder 1970, p. 115.
6. Ibid.
7. Ibid.
8. Ibid., p. 116.
9. E.g. Pierre Teilhard de Chardin, *The Future of Man*, Collins (Fontana) 1969, chapter III.
10. Cf. Helen Oppenheimer, *Law and Love*, Faith Press 1962, p. 82; 'Ought and Is', *Duty and Discernment*, pp. 17f., 22.
11. See above, p. 3.
12. Helen Oppenheimer, *The Character of Christian Morality*, p. 91.
13. See below, pp. 172–3.
14. St Augustine, *On the Psalms*, Third Discourse on Ps. 36.
15. Ibid., p. 312.
16. Ibid., p. 317.
17. Ibid., Second Discourse on Ps. 33.
18. See above, pp. 3–4.
19. Julian of Norwich, *Showings*, chapter 27.
20. Iris Murdoch, *The Sovereignty of Good*, p. 59.
21. *Early Letters of William and Dorothy Wordsworth*, (1787–1805) ed. Ernest de Selincourt, Clarendon Press 1935; letter dated 11 February 1805, pp. 446 *et seqq*.
22. Cf. Helen Oppenheimer, *The Character of Christian Morality*, pp. 94–5.

Chapter 20 Glibness, Gloom and Glory

1. Ps. 48.11–12.
2. See above, p. 20.
3. See above, pp. 19–20; Helen Oppenheimer, *The Character of Christian Morality*, p. 94.

4. See above, p. 163.
5. See above, pp. 107, 109.
6. Cf. Austin Farrer, *The Glass of Vision*, Dacre Press 1948.
7. See above, p. 170.
8. E.g. I. T. Ramsey, *Religious Language*, SCM 1957, chapter I; 'A Personal God', *Prospect for Theology*, ed. F. G. Healey, Nisbet 1966.
9. See above, p. 20.
10. Job 38–41.
11. Job 42.5–6.
12. See D. M. Emmet, *Function, Purpose and Powers*, Macmillan 1958, chapter VIII.
13. Johs Pedersen, *Israel*, Oxford University Press 1926, p. 182.
14. See above, p. 20 and note 4, and pp. 165–6.
15. E.g. I Cor. 15.4.
16. See above, p. 4.
17. Cf. Oscar Cullmann, *Immortality of the Soul or Resurrection of the Dead?*, Epworth 1958, chapter I.
18. Cf. H. A. Williams, *The True Wilderness*, Constable 1965, pp. 160–1.
19. Cf. John Austin Baker, *The Foolishness of God*, Darton, Longman & Todd 1970, chapter 10.
20. Milton, 'Samson Agonistes'.
21. Bertrand Russell, 'A Free Man's Worship', *Mysticism and Logic and Other Essays*, Allen and Unwin 1917, pp. 46–7.
22. See above, p. 5.
23. Edwin Muir, 'One Foot in Eden', reprinted by permission of Faber and Faber Ltd from *The Collected Poems of Edwin Muir*, p. 227.
24. George Herbert, 'Denial'.
25. See above, p. 20.
26. Julian of Norwich, *Showings*, chapter XXII, pp. 216–17.
27. Ibid., chapter XXIV, p. 221.
28. *Through the Looking Glass*, chapter II.
29. Edwin Muir, 'The Question', reprinted by permission of Faber and Faber Ltd from *The Collected Poems of Edwin Muir*, p. 122.

INDEX

Abortion, 13, 28, 37, 42, 45, 47, 61, 73, 78, 79, 95
Abraham, 91, 92, 177
Accedia, 174
Adam, 28, 30, 59
Addison, Joseph, 71
Adultery, woman taken in, 60
Aesthetics, 64, 163–4, 168, 181, 184, 188 *see* Taste
Affliction *see* Troubles
Agape, 74, 104–14, 116, 119, 137
Allah, 148
Alice, 126, 127, 128
Analogy *see* Personalism
Ancient Mariner, 67–8
Angelico, Fra, 169
Anglicans, 2, 15, 20
Animals, 65, 71, 79, 96–100, 102, 148, 167
Anscombe, G. E. M., 192n
Aquinas, 103, 128, 165
Aristotelians, 142
Athanasius, 140, 199n
Atheism, 98, 141, 158 *see* Sceptics
Augustine, 3–4, 5, 90, 103, 104, 105–6, 110, 113, 143–4, 152, 153, 159–60, 165, 166, 168, 169, 171–2
Austen, Jane, 90 *see* Mrs Bennett
Autonomy, 25, 28–32, 34, chs 5 and 6, 57, 58, 61, 63, 70
Ayer, A. J., 192n

Bach, 64, 142
Badness *see* Wickedness
Baier, K., 194n
Baker, J. A., 202n
Bambrough, R., 42, 57, 192n
Barth, Z., 136

Bathsheba, 181
Beatitudes, 103, 159, 182
Beethoven, 64, 71, 83
Benevolence, 15, 16, 23, 75–6 *see* Utilitarianism, Personalism, Agape
Benn, S. I., 43, 192n
Bennett, J., 38
Bennett, Mrs, 102
Bentham, 196n
Bernard, St, 113
Blackham, H. J., 190n
Blessing, 2, 30, 67, 90, 108, 120, 180, 181, 182, 188
Bloom, A., 92, 198n
Bloomsbury Group, 73
Blougram, Bishop, 158
Blum, L. A., 198n
Browning, E. B., 120
Browning, R., 62, 158, 174–5, 185, 189, 196n
Brunner, E., 133, 135
Burnaby, J., 104, 108, 112, 133, 167, 197n, 198n
Butler, Bishop, 15–16, 18, 22–4, 26, 165, 166

Caesar, 60, 80
Calvin, 138
Camus, 70
Canticle of the Sun, 7
Canute, 60
Carroll, Lewis *see* Alice
Catechism, Shorter *see* End of man
Charity *see* Agape
Christ, 5, 6, 103, 104, 108, 111, 128, 132, 137, 139, 142, 153, 154, 166, 182, 183, 184, 185, 186, 188
Cohen, B., 43

Coleridge *see* Ancient Mariner
Colossians, Epistle to, 148
Commandments, Two, 54, 93, 108
Conscience, 13, 15, 16, 22, 23–4, 26, 35, 38
Consequences *see* Utilitarianism
Contemplation, 45, 67, 121, 122, 141–2, 164, 168, 188
Contraception, 49, 80
Correctives, 4, 44, 114, 118–19, 121, 127
Cory, W., 201n
Creation, 5, 6, 7, 17, 27, 75, 76, 80, 84, 109, 126, 180
Creativity, 24, 27f., 29, 35, 55, 62, 64
Creator, 19, 31, 54f., 59, 60, 79, 107, 112, 113, 117, 120, 121, 133, 164, 178, 184
Crombie, I. M., 154
Cross, 5, 6, 103, 104, 121, 174, 182–3, 185, 187
Cullmann, O., 202n

Daniel, 183
Dante, 128, 169
Darcy, M. C., 143
Darwin, C., 98–9
David, 94, 181
Death, 4, 52–3, 92, 135, 170f., 182, 183, 188
Delight, 2, 3, 108, 112, 121, 123, 140, 163, 169, 170, 171, 178, 189 *see* Enjoyment
Dereliction, 100, 183–7
'Describing', 32, 38, 59, 67
Descriptivism, 39, 40 *see* Naturalism
Deutero-Isaiah, 149
Diamond, C., 196n
Dignity, 95, 97, 196n
Divergence, diversity, 30, 39–42, 46, 65, 72–3, 74, 161, 162 *see* Relativism
Dodd, C. H., 197n
Dunstan, G. R., 197n
Duty, 14, 25, 31, 32, 36, 42, 47, 50, 55, 58, 69, 71, 72, 124, 141, 164, 165, 178 *see* Integrity

Education, 37, 40, 41, 44, 50, 52, 62, 192n, 195n
Election, 100, 118
Elphinstone, A., 190n
Emmaus, 182
Emmet, D., 44, 191n, 202n
Emotivists, 33
End of man, 6, 30, 93, 103, ch. 18
Enemies, 21, 126–30, 133
Enjoyment, 2, 7, 62, 65, 70, 101, 120, 122, 126, 141, ch. 18 *see* Delight
Equality, 81, 82, 86, 94–5
Eros, 104–9, 111, 112–13, 116, 134, 137
Esau, 181
Eucharist, 91
Euphoria, 170f., 174, 176, 177, 182, 183, 184, 185
Euthanasia, 47, 73, 96
Evaluating, 32, 33, 34, 38, 52–3, ch. 7, 70, 101
Eve, 28, 30, 54
Evil *see* Wickedness
Existentialism, 35–6

Facts (and values), 21, 31–5, 37, 40, 51–5, 57, 59–62, 65, 67, 69, 76, 185
Faith, 1, 9, 12, 24, 31, 52, 78, 93, 98, 102, 103, 108, 127, 133, 138, 139, 152, 167, 172, 182, 186, 188
Fanatics, 39, 42, 49, 50
Farrer, A., 2, 54, 58–9, 142, 143, 168–9, 179
Fascist, 130
Fatherhood of God, 22, 93, 94, 108, 112, 118, 134, 136, 138, 156, 188
Findlay, J. N., 157–9, 164
Foot, P., 191n, 192n
Forgiveness, 6, 127–9
Forster, E. M., 129
Francis, St, 7, 91, 118, 128
Frankena, W. K., 193n
Freedom, 28, 29, 30, 36, 40, 41, 54, 56–7
Friendship, 78, 89, 115, 125, ch. 15, 140, 145 *see* Philia
Fromm, E., 90
Fruit of spirit, 86–7, 88f.

Geach, P., 149–50, 154
Gift of God *see* Reward
Gilby, T., 165
Glorify and enjoy *see* End of man
Gods, 142 *see* Idolatry
Golden Rule, 12, 16
Goliath, 32
Goodness as indefinable, 18, 31
Goneril and Regan, 117
Grace, 1, 25, 26, 36, 151, 181
Greed, 6, 54, 90, 108, 117, 121, 122, 137
Grief *see* Troubles
Gustafson, J. M., 191n
Guthrie, W. K., 200n

Halmos, P., 44
Handel, 78
Hare, R. M., 34, 36, 37, 38–40, 42, 48, 56–7, 66, 69, 70, 193n, 194n, 195n
Harrison, J., 191n
Hart, H. L. A., 42, 61, 191n
Hatred, 54–5, 164
Heaven, 3–4, 6, 34, 100, 103, 116, 123, 125, 134, 139, 161, 162, 163, ch. 19, 182, 187, 189, 197n
Heber, Bishop, 199n
Hepburn, R. W., 31, 194n
Herbert, George, 100, 110, 186
Hick, J., 194n
Himmler, 83
Holland, R. F., 194n
Hooligans, 38–40
Hospitality, 91, 132
Huckleberry Finn, 38, 41
Human nature *see* Natural Law
Humanae Vitae, 191n
Humanism, 5, 8, 19, 30, 36, 37, 48, 80, 81, 94, 161, 176, 181
Hume, D., 31, 32

Idealism, 150
Idolatry, 143, 145, ch. 17, 157, 158, 160
Ikons, 151
Image of God, 27, 47, 54, 80, 84, 110, 112, 138, 139, 140, 156, 157

Inasmuch saying, 150, 168
Incarnation, 7, 8, 102, 140, 154
Inertness, 27, 29, 33, 71, 87, 118
Integrity, 14, 16, 23, 73, 75, 161, 170
Intuitionism, 49, 66f.
Isaiah, 58

Jacob, 92, 181
Jenkins, D., 195n
Job, 107, 170, 172, 178, 180
Jonathan, 78, 181
Judas, 28
Judging *see* Evaluating
Julian of Norwich, 112, 113, 172, 187–8

Kant, I., 29, 72, 74, 95–7, 124
Keats, 54, 101
Kerner, G. C., 193n
Kingdom of heaven, 6, 29, 103, 123, 183
Kipling, 143
Kirk, K., 195n
Knox, R., 1

Lee, R. S., 192n
Leibnitz, 96–7
Lewis, C. S., 20, 134–5, 191n, 194n
Lewis, H. D., 150–1, 200n
Liberation theology, 138
Lifestyles *see* Divergence, Ways of life
Linden, E., 196n
Locke, J., 195n
Lost coin, 81
Love, 75, 76, 81, 83f., 85f., 93, 102, 115, 117f., 122, ch. 14, 169–70
see Agape, Benevolence, Enemies, Eros, Friendship, Neighbours, Partiality, Philia, Self, Unconditional
Luther, 106, 149

Macbeath, A., 191n, 195n
Macbeth, 28, 115, 117
MacKinnon, D. M., 194n
Maclagan, W. G., 198n

Maclaren, E., 196n
MacTaggart, 195n
Malice *see* Hatred, Wickedness
Manichees, 110
Marcel, G., 1
Markall, G., 195n
Marriage, 111, 134, 142, 160, 171, 197n
Mascall, E. L., 197n
Martyrdom, 143, 149, 183, 185
Mercenary, 1, 3, 5, 6, 13, 18, 35, 121, 159, 160, 161 *see* Reward
Mercy, 119
Merit, 83, 86f.
Michelangelo, 79, 94
Midgley, M., 96–7, 195n, 196n
Mill, J. S., 12, 32
Milton, 1, 52, 54, 128, 183, 202n
Misery *see* Trouble
Mitchell, B., 193n, 195n
Moral problems, 13, 14, 22–4, 27, 28, 29, 42, 45, 46, 60, 73
Moore, G. E., 32
Mounce, H. O., 190n, 191n, 195n
Mozart, 58, 128
Muir, E., 53, 184, 189, 194n, 202n
Murdoch, I., 66–7, 97, 142, 172, 194n

Nash, O., 118
Nathan, 94
Natural law, 11, 15, 17, ch. 3, 26, 27, 35, 166
'Naturalism' and 'non-naturalism', 32, 34, 38–9, 76
Naturalistic fallacy, 31–2
Nazis, 28, 128
Neighbours, 10, 132, 133, 136, 138
Newson, E., 195n
Nietzsche, 42
Noah, 81
Nygren, A., 104–9, 137, 198n

Obedience, 27, 28, 31, 32, 52, 108, 165, 178, 182
O'Donovan, O., 197n
Oman, 25
Oppenheimer, H., 191n, 192n, 193n, 195n, 196n, 198n, 199n, 200n, 201n

Otherworldliness, 3, 4, 74, 103, 163f., 171, 172, 174, 182
Others, Good to, 103, 118 *see* Benevolence
Ought and Is *see* Fact, Evaluation, Naturalistic fallacy
Owen, Wilfrid, 53

Pantheism, 36
Parenthood, 22, 62, 86, 89, 99, 134 *see* Fatherhood of God
Partiality, 118, 120, 124, 125, 131, 134, 135, 137, 138
Paul, St, 103, 162, 164
Paul VI, 191n
Pearl of great price, 103
Pedersen, J., 180
Personalism, 72–6, 79, 94, 140, 143, 144, 148, 150, 152, 153, 158, 162, 168, 169
Philia, 111, 112
Phillips, D. Z., 190n, 191n
Philosophy and philosophers, 2, 15, 28, 29, 31, 32, 33, 34, ch. 5, 48, 54, 59, 65, 70, 76, 169, 179, 196n
Picasso, 184
Pie in the sky, 3, 170, 188
Platonic tradition, 105, 106
Praise *see* Worship
Prejudice, 12, 29, 40, 59, 64, 67, 94, 125
Prescriptivism, 33, 38–40, 41, 42, 56, 66, 69, 101
Principles, 12, 14, 23, 24, 28, 36, 38, 41, 43, 48, 56
Protestants, 42, 86, 106, 145, 158, 176, 191n
Psalms, 7, 20, 115, 117, 148, 166, 171, 175, 177, 178, 179, 180, 185, 201n

Racism, 37, 39, 43, 49, 94, 130
Ramsey, I. T., 4, 69, 145, 179, 191n, 202n
Rape, 13, 49
Relativism, 20, 21, 49, 50, 62, 66, 72, 114 *see* Divergence

Resurrection, 4, 92, 102, 134, 135, 174, 178, 182, 183, 184, 186, 188, 189 *see* Heaven

Reward, prize, gift of God, 3, 4, 5, 6, ch. 2, 76, 87, 90, 93, 103, 107, 108, 113, 114, 116, 120, 132, 157, 159, 162, 164, 165, 177, 179, 180, 181, 182 *see* Mercenary

Rich young man, 28, 166

Richard II, 181

Richard III, 128

Robinson, N. H. G., 193n

Robinson, R., 141

Roland, Childe, 174–5, 185, 189

Roles, 88, 89, 90, 191n

Rubens, 64

Rules, 20–1 *see* Principles

Russell, Bertrand, 184, 188

Sacraments, 90f., 150, 154, 181

Sacrifice, 6, 11, 21, 24, 144, 149, 164

Samaritan, Good, 136, 138

Saul, 181

Sceptics, unbelievers, 5, 6, 7, 8, 12, 14, 19, 26, 30, 31, 34, 42, 74, 75, 80, 82, 93–4, 141

Scylla and Charybdis, 44

Self-centredness, 82
  -consciousness, 98, 101
  -denial, 16, 102, 103, 104
  -interest, 18, 75, 167
  -love, 15, 16, 23, 83, 103, 106, 107, 115, 116, 117
  -realization, 30, 114, 115
  -sacrifice, 1, 75, 182

Selfishness, egoism, 2, 5, 6, 10, 11, 13, 19, 74, 86, 87, 99, 102, 104, 107, 110, 114, 115, 116, 117, 120, 121, 124, 131, 157, 159, 164, 165, 169

Sentimentality, 102, 112, 117, 129, 130

Sex, 39, 47, 49, 50, 82, 133, 167 *see* Contraception, Rape

Sextus, false, 49

Shakespeare, 28, 60, 115, 117, 126, 128, 181

Shelley, 3, 200n

Shylock, 60

Sin, sinners, 2, 94, 110, 116, 128, 129, 130, 137, 143, 144, 150, 152

Sisyphus, 87

Smart, N., 144, 150, 151, 154

Snobbery, 77–8, 94, 148, 168

Solomon, 60

Soul, 92, 98, 100, 101, 105

Southey, 12

Stalley, R. F., 193n

Stalker, D. M. G., 200n

Stephen, St, 183

Stevenson, C. L., 192n

Strawson, P. F., 49, 193n

Sugarman, B., 40, 192n, 193n

Suicide, 170

Swinburne, R. G., 194n

Taste, 33, 46, 47, 63, 64, 65, 69, 73, 124, 125, 126f.

Teilhard de Chardin, P., 2, 143, 169

Telfer, E., 197n

Temptation of Christ, 153

Terence, 198n

Teresa of Avila, 83

Terrorists, 39, 128

Thomas, St *see* Aquinas

Tintoretto, 64

Titus, 158

Tolerance, 41, 43, 46, 49, 50, 55, 64, 65, 119, 122, 148

Traherne, 108, 109, 117, 121, 138–9

Transcendence, 136, 145, 147, 155, 157, 165, 166, 189

Trinity, 11, 114

Trobriand Islanders, 73

Troubles, sorrows, 6, 13, 15, 50, 53, 112, 129, 164, 170, 171, 172, 173, 177, 178, 179, 182, 183, 184, 186, 190n *see* Dereliction

Turpin, Dick, 128

Twain, Mark *see* Huckleberry Finn

Unbelievers *see* Sceptics

Unconditional, unmotivated, 79, 93, 105, 109, 110, 119, 120, 121, 131, 133, 136, 137

Universalizability, consistency, 33, 36, 39, 40, 78

Unjust Steward, 128
Utilitarianism, 11, 12, 13, 14, 15, 16,
   22, 23, 24, 28, 35, 40, 72, 73, 74, 165

Value-free, 43–4, 71
Vanstone, W. H., 190n, 200n
Vision of God, 156, 157, 159, 160, 161,
   162, 164, 166, 167, 168

Wanting, 3, 11, 15, 23, 47, 72, 83, 87,
   93, 102, 103, 104–5, 108, 109f.,
   ch. 13, 124, 169, 189
Ward, K., 141–2, 191n, 194n
Washoe, 100 *see* Linden, E.
Watkins, S. W. N., 193n
Ways of life, 21, 45, 49, 50, 55, 56, 57,
   64, 72–3 *see* Divergence
We, 9–10, 11
Webb, C. C. J., 150

Weil, S., 66
White stone, 92, 100
Wickedness, 11, 14, 49, 55, 115, 117,
   127, 128, 129, 131, 147–8, 171, 184
Wilbye, 195n
Will of God, 12, 28, 29, 30, 31, 32, 34,
   36, 42, 49, 54, 122, 124
Williams, B., 14, 16, 22–4, 43
Williams, Charles, 116
Williams, H. A., 142, 202n
Williams, N., 40, 192n, 193n
Wilson, J., 40, 192n, 193n
Witches, 21
Woods, G. F., 18, 191n
Wordsworth, 11, 170, 172–4, 179
Work, 29, 87, 88, 89, 119, 120, 136
Worldliness, 6, 90, 137, 161, 162
Worship, 5, 20, 103, 107, 116, 123,
   chs 16–18
Wright, D., 41, 193n